Some aspects of a local Christian congregation are like a business, such as insurance, building maintenance, taxes . . . and conflict. Even more aspects of a local Christian congregation are like a family, including connectedness, affection, mutual help . . . and conflict. The world and human nature will nearly always make one of two choices when faced with conflict: fight or flight. Neither of those work in the end because only God's healing Word can truly resolve conflict. *Built on the Rock* skillfully includes God's Word and many case studies, all applicable for every Christian and every Christian congregation.

—*Rev. Dan P. Gilbert*
President, Northern Illinois District, LCMS

Ted Kober reveals the Lord's prescription for a healthy church: abiding in God's Word. Ted's vast experience in assisting conflicted congregations and his examining of healthy congregations provide ample case studies to prove that the Reformation *sola*, Scripture alone, is still the potent, divine medicine to strengthen unhealthy congregations and to keep healthy congregations strong in Christ.

—*Rev. Scott C. Sailer*
President, South Dakota District, LCMS

Rarely does a book encourage, instruct, challenge, and uplift its readers. *Built on the Rock* did all of these things for me—as a Christian, a pastor, and a theologian. Kober calls the Church back to foundational truths about sin, confession, and forgiveness in our life together in Christ. While there are practical insights as well, Kober most importantly appeals to the Gospel as the source of our life together. Whether your church is conflicted or healthy, *Built on the Rock* will offer truth and encouragement to you, rooted in the Good News of Jesus Christ.

—*Rev. Dr. Jeffrey Gibbs*
Professor of Exegetical Theology
Concordia Seminary, St. Louis, MO

I have known Ted Kober for many years, and some of his publications were resourced in my PhD dissertation on reconciliation. He is a man of great detail and once again shows himself to cover every aspect of what a healthy congregation looks like and how it lives out its baptismal regeneration. This book is a basic catechism on the topic of true reconciliation in the parish. Ted uses a plethora of Bible texts to generate his points along with excellent examples from congregations who have exhibited ill health. The two major themes of the book are (1) the more a congregation is in Bible study, the greater opportunity it has to express a healthy witness of the faith, and (2) the congregation that is willing and able to confess its sin to God and the ones they have offended is the one that not only desires forgiveness but also desires to extend it to the repentant.

Ted spends equal amounts of time addressing the laity and the clergy from each aspect of the two main points. He is fair to each and sound in his applications. I think this book is going to be a great asset to the entire Church and a blessing to the overall confession of the Lutheran Church to our neighbor as well as to the world. Each chapter concludes with Bible study format of questions and discussion topics. I highly recommend it for church and pastor libraries as well as bookshelves in the homes of our members.

—*Rev. Dr. Brian Saunders*
President, Iowa District East, LCMS

Wherever there are sinners, conflict will take place. The evil one uses conflict to discourage and divide, to drive people away from the Church. In his book *Built on the Rock*, Ted Kober demonstrates why so many respect him as an expert in Christ-centered reconciliation. Too often when there is conflict in the local parish, Christians forget and neglect the Word of God. Kober addresses the need for God's people to be in the Word of God. He displays not only a grasp of conflict dynamics but also the understanding that in the church it is not merely a matter of conflict resolution, but most appropriately a matter of reconciliation that comes through confession and absolution as sinners stand together at the foot of the cross. Ted emphasizes, and rightly so, that the Church is "not just another organization," but rather the Body of Christ, a place in which God's Word blesses and guides, and a place in which there is accountability to God and one another. Kober places special emphasis on "living lifestyles of reconciliation," a confession that is too often neglected in this narcissistic age. There is much here for laity and pastors alike.

—*Rev. John C. Wille*
President, South Wisconsin District, LCMS

A healthy congregation is a place of grace. Ted Kober's prescription for church health, a strong dose of God's Word and the healing touch of humble confession and forgiveness, is the Holy Spirit's own cure for a church in crisis, or a church seeking to avoid one! I strongly recommend a careful study of *Built on the Rock* for pastors and leaders who know that church health always precedes fruitfulness. You'll discover Christ-centered, practical advice to help you "maintain the unity of the Spirit in the bond of peace" (Ephesians 4:3).

—*Rev. Dr. Darrell Zimmerman*
Program Director, Grace Place Wellness Ministries

Ted Kober's book is a wake-up call for the Church! *Built on the Rock* shows just how important it is for a healthy congregation to continually grow in God's Word. Biblical illiteracy has engulfed many churches and created a lethargy toward studying God's Word, which leave that ministry at risk for attacks by the evil one. Sharing biblical wisdom and practical strategies along with exercises to benefit both leaders and members of congregations, he provides a clear direction for those who desire to strengthen their ministry and grow as a healthy church. This book is a tremendous resource that I would recommend to any congregation that desires their ministry to be built upon the Rock!

—*Rev. Gregory S. Walton*
President, Florida-Georgia District, LCMS

This is an important and needed book. It will likely engage you (it is interesting), challenge you (it raises important spiritual issues), convict you (because it sets a high but fundamental bar for congregational leadership), and encourage you (it is hopeful). Kober makes an effective case: a congregation's spiritual health is "based on how well her members, especially the leaders, are rooted in God's Word and live lifestyles of reconciliation" (p. 17). He returns again and again to the implications of focusing on Jesus and actively studying and applying the Scriptures as signs of health in a congregation.

—*Rev. Bruce M. Hartung, PhD*
Professor Emeritus, Practical Theology
Concordia Seminary, St. Louis, MO

One of the many "inevitables" in life is *conflict*. The question is not whether conflicts will come but how we will respond to them. Ted Kober helps us understand not only that "every church deals with conflict," but that "in conflict, a congregation's true health is exposed." This book is a tremendous resource and guide to assist congregations in being prepared to deal with conflicts. He gives us the key: be *built on the Rock*. Take every opportunity to involve the congregation in Bible study. They won't be inoculated against conflict, but the congregational immune system will be strengthened to deal with it. The workbook style provides an excellent format for congregational study and will be a blessing in all of our relationships. A must-read!

—*Rev. Dr. Donald J. Fondow*
President, Minnesota North District, LCMS

This is a book for the whole church—for pastors and lay leaders alike. Ted Kober has authored an exceptionally practical, well-written book. He holds the reader's attention with real stories that could come from any congregation. They provide the evidence to show us what we already intuitively know: congregations that study the Word of God together are healthier than those that don't! What Ted teaches us is that healthy congregations are more able to weather the inevitable conflicts that will come. It is a wonderful reminder of the promise of Isaiah 55:11, "so shall My word be that goes out from My mouth; it shall not return to Me empty, but it shall accomplish that which I purpose, and shall succeed in the thing for which I sent it."

—*Rev. Dr. Steve Turner*
President, Iowa District West, LCMS

TED KOBER

BUILT ON THE ROCK

THE **HEALTHY** CONGREGATION

CONCORDIA PUBLISHING HOUSE • SAINT LOUIS

Published by Concordia Publishing House
3558 S. Jefferson Ave., St. Louis, MO 63118–3968
1-800-325-3040 • cph.org

Library of Congress Cataloging-in-Publication Data

Names: Kober, Ted, author.
Title: Built on the rock : the healthy congregation / Ted Kober.
Description: St. Louis : Concordia Publishing House, 2017. | Includes bibliographical references and index.
Identifiers: LCCN 2017043613 (print) | LCCN 2017047187 (ebook) | ISBN 9780758658074 | ISBN 9780758658067 (alk. paper)
Subjects: LCSH: Church. | Spiritual formation. | Church--Marks. | Lutheran Church--Doctrines.
Classification: LCC BV600.3 (ebook) | LCC BV600.3 .K63 2017 (print) | DDC 250--dc23
LC record available at https://lccn.loc.gov/2017043613

Manufactured in the United States of America

3 4 5 6 7 8 9 10   27 26 25 24 23 22 21 20

DEDICATION

I dedicate this book to the glory of God in thanksgiving for my pastors from Trinity Lutheran Church in Billings, Montana. From my earliest years, they taught me God's Word and encouraged me to build my faith on Christ, the Solid Rock:

Rev. Dr. Paul M. Freiburger, Pastor (1929–76), Assistant to the Pastor (1976 into the early 1990s)

Rev. Lloyd C. Warneke, Pastor (1976–82)

Rev. Harold V. Huber, Assistant Pastor while LCMS Montana District President (1978–84)

Rev. Dr. Richard L. Thompson, Pastor (1984–93)

Rev. Albert G. Pullmann, Assistant Pastor while LCMS Montana District President (1985–89)

Rev. Dr. Elwood E. Mather III, Assistant Pastor (1992–96)

Rev. David L. Poovey, Pastor (1995–2002)

Rev. James A. Haugen, Associate Pastor (2000–2003)

Rev. Daniel W. Rinderknecht, Pastor (2003 to present)

Rev. Timothy Richholt, Associate Pastor (2004–14)

Rev. Daniel Paul Keinath, Associate Pastor (2015 to present)

CONTENTS

ACKNOWLEDGMENTS

Many have influenced me in my spiritual walk and thus in the writing of this book. I praise God for the gifts given me through these fellow saints. I especially want to express my thanksgiving for a few of them.

I appreciate the many with whom I have worked from Peacemaker Ministries, including its founder, Ken Sande. I am especially thankful for two brothers in Christ who with me cofounded Ambassadors of Reconciliation: Rev. Ed Keinath and Rev. Bruce Zagel. These two men served with me on many of the cases that helped shape my thoughts for this book, and their insights are reflected throughout. Without the support and encouragement of my co-worker Dwight Schettler, I would not have had the opportunity to write this book, for he assumed many of my responsibilities at Ambassadors of Reconciliation while I was focused on writing. The Board of Directors for Ambassadors of Reconciliation have provided encouragement, moral support, and wisdom since the founding of the ministry. Individual members of the board also served with me on cases and teaching assignments. Other colleagues from Ambassadors of Reconciliation and the network of Christian conciliators throughout the world continue to influence my perspectives on what makes a church healthy.

I am grateful for my grandmother Julia Kober, whose example inspired my faith and trust in God in my younger years. I am grateful to the pastors who have served—and continue to serve—me in my own congregation. I have been blessed to learn from godly leaders throughout The Lutheran Church—Missouri Synod and her partner churches. I thank my editor, Rev. Scot Kinnaman, who first asked me to write this book. I appreciate the pastors and district presidents who participated in my study of healthy congregations.

God blessed me with a godly wife. Sonja continues to be my best friend, my dearest sister in Christ, and my greatest supporter. Our conversations about our Lord and His Word continue to challenge and encourage me.

For these and many more, I thank the Giver of all good gifts. "Bless the LORD, O my soul, and all that is within me, bless His holy name!" (Psalm 103:1).

Preface

The first time it happened, I could hardly believe what we were witnessing. My colleague and I were meeting with twelve elders of a conflicted church. We asked them to look up a passage of Scripture. Half of them had no idea where to find the Gospel of John. Some were paging through the Bible, beginning with Genesis. One had landed on 1 John. These leaders were obviously unacquainted with the Bible.

Working with more churches over the years, I became less surprised. My expectations changed as I began to recognize a pattern: the leaders of churches struggling with destructive conflicts knew almost nothing about the Bible. And their members were even less familiar. Biblical illiteracy had led to spiritual immaturity, and these churches became unhealthy because their leaders and members had become disconnected from the Rock on which they were built.

In Matthew chapter 7, Jesus contrasts two men who built a house. He says,

> Everyone then who hears these words of Mine and does them will be like a wise man who built his house on the rock. And the rain fell, and the floods came, and the winds blew and beat on that house, but it did not fall, because it had been founded on the rock. And everyone who hears these words of mine and does not do them will be like a foolish man who built his house on the sand. And the rain fell, and the floods came, and the winds blew and beat against that house, and it fell, and great was the fall of it. (vv. 24–27)

The Christian congregation can be securely founded upon Christ, the Rock, or she can be built on shifting sand. When the storms of conflict come against her, the church's bond to the Rock is exposed. On one hand, a healthy congregation will be found solidly connected to Christ and His Word. And while storms cause damage, the church built on the Rock remains strong. On the other hand, the tempests of conflict within an unhealthy church inflict severe damage, tearing the church apart, sometimes even destroying it. These storms expose a church who has placed her trust more in worldly means than in the Means of Grace.

So how should the leaders of Christ's churches seek to build and sustain healthy congregations?

A number of current resources on healthy churches apply a psychological approach based on family systems theory. This methodology views the church as a system of interconnected and interdependent individuals. No individual can be understood in isolation from the system. This approach builds its philosophy on assessing and improving the emotional health of the leaders and members. Family systems theory can be insightful for describing how people respond within groups. Recognizing these dynamics can prove helpful for leaders as they seek ways to function within those systems. While useful for describing human behavior, psychology typically depends on human wisdom when prescribing the answers, neglecting the power of the cross. Solutions based on psychology typically fail to direct people to God's Word or to confess sin and seek Christ's forgiveness for empowering changed behavior.

Other resources draw upon the latest management practices. Viewing churches as entities with managerial needs, these resources apply business and organizational principles to describe churches' challenges and to propose solutions. Because congregations employ people and own property and financial assets, these principles can guide churches in their business aspects, including defining mission and setting new directions. Yet, these management tools, too, depend on human reasoning that disregards the power of confession and God's forgiveness when dealing with people.

I acknowledge that family systems theory and sound business practices can provide useful information for understanding systems and administering organizations. Nevertheless, these resources should not become alternatives for the cross of Christ. Nor should they ignore or minimize the power of the Gospel to transform lives.

God's Word emphasizes the power of the cross for strengthening churches and preparing them for conflict—foolishness to the world's thinking. When addressing the conflicted congregation at Corinth, the apostle Paul exhorted her members to trust the power of the cross rather than worldly philosophies: "For Christ did not send me to baptize but to preach the gospel, and *not with words of eloquent wisdom, lest the cross of Christ be emptied of its power*. For the word of the cross is folly to those who are perishing, but to us who are being saved it is the power of God" (1 Corinthians 1:17–18, emphasis added; note the rest of chapters 1 and 2 of Paul's letter).

Paul also admonished: "But I, brothers, could not address you as spiritual people, but as people of the flesh, as infants in Christ. I fed you with milk, not solid food, for you were not ready for it. And even now you are not ready, for you are still of the flesh. For while there is jealousy and strife among you, are you not of the flesh and behaving only in a human way?" (1 Corinthians 3:1–3).

Notice that Paul did not approach this conflicted church with worldly philosophies or the latest business management practices. He did not identify the main issue as emotional, systematic, or organizational. Rather, he confronted the Corinthians' behavior from a spiritual point of view.

People often ask me as a church reconciliation consultant, "What is the most common issue over which churches fight?" I tell them the issues vary from place to place. But I find one common characteristic among highly conflicted churches: they have too few people, including leaders, in God's Word.

The healthy churches I encounter benefit from larger percentages of people in regular Bible study. Their leaders demonstrate scriptural knowledge and trust in Christ as they practice repentance through confession and forgiveness. Unhealthy churches have small numbers of people who know God's Word or apply it to their own lives. Leaders of these churches are skilled in justifying their actions, judging and accusing one another, and employing sinful means for dealing with their disputes.

One would think these basic truths—that Christ must be the foundation and that leaders and members must abide in God's Word—would be so obvious that people wouldn't need to be reminded of them. But the reality is that members and leaders alike often depend more on worldly wisdom to deal with the challenges of congregational life than what they confess by faith.

One might also expect that since our faithful Christian congregations profess to be people of the Word, such a book on this subject would be unnecessary. Sadly, however, I have discovered through years of experience that many in our churches are biblically illiterate or have too little knowledge of the Bible with which to guide their reactions. Furthermore, many who do know something about God's Word, including professional church workers, seem to have lost their trust in Christ's power for addressing new and ongoing challenges. The alluring wisdom of psychological theories and business management practices become attractive substitutes when what is really needed is simply getting back to the basics: looking to Jesus, the founder and perfecter of our faith; dwelling in God's Word; and living as reconciled children of God in mutual confession and forgiveness.

The result? Many congregations suffer from poor spiritual health.

In this book, I define healthy congregations from a spiritual maturity perspective. Healthy churches are those whose leadership and membership are solidly grounded in Christ, nourished by God's Word, and able to apply it to their lives. Their spiritual maturity evidences itself when they practice confession and forgiveness in their relationships with one another.

Church leaders and members who are unfamiliar with God's Word and fail to apply the Word to themselves are spiritually immature. The result? Their churches are unhealthy. The lack of spiritual maturity is shown in their inability to admit their faults and forgive one another. The consequences? Great harm is done to individuals, the church as a body, and its public witness.

Thus, I present the concepts of this book as the fundamental place for church leaders to begin when addressing the health of their congregations.

The book features fifteen chapters organized in four parts.

PART 1: THE FOUNDATION FOR HEALTH

In the first four chapters, I explore how one can look beneath the symptoms to uncover the root cause of poor health in churches. The lack of a church's health becomes revealed in conflict. I will describe how corporate health is rooted in the spiritual health of individuals, especially the leaders. At the core of the issue, I will describe how idols of the heart lead people to sin in conflict. The more they worship their idols, the worse their conflict is with God and others. This diagnosis provides a spiritual foundation for understanding what is needed for treating the underlying causes of poor health in churches.

> Healthy churches are those whose leadership and membership are solidly grounded in Christ, nourished by God's Word, and able to apply it to their lives.

14

PART 2: RESTORING HEALTH AND NURTURING SPIRITUAL WELLNESS

In chapters 5 through 8, I describe how to restore health by addressing the idols of the heart. Healing begins with confession and forgiveness. However, in order to sustain good health, churches need to be focused on God's Word and Sacraments. *The emphasis will be on commitment to being in God's Word, which is the first focal point of the book.* Church members and leaders mature in their faith as they practice confession and forgiveness. Lack of repentance demonstrates self-justification, another form of idolatry. Repentance gives witness to one's faith in Christ and the power of His forgiveness. *Thus, the second key focal point is the practice of confession and forgiveness, including private absolution.*

In chapter 6, I identify the true enemy of congregational health. In the following chapter, I describe four threats to spiritual wellness: the unrepentant pastor, the unrepentant lay leader, the fix-it mentality, and widespread biblical illiteracy. This chapter serves to reinforce the two key focal points of the book through antithesis.

PART 3: HEALTHY SPIRITUAL LEADERSHIP

In this section, you will be guided in what church leaders can do to bring their congregation to spiritual health. The first chapter of this section highlights biblical qualifications for serving as a church leader. The second chapter reinforces the importance of spiritual leadership. Private absolution for leaders (lay and pastoral) is identified as a vital factor contributing to church health. Ministering to the professional church worker is also discussed. Finally, the role of organizational structure in congregational health is addressed. While necessary for sound business operations, organizational structure must not overshadow the leadership's desire for a healthy church.

PART 4: PRACTICAL APPLICATIONS FOR IMPROVING SPIRITUAL HEALTH

In the last three chapters, you will be given direction for improving and sustaining the spiritual wellness of the membership. These chapters include practical and specific ideas for achieving health among the members of your church.

REFLECTION

Throughout the book, I provide questions for reflection. My hope is that as you utilize these either in personal reflection or in conversation with other leaders, you will find practical ways to strengthen the health of your congregation.

I have served as a Certified Christian Conciliator™ since 1992 (1992–2004 with Peacemaker Ministries; 2005 to present with Ambassadors of Reconciliation). During this time, I have worked together with several colleagues in serving thousands of Christian ministry leaders in multiple countries, offering training in reconciliation and providing consultation services.

In simpler cases, a church or another ministry may be assisted by a single reconciler. In more complex situations, a team of two to six reconcilers work to guide the reconciliation process. Reconciliation consultation usually begins with a Bible study on peacemaking and may include conflict coaching, data gathering, evaluation, mediations, leading groups in reconciliation exercises, and reporting to the church or its leaders with our observations, conclusions, and recommendations.

Throughout this book, I share experiences drawn from actual cases. Examples reflect the kinds of issues that arise in real-life situations. However, unless I indicate otherwise, individual names, churches, and situations are fictional.

Events I describe from my own life experiences are true accounts. Except where I specify otherwise, names and details are changed to protect confidences.

My prayer for writing this book is from Psalm 19:14:

> Let the words of my mouth and the meditation of my heart
> be acceptable in Your sight,
> O Lord, my rock and my redeemer.

In Christ's service, Ted Kober

PART 1

THE FOUNDATION FOR HEALTH

How often have you heard of someone you know who experienced a heart attack and you thought, "Wow, I thought he was so healthy!" Someone may appear fit and robust until experiencing a health crisis. He may have not smoked or abused alcohol. He may have looked great. However, his apparent health may have been deceiving.

Inherited vulnerabilities, hypertension, high cholesterol, built-up plaque, or other risk factors may have been culminating over time, leading up to what seemed like a surprise attack. On the outside, the person appeared fine. But on the inside, an increasingly poor health condition was intensifying stress on the body, until it suffered cardiac arrest.

Likewise, a church may seem healthy by her apparent characteristics: a vibrant leader, a friendly atmosphere, an inviting new edifice, growth in worship attendance, a strong financial base, and stimulating worship experiences. But should a conflict erupt that leads to a crisis, the congregation's hidden spiritual heart disease will be exposed. The result? The surprisingly unhealthy church experiences a heart attack, and it struggles to survive.

To understand and promote health in a congregation, one must properly diagnose what contributes to the church's health or lack of it. If you fail to diagnose the foundational issue, you might help a church take on a healthy appearance. She may possess many qualities that healthy churches exhibit. But the real danger will be left untreated, leaving the church vulnerable to a major heart attack. The church may be infected with idols of the heart. If left unchecked, the congregation will suffer a major crisis in its next conflict.

The foundation for a church's spiritual health is based on how well her members, especially the leaders, are rooted in God's Word and live lifestyles of reconciliation—reflecting our forgiveness from Christ in the way that we confess our sins to one another and forgive one another.

CHAPTER 1

THE ULTIMATE TEST OF SPIRITUAL HEALTH

My hope is built on nothing less

Than Jesus' blood and righteousness;

No merit of my own I claim

But wholly lean on Jesus' name.

On Christ, the solid rock, I stand;

All other ground is sinking sand. (*LSB* 575:1)

Every church deals with conflict—it's a given that goes back to Genesis 3, where Scripture records how man fell into sin. Conflict in an unhealthy church can tear her apart. But conflict in a healthy congregation can provide opportunities for growth in spiritual maturity, increasing her dependence on Christ, her head. Conflict will either diminish or enhance the overall mission and ministry of the local congregation. What makes the difference is how the church's members, beginning with her leaders, respond to it. Their spiritual maturity or lack of it will determine their individual and corporate responses.

Conflict provides the ultimate test of spiritual health.

Consider two churches faced with conflict and how differently they responded.

Case Study: St. Mark's Church

How Could This Happen to Our Church?

The leaders at St. Mark's Church and School found themselves in a crisis that seemed to evolve in just three months. The long-term beloved principal resigned her position due to the effects of job-related stress on her health. The cherished organist left his position to take a new job at a church with a much-inferior organ. Four of the nine council members tendered their resignations. Seventeen families, including the treasurer's, formally transferred their memberships to new churches. Overall worship attendance dropped noticeably. Weekly offerings declined by 25 percent. Gossip had spread rumors about everyone in leadership. A new blog provided means for filing complaints, initially by families who left the church. But several of the recent anonymous posts were from people still attending, including some of the elected lay leaders.

The elders firmly stood behind Pastor Jackson and his twelve years as senior pastor. The school board opposed Pastor Jackson, calling for his removal. They blamed him for the principal's departure. Council members were divided on their support for Pastor. The polarization among the leadership represented the disunity in the church.

During the initial call from the chairman of the elders, the reconciliation consultant learned that the congregation experienced significant growth under Pastor Jackson's leadership. In fact, the elder asserted, their congregation was recognized as the fastest-growing church in their district. St. Mark's was recently commended as a model church for its evangelism efforts. The denomination's regional leadership spoke on St. Mark's success of articulating its mission and committing to a mission focus. Until a few months prior, their average worship attendance was just over 600 per weekend. Only ten years earlier, average worship attendance was just 155. But when the head elder called the consultant for guidance, worship attendance during the previous Sundays had dropped to 445.

The elder chairman bemoaned that this could happen to such a healthy church. He could hardly believe their church was in turmoil.

The reconciler asked, "How many different adults attend Bible study during the week?" He took time to count, since no formal statistics were recorded.

"Let's see. Sunday morning used to be around thirty-five, but it has also dropped off—maybe twenty-five or so recently. Our most-attended worship service is during that same time slot. I don't attend the men's or women's Bible studies during the week. I think a faithful group of six or seven attend the men's, and the women have about fifteen. There's one small group that meets in a home. I would say about fifty to sixty people total. Of course, some of those who attend the Sunday morning class also attend one of the other studies."

"How many of those attending Bible study are elected leaders from your various boards?"

"I'm not really sure—maybe fifteen to twenty?"

"How many elected lay leadership positions do you have?"

"Before all these resignations, we had seventy-five people elected to different boards."

"So that would mean that about one-fourth of your elected leaders attend Bible study, and three-fourths do not."

"That's probably right."

"How many of your church and school staff attend Bible study?"

"I don't really know. On Sunday morning, I see two or three of the church staff. But come to think of it, I haven't seen any of the teachers in our Sunday Bible class. Two of them teach Sunday School. Schoolteachers wouldn't be able to attend the weekday studies because they're in class."

After years of working with conflicted churches, our trained reconciliation consultants have learned to ask about Bible study attendance. It's a quick way to assess a congregation's spiritual maturity. Many churches suffer from the same weakness.

After considering their options, St. Mark's Church and School invited a reconciliation team to assist them. The process began with a full-day Bible study seminar on peacemaking.

During the seminar, the attendees' biblical illiteracy became apparent. Most struggled to look up passages from well-known books of the Bible. Bible stories the reconciliation team assumed were well known had to be explained because so many people were unfamiliar with them.

Reconciliation work continued as the team members met with various leadership groups and individual families.

As the reconciliation team met with the elders, they passed around Bibles from the church's pews. (The elders were unaccustomed to bringing Bibles to their meetings.) For an opening devotion, they were asked to look up a passage from 2 Corinthians 5. Three of the ten elders starting flipping through the Bible without finding it. Another went directly to the table of contents. One opened to Colossians, but couldn't find chapter 5. Half of the elders could not find 2 Corinthians. According to their bylaws, the elders were responsible for overall spiritual welfare of the church.

Later, the reconcilers asked the school board members to look up a passage from <u>Romans.</u> Only a third of them knew where to begin. The school board chairman had to go back to the table of contents three times before he found Romans. The experience with the council members was similar. *Most of the elected leaders struggled to find common books of the Bible.*

In the days following, the reconcilers held 120 meetings with member families. People poured out their hurts, blaming particular leaders. A number of folks were angry. Many shared complaints. Virtually none of these people believed they had contributed to the conflicts, including the pastor and other leaders. People's stories included conflicting information about significant events. As observers, the team wondered if these people were truly from the same church. Gossip and slander had so tainted their memories that there were few common descriptions of the same occurrences. Emails, Facebook entries, and the blog provided ample opportunity for backbiting and tearing down. <u>Paul warned</u> about such behavior when he wrote, "<u>But if you bite and devour one another, watch out that you are not consumed by one another</u>" (Galatians 5:15).

Although the members did not realize it, St. Mark's Church and School had been suffering from poor spiritual health for some time. So when a few igniting events occurred, people immediately reacted from their old Adam natures, and the congregation found itself in crisis. The church could be compared to an individual who doesn't take care of his body for an extended time—high cholesterol and plaque build-up may not show outward signs of poor health until the body has a major exertion that triggers a heart attack.

Case Study: St. John's Church

Hope in Spite of a Leader's Failure

St. John's Church also experienced a major event that could ignite conflict, but the leaders and members responded very differently than those of St. Mark's.

Two teenage girls were using the youth minister's tablet to order pizza online. All of a sudden, pornographic pop-ups filled the screen. The girls didn't speak to the youth leader about it but instead told their parents, who went immediately to Pastor Smith.

As the pastor met with him, the youth minister broke down and cried, admitting his longtime habit. He had been struggling with an addiction to Internet pornography since age 12. He willingly gave up his tablet and computer for further investigation, telling the pastor he could expect to find some inappropriate emails as well. The single youth minister had been exchanging sexually explicit emails with a young married woman from the community.

Pastor Smith pronounced God's forgiveness to his staff member and prayed with him. He reminded the youth leader that though Christ's forgiveness is assured, he will likely suffer earthly consequences. The full-time youth leader offered to resign, but the pastor asked him not to do that until the situation could be fully addressed. The youth minister agreed to stay at home until further notice.

Over the next several days, Pastor Smith met with a number of people— the youth minister, the girls and their parents, the district supervisor, and the elders and church officers. The church leadership decided to place the youth leader on paid leave until things had been resolved. News spread throughout the church about the situation. Many expressed their sadness or disappointment. A few were angry. Most of the youth parents expressed support for the youth minister and their desire for him to remain on staff. He had been so appreciated by their teenaged children. However, a few demanded his termination, stating that he was a poor example for their youth.

Pastor Smith arranged a meeting between the youth worker and the girls involved, with their parents. The youth leader confessed his sin directly to them, asking for forgiveness. The girls readily forgave him, as did one girl's parents. But the other girl's father became indignant, and his wife remained silent. The father insisted the young man be terminated.

Over the next couple of weeks, three opposing positions evolved among members. A few said the youth worker must go. Many hoped he would stay. A third group expressed ignorance or ambiguity about what should happen next.

The congregation's leaders reached out for reconciliation help.

In the first call with the pastor and elder chairman, the reconciliation consultant learned the following information. The congregation had an average Sunday worship attendance of 375. They had experienced moderate growth in membership over the past years, peaking around 410. But the recent closure of the nearby military base and two other major businesses had led to several members leaving town. Although they had grown for a few years, their current worship attendance was similar to what it had been six years prior. In the few weeks since the discovery about the youth leader, neither attendance nor offerings had experienced any significant change. No elected leaders had resigned.

When asked about Bible study attendance, Pastor Smith answered that Sunday mornings offered three Bible studies with about 75 people total attending. Eight small groups met throughout the week, with a total participation of 55. He indicated that some who attended Sunday mornings also attended the small groups, but he also noted that not everyone attends each week. Several members traveled extensively for work, including weekends. He estimated that at least 110 different people attended at least one study per week. When asked, the elder chair indicated that elected lay leaders were expected to attend Bible study. All the elders actively participated, but he acknowledged that about 20 percent of the other lay leaders were not involved.

When the reconciler arrived on-site, he found a leadership team that knew their Bibles. He met with the elders, council, and youth board in a common meeting. Most had Bibles with them. When he asked them to look up various verses, they had no difficulties finding them. A few even suggested other passages that came to mind during the discussion.

Reconciliation work began with teaching the congregation in a full-day Bible study on peacemaking. During the seminar, few had problems locating Bible passages. Their questions and comments reflected spiritual maturity.

The youth minister feared meeting with the consultant, but he was ready. His contrition was evident as he expressed his willingness to do whatever was necessary, including stepping down. His pastor and elders were encouraging him to stay, but he was uncertain what to do.

After meeting a few others, the reconciler met again with Pastor Smith and his lay leaders. Together, they reviewed scriptural qualifications for a church leader in 1 Timothy 3 and Titus 1. They reflected on what the Bible teaches regarding confession and forgiveness as well as earthly consequences. They also discussed how best to care for the youth leader as well as for the youth, their parents, and the rest of the congregation. If there were no consequences, the unintended message could be that sexual sin using technology is okay. On the other hand, how could the congregation experience the power of forgiveness? Even with forgiveness, had this moral failing disqualified the young man from service in their church?

In the end, the youth leader decided to make a public confession to the congregation. A special service was arranged for members only where he could confess his sins and the pastor could pronounce God's forgiveness. Pastor Smith led the congregation in a devotion that focused on forgiveness through Christ. The youth minister confessed that his sinful behavior provided a poor example to the youth he served. In his confession, the youth leader asked to be released from his position because he had violated the people's trust in his leadership. He could not be described as a man above reproach or having a good reputation with outsiders (ref. 1 Timothy 3:2, 7). He told the congregation he was seeking professional help and needed time away to focus on healing. The district supervisor had committed to working with him to eventually restore him to ministry.

His public confession, the pronouncement of forgiveness, and his asking for release of his position all brought calm to the congregation. The factions that had begun to form became unified as together they grieved over the fall of one of their leaders. But they were all reminded of God's promises and provision, especially in the challenges of life.

EXPOSED!

In conflict, a congregation's true health is exposed.

As noted in the description of the first church, the leaders and their members responded to conflict not just in *unhealthy* ways, but with *sinful* thoughts, words, and actions. As individuals began to resign and gossip spread, people with differing positions became polarized. More sin followed. Although the church initially appeared strong because of growth in numbers, the veneer of good health dissipated as her numbers fell.

Several people resigned leadership positions. Congregants voted their disapproval by their feet (avoiding worship) and their pocketbooks (withholding offerings). Avoiding worship is a sin against the commandment "Remember the Sabbath day by keeping it holy." Withholding offerings is a form of stealing from God, a sin against the commandment "You shall not steal." Extensive gossip was not only a sin against "You shall not give false testimony against your neighbor" but also against the First Commandment, "You shall have no other gods." Those who gossip make themselves gods, judging and condemning those whose reputations they destroy. People resisted confessing their own sins and accused one another instead. In light of their conflict, the church struggled to heal because her congregation suffered from poor spiritual health.

The second church initially struggled with some sinful responses as well. But her leaders remained calm and steadfast. They demonstrated mature faith in God by seeking help based on the Bible. They were teachable, trusting in God and His Word despite pressures from vocal individuals. As leaders discussed how best to respond, they found hope in Christ and His forgiveness. Although many were saddened by the youth leader's resignation, they rallied around him. They forgave him, yet they recognized that sin brings about earthly consequences. In spite of the moral failure of a key leader, the church was able to heal because it was healthy and spiritually mature. People with differing positions reconciled their relationships as they shared forgiveness with one another.

In working in reconciliation ministry for more than twenty years, I have observed one commonality among highly conflicted churches: they have too few people, especially leaders, in Bible study. A quick litmus test often reveals the underlying cause of the church's poor health—they have fewer than 20 percent of their average weekly worship attendance in adult Bible study. Further examination will confirm the initial diagnosis—a significant lack of basic biblical knowledge.

I can recall only a few cases where highly conflicted churches had a higher percentage of members in Bible study. Although these churches had more than 20 percent of their people in Bible study, their members were unable to apply the Scriptures to their own actions. Instead, they used legalism to accuse one another (see Matthew 7:1–5). There was little evidence of personal application, individual repentance, or forgiveness for others' wrongs.

When I first began consulting with conflicted churches, I was appalled that a congregation's key leaders, including her elders, could know so little about the Bible. When a congregation's leaders struggle to find familiar books such as Psalms, the Gospels, or the Epistles, it exposes biblical illiteracy. I could not believe they often did not even know whether a major book was in the Old or New Testament. Some real-life examples from different churches include the following:

- In a board of eleven elders, not one knew where the Book of Romans could be found.
- Only one elder of eight could identify any of the Ten Commandments. Others could not even informally describe any of them.
- In a church council, fewer than half of the fourteen members could easily find the Gospel of John.
- In a school board of eight people, only two could easily locate Matthew.
- The chairman of one church council gave up trying to find Ephesians, slammed the Bible shut, and shoved it to the center of the table.

When visiting another church, I was asked to lead the Sunday morning adult Bible class. In this congregation, which had an average worship attendance of 250, about thirty people showed up for Bible study. I was told that this was about double the normal attendance, attributed to the fact that there was a guest speaker. When I asked people to look up the first passage, the class had to be paused until church leaders could find enough Bibles for them to share. I don't know what these people did in their normal Bible study hour, but only two people had a Bible. The teaching progressed slowly because I had to allow so much time for people to look up passages. The church's lack of commitment to being in the Word was revealed.

My assumptions about biblical knowledge among the members—and especially the leaders—of Christian churches were shattered. My automatic expectations have since been adjusted. Fortunately, many churches benefit from a leadership that is familiar with the Bible. But I no longer assume that is the case just because a church is Christian.

For years, consultants and psychologists have studied church health and postured theories on how to improve it. Many of their observations accurately describe how a church might function as a system or organization.

But changing that system can often prove to be a mystery. I believe that this may be because we have misdiagnosed what is needed.

As consultants, we sometimes fall prey to our own presumptions. We assume the leaders and members of a church are familiar with God's Word because we think that they read it, study it, and apply it. We take for granted that they remember they are children of God, forgiven in Christ, and thus reflect His love for one another. Such assumptions can lead us to miss the underlying cause of the symptoms of poor health. Accordingly, the plans for changing that system based on these presumptions ultimately miss the mark.

The Bible addressed these issues centuries before. The answers to improving congregational health have been in the Bible for all time, hidden in plain sight.

Disagreements among God's people are part of every church's experience. But conflict need not result in a church being torn apart. A spiritually mature church can lean on Christ as she takes on the challenges that church life brings.

Dietrich Bonhoeffer stressed the importance of speaking God's Word to one another, especially in the face of conflict: "Where Christians live together the time must inevitably come when in some crisis one person will have to declare God's Word and will to another."[1]

When a church's leaders absent themselves from God's Word, they become ill equipped in their responsibilities. How can they declare God's Word to another if they themselves are not in the Word? When a crisis comes, such spiritually immature leaders will depend on other sources to deal with the difficulties. Their resources may include what they have learned from secular education, psychology, philosophy, business, and the like. Or they may react in ways that are influenced by various media, such as television, the Internet, social media, news

> The answers to improving congregational health have been in the Bible for all time, hidden in plain sight.

sources, and other publications. Perhaps their wisdom will flow from their personal experiences, including how they were raised, how they address marital disputes, how they handle their children, what they learned from resolving conflict at work, or how they settle claims from accidents or disputes with neighbors. In any case, the world's wisdom will dominate their responses to conflict in their church. God's Word will not even play a minor role in their actions or decisions.

Timothy Mech observes that what is needed for addressing root problems of the Church today has been available to us all along:

> The answer to the challenge for the Church in this self-absorbed culture is found where it has always been found, in the Word of God. Interesting, isn't it? That almost all of the problems we face in the church and in everyday life have to do with our being disconnected from the Word of God in one way or another? We need more of the Word of God in our lives, not less.[2]

Leaders who fail to be regularly nourished by the Word of Christ become immature in their faith, and the health of their church deteriorates—for members often follow the example of their leaders. These leaders may even include pastors who neglect their own personal devotional life. Even clergy can look to worldly ways rather than God's direction when responding to crises in the congregation.

Conflict will eventually test the health of a church. Despite all the visible signs of a vibrant ministry, conflict will reveal what or whom the people ultimately trust for their direction.

God calls His leaders to equip the saints so that they will become *spiritually* mature, individually and corporately. Although some may describe this behavior as emotional intelligence, the Bible does not name this wisdom or ability to love and forgive one another as *emotional*. Spiritual maturity includes controlling one's emotions and attitudes, but it is much more. Spiritual maturity reflects an active, living faith in Christ and dependence upon the Bible for direction and wisdom.

Conflict will eventually test the health of a church. Despite all the visible signs of a vibrant ministry, conflict will reveal what or whom the people ultimately trust for their direction.

Notice how Paul encourages the Church in Colossae to "set your minds on things that are above, not on things that are on earth" (Colossians 3:2):

> Put on then, as God's chosen ones, holy and beloved, compassionate hearts, kindness, humility, meekness, and patience, bearing with one another and, if one has a complaint against another, forgiving each other; as the Lord has forgiven you, so you also must forgive. And above all these put on love, which binds everything together in perfect harmony. And let the peace of Christ rule in your hearts, to which indeed you were called in one body. And be thankful. Let the word of Christ dwell in you richly, teaching and admonishing one another in all wisdom, singing psalms and hymns and spiritual songs, with thankfulness in your hearts to God. (Colossians 3:12–16)

Letting "the word of Christ dwell in you richly" is necessary for spiritual maturity. How can members teach and admonish one another with all wisdom if the Word is not dwelling in them richly? How can they forgive and love one another if they are not regularly in God's Word? How can the peace of Christ rule their hearts if they are unfamiliar with the Bible?

Spiritual maturity that leads to brotherly love requires nourishment from Christ, the living Word. Paul explains:

> And He gave the apostles, the prophets, the evangelists, the shepherds and teachers, *to equip the saints for the work of ministry, for building up the body of Christ, until we all attain to the unity of the faith and of the knowledge of the Son of God, to mature manhood, to the measure of the stature of the fullness of Christ,* so that we may no longer be children, tossed to and fro by the waves and carried about by every wind of doctrine, by human cunning, by craftiness in deceitful schemes. Rather, *speaking the truth in love, we are to grow up in every way into Him who is the head, into Christ,* from whom the whole body, joined and held together by every joint with which

it is equipped, *when each part is working properly, makes the body grow so that it builds itself up in love.* (Ephesians 4:11–16, emphasis added)

God's people mature in faith as we individually and corporately "grow up in every way into Him who is the head, into Christ." Then, the Body of Christ grows as it builds itself up in love. Maturing in faith depends on being connected regularly to Jesus through His Word.

Paul indicated that bearing good fruit comes from spiritual wisdom and understanding, gained from our increase in the knowledge of God.

And so, from the day we heard, we have not ceased to pray for you, asking that *you may be filled with the knowledge of His will in all spiritual wisdom and understanding,* so as to walk in a manner worthy of the Lord, fully pleasing to Him: *bearing fruit in every good work and increasing in the knowledge of God.* (Colossians 1:9–10, emphasis added)

How does one increase in the knowledge of God? By abiding in the Bible. Often. In personal devotions and in studying with others.

SPIRITUAL IMMATURITY IS TREATABLE!

If your congregation is lacking in its health, the good news is that this condition is curable. Your congregation can grow in spiritual maturity and increase its health by increasing Bible study among leaders and members. The key to becoming and maintaining the health of a Christian church depends on the members being rooted in the Word of Christ.

We can trust God to do what He promises in His Word. His Word will not be fruitless:

For My thoughts are not your thoughts,
  neither are your ways My ways, declares the LORD.
For as the heavens are higher than the earth,
  so are My ways higher than your ways
  and My thoughts than your thoughts.

For as the rain and the snow come down from heaven
    and do not return there but water the earth,
making it bring forth and sprout,
    giving seed to the sower and bread to the eater,
so shall My word be that goes out from My mouth;
    it shall not return to Me empty,
but it shall accomplish that which I purpose,
    and shall succeed in the thing for which I sent it.
(Isaiah 55:8–11)

Reflection

Reflection

Considering this chapter, reflect on these questions personally or discuss them with the leaders in your congregation.

1. As you reflect on this chapter, apply the following questions to your congregation.

    a. How many people regularly attend Bible study?

        25% – 50%

    b. How many of our leaders easily locate the most familiar books of the Bible?

    c. Is my example of personal devotion to God's Word what it should be?

    d. In what ways have I failed as a leader of Christ's Church?

2. If you find yourself guilty of failing to address the unhealthy practices described in this chapter, I have good news for you.

    God knows how you fail to live up to His standards as a leader of His Church. He sees your weaknesses and recognizes your neglect of His Word. He is more aware than you how you lean on worldly wisdom more than the foolishness of the cross.

    Nonetheless, He loves you. He cares so much about you that He sent His one and only Son into this world to take the full punishment for your sins, including your failures as a church leader.

Because of the promises of Scripture, you can be comforted that for Christ's sake, you are forgiven! "For our sake He made Him to be sin who knew no sin, so that in Him we might become the righteousness of God" (2 Corinthians 5:21).

3. Take time today to meditate on God's gift of forgiveness. Jot down what encourages you most from the following passages:

    a. Psalm 32:1–5

    b. Isaiah 53:6

    c. John 3:16

    d. Romans 5:1–11

    e. "And the peace of God, which surpasses all understanding, will guard your hearts and your minds in Christ Jesus" (Philippians 4:7).

4. Paul encourages all of us as leaders: "What you have learned and received and heard and seen in me—practice these things, and the God of peace will be with you" (Philippians 4:9). Having been reminded of the peace that is yours through Christ (4:7), put your faith into practice. Write down three to five ideas that will help equip you as a leader in your church.

CHAPTER 2

TESTING MY CONCLUSIONS

The man is ever blessed
    Who shuns the sinners' ways,
Among their counsels never stands,
    Nor takes the scorners' place.

But makes the Law of God
    His study and delight
Amid the labors of the day
    And watches of the night.

He like a tree shall thrive,
    With waters near the root;
Fresh as the leaf his name shall live,
    His works are heav'nly fruit. (*LSB* 705:1–3)

There are many authors who postulate about what makes a church healthy. However, working for more than two decades with church conflict and reconciliation, I have encountered an underlying cause affecting church health that is not recognized by most writers on this topic as foundational. I observed that the health of a congregation is directly related to how richly the Word of Christ abides in her people, especially her leaders.

Paul writes: "Let the word of Christ dwell in you richly, teaching and admonishing one another in all wisdom, singing psalms and hymns and spiritual songs, with thankfulness in your hearts to God" (Colossians 3:16). When the Word of Christ dwells richly within a church's members, they respond to conflict in healthy ways that reflect that indwelling. They respect one another in the midst of disagreement. They reference the Bible when making key decisions. When disputes become heated, they reconcile with one another through confession and forgiveness. They demonstrate spiritual maturity and congregational health.

But what if they don't abide in God's Word? How will that be reflected in their life together? Their responses to conflict are guided more by their sinful nature than their Christ nature. Instead of teaching and admonishing one another in God's wisdom, they apply the wisdom of the sinful nature, tearing one another down and using personal attacks. Instead of talking directly to those with whom they disagree, they gossip and slander. Anger fuels sinful words and actions. Murder takes place in their hearts. Factions form as polarized groups attempt power plays. Self-justification trumps confession and forgiveness.

When working with people from both healthy and unhealthy churches, it doesn't take long to recognize which ones are grounded in God's Word.

Some resources identify "spirituality" or similar characteristics as one of several traits necessary for a healthy church. In contrast, my experiences led me to conclude that spiritual maturity rooted in God's Word is not one of several characteristics but is the most essential quality that correlates to the health of a congregation.

So could my observations be tested by studying healthy churches? Has anyone else made similar observations?

I implemented a qualitative study[3] to learn directly from the pastors of healthy churches.

And I also reviewed an extensive research project on individual spiritual health conducted by Greg Hawkins and Cally Parkinson that I believe supports my findings.

EXAMINING THE HEALTHY

I contacted ten ecclesiastical supervisors from my own church body, The Lutheran Church—Missouri Synod. I chose experienced supervisors who had been in their position for at least a few years, because I felt they would be best qualified to know the churches in their regions.

I described my intent to study healthy churches by interviewing pastors of healthy congregations. I asked the supervisors for two or three names of churches within their districts that they considered healthy.

When asked how I define healthy churches, I advised them to use their own judgment. I wanted to avoid biasing the supervisors with my past experiences.

From the references, I eliminated pastors I knew well. I ended up meeting with pastors from eleven churches, including two from one district. I did this to make certain I talked with at least ten pastors. When I first contacted these pastors, I described the project and indicated that their ecclesiastical supervisor had referred me to them. I met with each one in person at his church. Interviews lasted between one and two hours. I provided the following questions in advance of our meetings:

1. What has been your average worship attendance for the last ten years? What are the trends you have observed in attendance?

2. What are your congregation's total number of baptized and communicant members? Are there any trends you have observed in membership changes over the last ten years?

3. What is the total number of individual adults who regularly attend Bible study during the week? (This may be different from the total attendance of Bible studies throughout the week, since some individuals may attend more than one Bible study, and others may not attend every week but are regularly involved.) Have there been any trends in the attendance over the last few years? How many lay leaders do you have? How many lay leaders are involved in Bible study?

4. Describe your Bible study opportunities, including descriptions of what is done during your Bible studies.

5. Briefly describe your congregation's organizational structure.

6. What do you believe are contributing factors that make your church healthy?

7. What are some of the greatest strengths of your church?

8. Every church encounters conflicts, whether between key leaders or among the membership. Describe a situation involving a serious conflict and how your church responded.

9. If you could change anything in your church, what would it be?

10. What do you hope to do to maintain or improve the spiritual health of your church?

11. Is there anything else you would like to share?

Before and even during the interview, I did not define what I meant by healthy churches. Interestingly, about half of the pastors were surprised that their ecclesiastical supervisor thought of theirs as a healthy church. None of them indicated they were in crisis, but all were well aware of challenges in their own churches. Only a few readily agreed their congregations were healthy.

WHAT I LEARNED

I enjoyed personally meeting the pastors and visiting their church sites. The interviews gave opportunity for open-ended discussions on the joys and challenges of congregational ministry. I welcomed learning how differently these churches served their own members, their communities, and beyond. At the conclusion of each survey, I shared my observations and what I was learning from the project.

I appreciated the diversity among the pastors. Although every pastor demonstrated leadership qualities, each one exhibited unique characteristics. Some were charismatic, others more stoic. Personalities ranged from laid-back to intense. Leadership styles varied from personal involvement in many decisions to limiting direction to big-picture items. Their ages ranged from mid-30s to mid-60s.

The congregations also represented a diverse spectrum. I visited congregations in rural, suburban, and urban settings. Churches ranged from 39 to 157 years old, with an average age of 87. Average weekly worship attendance varied from 95 to 1,300, with the average attendance of 514. Most congregations had experienced numerical growth in attendance over ten years, but a few had plateaued or declined. Worship service styles ranged from traditional to contemporary, with several offering more than one style. Organizational structures for lay leadership included a multiboard system, a structure with only a few boards, and a model led by a single policy-based governance board. (Note: These churches were from one denomination that utilizes a congregational structure where laity and clergy work together in congregational decision-making.)

What Was Not Common

What some writers have identified as characteristics identifying healthy churches were evident in most of the churches. Nevertheless, characteristics some writers claimed were *necessary* were sometimes absent or not articulated by the pastors. I was unable to identity obvious commonality for some of these "necessary" traits, such as attendance growth, visionary senior pastors, a particular governance structure, or a focus on missions.

Take numerical growth, for example. Seven of the eleven churches had experienced growth in their average worship attendance when comparing current attendance to the average of the previous ten years (see Table 1).

TABLE 1

HEALTHY CHURCH SURVEYS

AVERAGE WORSHIP ATTENDANCE

Church	Last 10 years Avg. Worship Attendance	Current Avg. Worship Attendance	Amount of Increase (Decrease)	Percent of Increase (Decrease)
Church 1	152	150	(2)	(1%)
Church 2	438	388	(50)	(11%)
Church 3	99	95	(4)	(4%)
Church 4	292	305	13	4%
Church 5	358	404	46	13%
Church 6	1045	1150	105	10%
Church 7	355	524	169	48%
Church 8	728	625	(103)	(14%)
Church 9	230	245	15	7%
Church 10	449	465	16	4%
Church 11	1280	1300	20	2%
Averages	**493**	**514**	**21**	**4%**

While healthy churches often experience numerical growth, four of the eleven churches I met with had not. And yet, they were identified by their ecclesiastical supervisors as healthy. (After my interviews, I deduced that each of the pastors I met with led churches that I consider to be spiritually mature, healthy churches.)

I acknowledge that attendance statistics may be important indicators. However, statistics alone don't tell the whole story—more questions need to be asked.

As I inquired about the static or declining worship attendance, there were reasonable explanations for those trends. In one case, an economic depression caused by significant loss of jobs in the community resulted in many families moving away. In another church, several families left to join a church plant. In the church with a current average worship attendance declining to ninety-five from the ten-year average of ninety-nine, the pastor reported forty funerals of regular attending members in eight years. Considering those saints who have entered heaven, one could even recognize growth in attendance.

A few pastors (including those with growth in attendance) noted that over the last ten years, people's personal definition for regular worship attendance had decreased from three or four weekends per month to two times per month. This affects average worship attendance but does not necessarily reflect the total number of people considered active in the church.

Other characteristics that did not prove common among these churches include the following:

- **Visionary Senior Pastors**—Some pastors I met would certainly be described as visionary. But I also interviewed a few who would probably not meet the qualifications of those who state that a visionary senior pastor is required for a church to be healthy.

- **Governance**—Some consultants assert that a particular governance structure is necessary in order for a church to be healthy. I am an advocate of having well-defined structure to minimize confusion over roles and authority, but I also believe that one type of structure does not fit all. I observed in this project that the governance structures varied widely—there did not appear to be evidence that would point to a specific governance model as necessary for church health.

- **Mission Focused**—I agree that church members ought to define and support their specific mission. Yet, how these churches defined their missions and how much emphasis was placed on them did not appear to show any specific commonality. Some pastors did not even mention their church's defined mission statement.

- **Style of Worship**—One of the characteristics sometimes referenced as necessary for a healthy congregation is "inspiring worship," but whether a worship service is considered inspirational is a subjective viewpoint difficult to define for everyone. I did not personally attend any worship services of the churches surveyed, so I could not personally attest to this trait. However, the pastors talked about their worship services, and I did learn that their styles of worship varied. I was unable to recognize any trend among them reflecting a specific style of worship (e.g., traditional, blended, or contemporary). Based on what they shared, though, I believed that the subject churches invested significantly in the planning and leading of worship.

A COMMON THEME

While few commonalities emerged, there was a repeating theme offered throughout the interviews without my prodding. Most pastors emphasized the necessity of connecting people with the Bible more than just during worship. The statistics from all the churches supported this trend when contrasted with unhealthy churches suffering from destructive conflicts.

Accurately measuring how many church members regularly study God's Word is problematic. Some people may read the Bible daily or do daily devotions, but they may not attend one of the church's Bible studies. Others may engage the Word through Bible studies not connected with their church.

However, I believe that those who are faithful students of the Word appreciate the importance of participating in Bible study with other believers. A church's Bible study attendance may not capture all who are regularly in God's Word, but it is a measurable indicator that can be compared to other churches'.

Another limitation with using a percentage of adult Bible study compared with worship attendance is the reality that children are part of a church's worship attendance but not adult Bible study. Nevertheless, using a percentage of adult Bible study attendance to worship attendance does provide an indicator that can be used for comparative purposes.

When working with churches I found to be unhealthy, I developed a rule of thumb based on years of observations. I calculate the total number of adults in Bible study divided by the church's average worship attendance. When the total is less than 20 percent, I tend to find that church to be unhealthy, demonstrating spiritual immaturity. Many of the churches where I have worked had percentages less than 10 percent. When our reconciliation teams worked on-site with such congregations, we observed that their members, and especially their leaders, demonstrated biblical illiteracy. The majority struggled when looking up Bible passages, and they displayed ignorance of basic biblical knowledge. They revealed their unfamiliarity with the Bible.

Consider Table 2. Note the percentage of people attending Bible study compared with the average worship attendance.

TABLE 2

HEALTHY CHURCH SURVEYS
BIBLE STUDY ATTENDANCE

Church	Avg. Worship Attendance	Total Adults in Bible Study	% Adults to Avg. Worship
Church 1	150	65	43%
Church 2	388	125	32%
Church 3	95	50	53%
Church 4	305	75	25%
Church 5	404	118	29%
Church 6	1150	600	52%
Church 7	524	275	52%
Church 8	625	200	32%
Church 9	245	85	35%
Church 10	465	199	43%
Church 11	1300	500	38%
Averages	**514**	**208**	**39%**

The churches I surveyed all exceeded my 20 percent rule-of-thumb percentage. Note that among the eleven churches, the percentage ranged from a low of 25 percent to a high of 53 percent, with an average of 39 percent. (The pastors whose churches recorded the lowest percentages admitted Bible study attendance needed addressing. And yet, their percentages still exceeded that of unhealthy churches.)

In Table 3, you can see what percentage of lay leaders attended Bible study.

TABLE 3

HEALTHY CHURCH SURVEYS

Bible Study Attendance among Leaders

Church	Total Number of Elected Leaders	Total Number of Leaders in Bible Study	Percent of Leaders in Bible Study
Church 1	26	8	31%
Church 2	40	28	70%
Church 3	29	10	34%
Church 4	22	20	91%
Church 5	21	17	81%
Church 6	11	8	73%
Church 7	55	41	75%
Church 8	9	9	100%
Church 9	15	13	87%
Church 10	32	26	81%
Church 11	10	10	100%
Averages	**25**	**17**	**75%**

Note that among the leadership, the percentages are even higher, varying from a low of 31 percent to 100 percent, with an average of 75 percent. Nine of the eleven churches surveyed had at least 70 percent of leadership Bible class attendance. (Again, those with lower percentages told me they needed to address that weakness.) Those reporting 100 percent leadership involvement in Bible study require anyone serving in a lay leadership role to regularly attend Bible study in addition to worship. These congregations established biblically sound standards that their church leaders must uphold in order to serve. They have committed themselves to being guided by people who are "full of the Spirit and of wisdom," as the apostles taught in Acts 6:3.

Throughout the surveys, ten of the eleven pastors specifically spoke about the importance of people being in God's Word. In answer to my question "What do you believe are contributing factors that make your church healthy?" pastors replied with a variety of answers: quality staff, gifted laity, focus on relationships within staff and membership, and dealing with conflict or difficult issues openly and in healthy ways. But the most common answer related to their members being in God's Word. Below are some of their replies (comments in brackets are mine):

- [Bible studies tied to] sermons based on one of that week's [Scripture] lessons, with each lesson having daily readings with simple questions (a weekly class covers more)
- Bible.IS [an online program] Bible reading for every day
- Bible study
- The Word of God
- Strong love for God's Word; leading people to walk in His ways (especially among a majority of leadership)
- LifeLight Bible Study Series [an in-depth Bible study from Concordia Publishing House]
- Challenge people (including reading through the Bible for the first time)
- Aggressively working to having people together in Bible study
- During Lent, Bible study attendance grows to 350 [which was 56 percent of their average worship attendance]
- Good pastors in the past who focused on prayer and being in the Word
- Don't dumb down the Word or water it down
- Being in the Word through sermons and Bible study
- Having various options for Bible study.
- Being in the Word

Each church I surveyed offered multiple opportunities for people to participate in Bible study. Options included Sunday morning studies (usually more than one), weekday studies at church and in member homes (times ranging from early morning to evening), Bible studies for special seasons (such as Lent), and personal reading plans or Web-based programs.

Each church offered more than one type of study too. Options included going through books of the Bible verse by verse, topical studies, reading Christian books and comparing them with the Bible, and discussing current events relative to what the Bible says. Some offered intensive studies requiring homework between sessions. A few of the churches designed their own Bible studies to coordinate with a sermon series or the appointed readings for a season. Bible study offerings often ranged from covering basics to in-depth studies, and class sizes varied from a few to more than a hundred.

Some pastors indicated that keeping people engaged in the Word is a never-ending challenge. Unless the pastor and lay leaders make it a priority and regularly encourage Bible study attendance, it can drop off or lose momentum. They shared with me that maintaining or increasing Bible study attendance is possible, but it takes constant effort.

THE CONFLICT TEST

Again, to test the congregation's health, I asked each pastor to complete a scenario: "Every church encounters conflicts, whether between key leaders or among the membership. Describe a situation involving a serious conflict and how your church responded."

I smiled when a few pastors asked if I planned to publish their answers in my book. Because some people think healthy churches shouldn't experience conflict, leaders feel awkward discussing their church conflicts. More important, however, pastors understand that many disputes have aspects that need to remain confidential. I assured them that I would not identify any specifics.

The reality is that every church experiences conflict. It's a given in this world tainted by sin, occupied by sinners, and tempted by Satan.

Moreover, necessary change often causes conflict. Remember, the Gospel itself creates conflict in a world affected by sin (note Jesus' words in Luke 12:49–53). Encouraging people to mature in God's Word will create conflict. Church building programs, changes in budgets, new ministries, closed ministries—all these can give rise to significant disagreements, where people's passions are exposed.

Conflict cannot be categorized as always good or always bad. But conflict is most certainly not neutral. How people respond to conflict reflects their spiritual maturity. The difference between a healthy church and an unhealthy church is not whether it experiences conflict, but rather how the leaders and members respond to conflict.

The serious conflicts shared with me were varied, just as I had experienced in my years as a reconciler. Disputes in the churches I surveyed arose due to various reasons: relocating the church, addressing multiple fund-raising events by the school, removing staff, undertaking a major building project, seeking financial support for a building proposal, planting a church, purchasing an organ, calling a new pastor, dealing with a staff member who struggled with addiction, addressing a church leader guilty of sexual misconduct, debating disagreements over debt, remodeling the sanctuary, addressing staff members involved in an affair, and dealing with members who regularly complained and tried to force change.

Yes, healthy churches can experience conflict! All churches do. The kinds of conflicts described were consistent with my reconciliation experience.

What I wanted to explore was not the details of the conflicts, but rather how leaders and members responded to these stormy events.

These kinds of occurrences can ignite harmful conflict, putting a church into crisis. In unhealthy churches, people respond with denial, unrestrained anger, power plays, resignations, cursing and shouting matches, gossip, withholding offerings, and leaving the church. In some cases, worship attendance dropped by 25, 30, or even 50 percent in just a few weeks. I am aware of churches that have had to close as a result of conflict. In severe cases, people make threats and can get into physical fights on the church property. I know church leaders who have sought restraining orders and church members who have called police for physical protection.

So I was encouraged to learn how leaders and members responded to the conflicts in these healthy churches. A small percentage of people responded in some of the sinful ways described above, but a much different response prevailed overall.

One pastor described an individual who created a lot of strife in the church. At one time, this man could stir up a lot of people and polarize them in a congregational meeting. People used to fear him because he was a bully. He once threatened physical harm to anyone who made changes to certain areas of the church building. But the church grew in its spiritual maturity, learning godly ways of responding. In response to one of his rants, an elder approached the man in private. He invited the man to come to an elder meeting to present his concerns. There, this man was treated with respect, even when the elders disagreed with him. After he left, the elders found ways to show care and love for this man. Others in the congregation acted in similar ways. In our interview, the pastor reported that the man is no longer able to upset large numbers of people.

Another pastor described a conflict over a building project. In congregational meetings, people voiced their differing views with passion, sometimes raising their voices. But when the meetings ended, several of those same people with different views came together to talk—not in anger or with threats, but with care. The pastor would see them laughing together and going out for coffee. He said people had the attitude of "Let's work on this together." He also noted, "They are people of forgiveness."

In one church, husband-and-wife longtime members had earned the reputation of being constant complainers. The couple often tries to spread their negativity and encourage cliques to form. However, because the people, especially the leaders, are spiritually mature, the couple is unable to gain traction or polarize people. How do the members handle them? The pastor says, "We continue to love them. We kill them with kindness. [Our leaders] don't legitimize bad behavior, but they seek to understand their point of view." This example came from a church that had a high percentage of leadership in Bible study.

In another congregation, strong opposing positions arose over changes in the church building. During their meeting, members recognized that there were intense feelings about the proposed changes. Although the bylaws required only a simple majority vote, the people believed they needed to build consensus. They passed a resolution requiring a two-thirds majority for this key decision. When leaders sensed the congregation was not yet ready, they delayed the vote until more unity was achieved. Throughout the process, people were encouraged to ask questions and raise objections. In the end, the final plan was approved by a 90 percent majority. The pastor told me, "Even those who were opposed were happy in the end."

One of my interviewees described a meeting at which people "got mad" as they deliberated two sides to an issue. As pastor, he told them that God could work with either decision they made. He reminded them who they were as children of God. They voted, and a decision was made. He reported that they now honor one another, for once the decision was made, even though there was disagreement, they have respected that decision. He used their conflict as a teaching opportunity, and because his members are spiritually healthy, they have responded to his leading.

One church was debating whether to plant a new church. The proposal would require several members to join the new congregation, meaning their financial contributions would go with them. Some members expressed concern that the sending church could not afford the loss. The church prepared for this major decision by walking through Scripture. People attended several Bible studies to guide them through their issues. The pastor told me, "The Spirit started to work through them." He said their spiritual maturity was reflected in how they treated one another, the mutual respect shown to one another, and that friends remained friends after meetings. It is possible to hold different opinions but still remain together. In the end, no one considered leaving the church. And the pastor also told me that no one approached him to complain about the other side.

In a case involving the infidelity of a well-loved staff member, the pastor described the steps taken to address those directly involved. He mentioned that confidences were protected and only general information was shared more broadly as needed. Many people were sad. Some were devastated. But the pastor indicated there was no gossip because of the way things were handled, and he was unaware of any one leaving the church because of the issue.

These churches responded in remarkably different ways than the churches in crisis I have served. I have witnessed how unhealthy churches deal with the same kinds of issues. The results are drastically different: personal harm to individuals, damage to the church as a body, and undermining the church's public witness. I have attended congregational meetings where opposing groups tried to shout down one another. I worked with a church that continued a controversial congregational meeting until two o'clock in the morning. (And not because they were spending time in the Bible!) I have seen gossip so widespread that it was impossible to ascertain even the most basic facts in a case. I have read emails containing verbal and physical threats. I am aware of innocent leaders whose reputations were so ruined by slander that their careers were ended.

So what's the difference? What prepares a church to deal with its disagreements in a God-pleasing manner? Moreover, what fails to equip a church to address its differences with civility?

Jesus says it plainly:

> I am the vine; you are the branches. Whoever abides in Me and I in him, he it is that bears much fruit, for apart from Me you can do nothing. If anyone does not abide in Me he is thrown away like a branch and withers; and the branches are gathered, thrown into the fire, and burned. If you abide in Me, and My words abide in you, ask whatever you wish, and it will be done for you. By this My Father is glorified, that you bear much fruit and so prove to be My disciples. (John 15:5–8)

ANYTHING ELSE?

When I asked about each church's greatest strengths, one pastor's second response was, "The Word of God is biggest." He added that he didn't want to mention it first because it sounds so cliché. He appeared somewhat apologetic for his thought. But it made me wonder: what would cause a pastor to be reluctant to point to God's Word as a strength? Church leaders often look for the latest psychological theory or management practice to strengthen their church. "Being in God's Word" is rather basic and doesn't sound innovative—it's too simplistic. In addition, the phrase "the church is all about Word and Sacrament ministry" has been used to justify churches that exhibit unhealthy symptoms. Just as this pastor was hesitant to point to the importance of connecting people to God's Word, do many other church leaders feel the same way?

When I asked my closing question of whether there was anything else they would like to share, one pastor reflected on his own needs: "Embrace the Word of God—I need it just as much [as my members]." He also added that he needed to daily apply Acts 6:1–7 to his life: "[I need to] devote myself to the Word and ministry of prayer." He recognized that to lead a spiritually healthy congregation, he, too, needed to focus on his own spiritual health.

Here are some other responses to that final question:

- Expect new members to be involved in worship and in the Word.

- Bible study has grown since I was here.

- We have healthy leaders. Most are in Bible study.

- The more we got people in the Word, the less conflict we experienced.

A HEALTHY WHOLE REQUIRES HEALTHY PARTS

The Bible compares the Church to a body, of which Christ is the Head. Some have described churches as organic institutions, where the congregations reflect attributes that mimic a living person.

Nevertheless, a Christian congregation is not simply a person unto itself. The congregation is comprised of individuals, and if most lack spiritual health, the congregation will not be well. If many members exhibit spiritual maturity, however, the entire church will reflect a corporate maturity. But even if the entire membership lacks spiritual health, if the leadership is spiritually healthy, the church will show signs of spiritual wellness.

For a congregational body to be healthy, its parts must be healthy. Thus, I reviewed with interest a study on individual spiritual growth and maturity—for if being fed regularly by God's Word affects individual spiritual health, then a church composed of spiritually healthy members will reflect that same condition.

UNEXPECTED RESULTS

One of the pastors I interviewed shared a book with me that reported the findings of an extensive research project conducted by Greg Hawkins and Cally Parkinson. Although the researchers were not focused on healthy congregations, they were researching what factors help individual Christians mature in their faith. I found that their conclusions affirm my premise on what makes individual parts of a church spiritually healthy—and, in turn, what affects the health of the congregation as a whole.

In their book *Follow Me: What's Next for You?* Hawkins and Parkinson describe their journey to utilize scientific processes for studying spiritual growth among Christ's followers. They identify what they learned in four years from 157,000 individual surveys representing more than five hundred churches. It was a study of what drives or hampers spiritual growth for individuals, and they say it led them to some unanticipated results.

They began their study by asking what people wanted most from their church. A top answer? To be challenged to grow in one's spiritual life.

As part of their work, they classified people into four groups along a spiritual continuum: Exploring Christ, Growing in Christ, Close to

Christ, and Christ-Centered. For each of the three stages between these four levels, they developed survey methods to determine what factors helped people grow from one level in their spiritual maturity to the next. They measured more than fifty factors—for example, personal activities, organized church activities, and core beliefs. Their intent was to discover which factors were most significant in helping people move from one level of spiritual maturity to the next.

Some of the anticipated outcomes included factors such as regularly attending worship services, meeting in small groups, learning through adult education, serving in a church ministry, participating in mission trips, and praying. But in their final analysis, the researchers drew a surprising conclusion: "Everywhere we turned the data revealed the same truth: spending time in the Bible is hands down the highest impact personal spiritual practice."[4]

They specifically focused on "reflecting on Scripture," which indicates more than a simple reading of a biblical text. "Reflecting on Scripture implies a contemplative process, one of thoughtful and careful deliberation."[5]

Hawkins and Parkinson further describe their findings: "When we threw all fifty-plus catalysts into the mix to assess which top five factors were the most influential catalysts of spiritual growth, reflection on Scripture was the only factor that appeared on all three lists."[6]

The authors assessed that reflection on Scripture was not only the most mentioned factor but also the key factor. "The Bible's influence seems to transcend all other factors—much like vanilla ice cream's popularity dwarfs all other flavors. The Bible is not just the vanilla when we look at personal spiritual practices; it's the vanilla when we look at *everything*."[7]

My personal experience is that churches in conflict demonstrate what happens when reflection on Scripture is not central to the members' individual practices. When they are not regularly reflecting on Scripture, they fail to exhibit the qualities of a mature Christian. Instead, their sinful nature dominates in their responses to conflict. The result? Major hurts to individuals as well as harm to the congregation. Such actions discourage those who are new or weak in the faith and provide a negative witness to those outside the church.

If a church's appointed or elected leaders are among those not in God's Word, the church will lack spiritual health.

I believe that the study described by Hawkins and Parkinson affirmed what I was observing in my work as a reconciler.

WHAT DOES THIS MEAN?

These two studies—my own and that of Hawkins and Parkinson—affirmed my own observations from the past twenty years: spiritually healthy individuals are those who regularly reflect on Scripture and apply it to their daily lives. When a church has a significant number of members, especially leaders, who are spiritually healthy, the church will exhibit spiritual health.

Being in God's Word is not just one of many factors that characterize a healthy church. It is the foundation on which its health is based. Churches whose members are founded upon Christ the Rock, the living Word, are able to weather the storms of conflict. Those who fail to dwell in Christ's Word are like those who built on shifting sand. The storms of conflict will cause great damage.

Without a significant percentage of leaders and members dwelling in the Word, other factors such as a dynamic leadership and growing numbers may be helpful for making a church a viable organization, just as they would for a service organization or a social club. But if a church wants to be healthy, she must be more than just another organization. She must be securely grounded in God's Word—not just by reference, but by practice.

What about churches where biblical illiteracy is widespread? Great news! That kind of illness is curable. The prescription is simple: *get people into the Bible*. God promises His Word will bear fruit (Isaiah 55:10–11).

> Being in God's Word is not just one of many factors that characterize a healthy church. It is the foundation on which its health is based.

Reflection

Reflection

Considering this chapter, discuss the following questions with the leaders in your congregation.

150

1. What has been your average worship attendance for the last ten years? What are the trends you have observed in attendance?

2. What are your congregation's total number of baptized and communicant members? Have you observed any trends in membership changes for the last ten years?

25 – 50 %

3. What is the total number of individual adults who regularly attend Bible study during the week? (This may be different than the total attendance of Bible studies throughout the week, since some individuals may attend more than one Bible study, and others may not attend every week but are regularly involved.) Have there been any trends in the attendance over the last few years?

    a. What percentage of the average worship attendance attends Bible study?

    b. How does your percentage compare with the healthy churches surveyed in this chapter?

4. How many lay leaders do you have? How many lay leaders are involved in Bible study?

    a. What percentage of your leaders are in Bible study?

b. How does your percentage compare with the healthy congregations surveyed in this chapter?

5. List your Bible study opportunities, including descriptions of what is done during each Bible study.

    Identify whether you could offer more studies or variety in studies.

6. Every church encounters conflicts, whether between key leaders or among the membership. Describe a situation involving a serious conflict.

    How did your church leaders and members respond to the situation?

7. Reflecting on this chapter, list some of the obvious indicators of spiritual *wellness* in your church.

8. List the less obvious indicators of spiritual *weakness* in your church.

9. What are you learning about the health of your congregation?

10. If you could change anything in your church, what would it be?

CHAPTER 3

THE UNDERLYING CAUSE

O bless the Lord, my soul,
Nor let His mercies lie
Forgotten in unthankfulness
And without praises die!

'Tis He forgives thy sins;
'Tis He relieves thy pain;
'Tis He that heals thy sicknesses
And makes thee young again. (*LSB* 814:2–3)

Psalm 103 (on which the hymn stanzas above are based) reminds us that healing and vitality flow from our God, beginning with the forgiveness of our sins. Meditating on the Word leads us to praise our God for His many blessings, including the gifts of forgiveness and healing.

Properly discerning the underlying cause for poor health is necessary before advocating what makes a church healthy.

CONTRASTING HEALTHY WITH UNHEALTHY CHURCHES

Healthy churches possess two main characteristics that distinguish them from the unhealthy:

1. Their members, especially the leadership, are regularly engaged in God's Word, as demonstrated by their familiarity with it and their desire to apply it to conflict.

2. Their members, beginning with the leaders, model reconciliation through confession and forgiveness.

Churches are not simply entities with only corporate identities and characteristics—they are composed of individual members. The health of a congregation depends on the health of its membership. The more spiritually mature the members of a church are, especially the leaders, the healthier the church. Churches whose memberships lack spiritual maturity suffer from a number of unhealthy behaviors and practices.

Spiritual health is not always easy to diagnose, though. One can find spiritually mature people in almost any church. Yet, it takes a minimum percentage of people with spiritual maturity to positively influence an entire organization. Having a majority of spiritually mature professional and lay leaders makes a difference, but churches can experience health by having a substantial number of influential members who regularly study God's Word and apply it to their lives.

So how does one diagnose the health of a congregation's members and leaders? Only God truly knows what is in a person's heart. Nevertheless, Jesus teaches that we will recognize spiritually healthy hearts by their fruit.

> For no good tree bears bad fruit, nor again does a bad tree bear good fruit, for each tree is known by its own fruit. For figs are not gathered from thornbushes, nor are grapes picked from a bramble bush. The good person out of the good treasure of his heart produces good, and the evil person out of his evil treasure produces evil, for out of the abundance of the heart his mouth speaks. (Luke 6:43–45)

Additionally, the psalmist distinguishes the wicked from the blessed man. Those who are blessed meditate on God's Word, and thus bear good fruit.

> Blessed is the man
> who walks not in the counsel of the wicked,
> nor stands in the way of sinners,
> nor sits in the seat of scoffers;
> but his delight is in the law of the LORD,
> and on His law he meditates day and night.

He is like a tree
> planted by streams of water
that yields its fruit in its season,
> and its leaf does not wither.
In all that he does, he prospers.
The wicked are not so,
> but are like chaff that the wind drives away. (Psalm 1:1–4)

How many spiritually mature members and leaders does it take to make a church healthy? Scripture does not give us a specific answer. My observation, based on reconciliation experience, has led me to develop a rule-of-thumb measurement—a healthy church has at least 20 percent of its average worship attendance participating in adult Bible study. As the percentage increases, so does the spiritual health of the church. Church health can be described on a spectrum, ranging from very unhealthy and unhealthy, to so-so, to healthy and very healthy. The larger the percentage of members who are biblically illiterate, the more immature the congregation will be and thus more vulnerable to unhealthy practices and conflict that results in crisis. The more people regularly reflect on God's Word, however, the more they will exhibit the fruit of the Spirit. The more the individual members exhibit that fruit, the healthier the church will be.

DIAGRAM 1

RESULTING HEALTH OF CONGREGATION

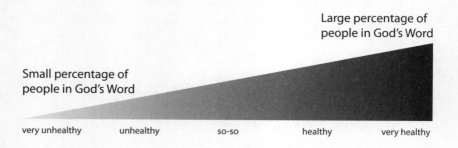

Large percentage of people in God's Word

Small percentage of people in God's Word

| very unhealthy | unhealthy | so-so | healthy | very healthy |

The manner in which congregants respond to conflict reveals their heart and level of spiritual maturity. I have been amazed at how differently churches address their conflicts.

In one church, gossip was so entrenched that their gossip about our reconciliation team reached my office before our team even began its work. It did not take long after arriving on scene to understand why. Their members were biblically illiterate and dealing with their conflict in sinful ways. In meeting with the elders, fewer than half could look up the most familiar books of the Bible. The church council was no better. The leaders obviously were unacquainted with Scripture. Following the worship service in which our team members were introduced, a woman approached me.

"Hi, I'm Connie. And I'm the church's best gossip! But that's okay—because we're all family here."

She was not joking. She was *proud* to crown herself the queen of gossip. She had no concept of what she had just revealed about her own heart. One who prides herself in sin is someone who is unacquainted with the Christ who died for that sin.

Unfortunately, she was not the only one who was unfamiliar with Scripture. The vast majority of people we met, including leaders, were biblically ignorant. Almost no one recognized how their responses to conflict were blatantly sinful. Accordingly, very few appreciated the atoning work of Jesus. We met a small number of people who knew the Bible well. But the number was too small to influence the church as a whole. Under the pressure of conflict, the church's poor health was revealed.

In a contrasting church, I met people who grieved over the moral failing of a staff member. They invited my assistance. As I met with them, the elders and board of directors easily found the Bible verses they were asked to look up. Although several had reacted sinfully to the situation, most were quick to repent. When God's forgiveness was proclaimed, they immediately responded with thanksgiving, confirmed in the way they forgave one another. They were eager to learn how God's Word could direct them in understanding how to balance mercy and

> The manner in which congregants respond to conflict reveals their heart and level of spiritual maturity.

justice. Although one of their leaders had fallen into a moral sin, the church suffered little loss in attendance or offerings. The church, including pastors and lay leaders, led one another to reconciliation by example. We worked with a few people who held on to their bitterness and anger, including one of the council members. Not surprisingly, those with bitterness showed a lack of Bible knowledge. Nonetheless, their negative attitudes did not infect the entire body. Tested in conflict, this church proved to be spiritually healthy.

DIAGNOSIS SIDETRACKS

When diagnosing health problems, one can easily get sidetracked and miss the main cause.

Upon returning home from working abroad in Ukraine, I experienced a growing pain in my back and arm that became disabling. As the pain increased and I lost feeling in my left fingers, I became desperate for relief. Would a therapist help? Could medication reduce inflammation? Should a chiropractor work it out? How could surgery fix it?

My doctor examined me and asked several questions, which I greatly appreciated. But I pressured him for a quick remedy. He suspected what was wrong but suggested further testing. He prescribed medication for temporary relief, but he wanted to look beyond the obvious symptoms to treat the underlying cause.

After a range of tests, he determined that I had ruptured two discs in my lower neck. The damaged discs were pinching the branch of nerves affecting my left shoulder, arm, and hand.

I had not realized I had injured my neck. While working in Ukraine, I was riding in a car and trying to sleep; we were driving through the night and it was a rough ride. The driver often swerved to miss potholes, but the car still violently hit several deep holes. While resting my head against the door window, a few jolts caused my head to hit the frame above. It must have been then that I damaged my neck. The pain increased slowly over a few weeks, especially while trying to sleep on the long flights back home.

Because my doctor didn't jump to a quick diagnosis to recommend immediate treatment, he was able to pinpoint the underlying issue with certainty. Treatment began with a neurologist injecting cortisone directly into the injured spinal cord. Within a few months, the pain was totally gone. Nothing I said or complained about sidetracked my doctor from doing what was most needed for successful diagnosis and treatment.

Reconciliation consultants work with churches that exhibit both healthy and unhealthy practices. It is not always easy to distinguish the underlying cause and what the results of the cause are. Healthy churches often exhibit a range of certain qualities, but such attributes on their own merit do not automatically make a church healthy. Some advocate that a church is healthy because she possesses these positive indicators. Thus, a consultant may reason that if an unhealthy church simply incorporates those characteristics, the church will turn healthy. An incomplete diagnosis of an unhealthy church may sidetrack a consultant, leading him to treat a symptom rather than a cause.

For example, I found a few characteristics that some say define a healthy congregation, but these characteristics may be present in *both healthy and unhealthy churches.* Here are some of those attributes:

- A clearly defined mission
- A well-defined structure as documented in the constitution and bylaws, policies and job descriptions
- Bold, visionary leadership
- Numerical growth (e.g., in membership, attendance, or offerings)
- Inspiring worship

A CLEARLY DEFINED MISSION

Focusing on mission is important. Many churches have lost their zeal for the Gospel or have forgotten why they established a congregation. In response, some consultants claim that defining the congregation's mission and calling it back to its purpose will make it healthy. But defining the mission by itself is not necessarily a sign of health.

I have worked with a number of churches in severe conflict that had defined mission statements.

One church had developed a wonderfully articulated mission. It was displayed throughout the building and repeated frequently in written communications. But the friction among the lay leadership led the frustrated pastor to resign, and many people left. In a few other cases, the pastor's passion for the church's mission became a source of destructive conflict among its members and leaders.

In another church fighting over its Christian school, the reconciliation consultant asked the leaders to describe the school's mission. People readily answered, "Following the Great Commission." The reconciler asked them what that meant. The answers included things such as these:

- We need to provide an alternative to public education!
- We've had a Christian school for one hundred years. The school's our mission!
- We want a private school so we can control what our kids are taught.

When the reconciler asked how the Great Commission was being fulfilled in their school, the answers revealed biblical ignorance. They were unable to describe how the school ministry was connected to the Great Commission in any way. In fact, they failed to describe any mention of Jesus at all! Instead, they focused on the attributes of private education, personal desires, and community pride. They were unified in describing their mission in a simple phrase, but they had no concept of what that phrase meant. As a result, their fight over the school and its funding had virtually nothing to do with the Great Commission. Identifying their mission failed to make them healthy.

Mission *is* important. And helping a congregation rally around a common vision can produce fruit. But a well-articulated mission does not automatically create health in a church.

A Well-Defined Structure

Poorly designed structure and the absence of well-written governing documents—such as the constitution, bylaws, policies, and job descriptions—can cause misunderstandings that lead to conflict. People struggle in a system where responsibilities and authorities are not clearly described in written governing documents. And yet, I have met with some churches that could use significant improvement in these areas but still maintain healthy attitudes toward one another and those outside their church. Amazingly, they seem to operate with mutual trust and without malice, notwithstanding inadequate governing documents. What makes the difference in these churches is their spiritual maturity. They work well together despite their poorly defined organizational structure. (By the way, I'm not justifying their weak systems—just describing how spiritual maturity can overcome other weaknesses.)

On the other hand, I have worked with churches that have invested extensively in well-laid-out structures, including comprehensive bylaws, policies, and job descriptions, yet still respond to conflict in destructive ways. One medium-size church boasted more than a hundred pages of governing documents that laid out its organization with detailed authorities and responsibilities. Yet, the church was being torn apart by its infighting. Her leaders knew almost nothing about the Bible, but they were well structured.

Well-organized structure *is* important. Nevertheless, good structure does not necessarily make a church healthy.

Bold, Visionary Leadership

If a church engages a bold, visionary leader, it will be healthy. At least that's what some advocate.

Certainly, visionaries can be inspiring and motivate people to new heights. Nonetheless, a visionary leader cannot supplant what God's Word alone can do. For it is the Word of God that transforms the hearts of people. As God's people engage themselves in His Word, His Spirit dwells within them.

Note how many examples are given in the Scriptures of leaders who would fail the tests of a visionary leader in the understanding of our world today. Moses did not develop his own vision of freeing the children of Israel from Pharaoh's oppression. On the contrary, he tried to talk his way out of the job. Which of the twelve disciples would pass the test of a visionary leader without God's Word?

Rather than appointing the most visionary leader (from a worldly point of view), God often chose the meek, even the lowly in society, to lead His people. Consider Esther or Abigail. Or the shepherd boy David.

A reconciliation team was invited to work with a congregation led by an energetic leader who personified the definition of a bold, visionary leader. He intentionally studied leadership practices in preparation to serve as the senior pastor. He inspired the congregation with his vision for growing the church and pressed forward with his initiatives. When members expressed concern over the way in which he was achieving goals in growing numbers, he told them to find another church and quoted a phrase from one of his management books: "You need to get off the bus." An increasing number of members began leaving the church, but the church council supported him because more people were joining than leaving and church finances were growing. The church's bottom-line statistics proved their pastor's success.

The elders, with whom he had developed close relationships, began to confront their pastor with Scripture, reminding him that a shepherd was to seek after those leaving the flock, not encourage them to get out. Tensions between the once-close spiritual leaders grew until the elders all resigned.

Visionary leadership *can be* important. However, unless that visionary leader is firmly grounded in God's Word, and unless the people following the leader test his message against that Word, it will fail to make a church healthy.

Numerical Growth

Many consultants base and evaluate a church's health by numerical growth in membership, attendance, or offerings. Numerical growth often is equated with church health. Actually, healthy churches frequently experience growth in numbers. That's because Christians who are nourished in God's Word and cultivate lifestyles of reconciliation bear fruit consistent with living in Christ. These people give positive witness to Jesus in their daily lives, especially by how they live. As a result, they attract others, increasing membership and attendance. Those who devote themselves to the study of God's Word commit themselves to first-fruit giving. Accordingly, as attendance increases, church offerings grow.

However, I remember a few churches that showed growth in all their essential numbers, but their leaders exhibited spiritual immaturity and a lack of biblical knowledge. Their growth may have been built upon a charismatic leader, a friendly culture, inspirational worship, ministries recognized for meeting special needs, or a beautiful building and furnishings. They may have been located in a fast-growing community. (By the way, these things in and of themselves may be great blessings!) But when major conflict erupted, such as a dispute over leadership or the moral failing of a leader, the church quickly became divided. Gossip and slander replaced care for one another. Major splits occurred. These financially strong churches suddenly found themselves in economic crisis. What once seemed healthy and strong can fall apart quickly under stress if it lacks a healthy foundation. Like a magnificent house built on shifting sand, the storms of conflict bring it down.

On the other hand, I have met people from healthy churches where their attendance, offerings, and membership may be static or even declining. Despite these statistics, they demonstrated their spiritual maturity in the way they cared for one another, ministered to people outside the church, and shared their faith with others.

Numerical growth *is* an important blessing of God that may result from a healthy church. Static or declining numbers should not be ignored, as they *may* indicate signs of poor health. But numerical growth alone does not prove a church is healthy, just as a decline in such numbers does not prove a church is unhealthy.

Inspiring Worship

One of the characteristics required for a healthy church, according to some, is inspiring worship services. The worship service is the place where a congregation is most visibly brought together. As one who travels extensively and worships in many churches, I can attest to the importance of the worship service. A poorly led worship service negatively affects the life of the congregation.

Nevertheless, how one defines "inspiring worship" varies significantly, depending on whom you ask.

I have attended worship services in churches that provide extremely well-led worship services. They may feature exceptional preaching, inspiring music and other arts, biblically faithful content throughout, people actively participating and not just spectating, and so on. But some of those same churches suffered severe crises that resulted in church splits or major losses of members, attendance, and finances. As we met with both leaders and members, the underlying cause was not lack of inspirational worship but rather spiritual immaturity. In such churches, too many leaders and members lacked the spiritual depth that comes from dwelling in Christ's Word more than just sixty minutes in worship on the weekend.

The corporate worship of congregations *is* important. Carefully planned and led worship services that are faithful to God's teaching are where God comes to His people through Word and Sacrament and they respond in praise and adoration. However, inspirational worship services by themselves do not indicate whether a church is healthy.

Having All These Qualities

What if a church has not just one or two of the qualities listed above but has all of them? Will that make it healthy?

One can list several qualities that characterize healthy churches, and many healthy congregations possess these qualities. I agree these qualities can be beneficial.

Sadly, I have met with unhealthy congregations that possessed all these qualities and more. At first glance, these churches were shining stars. They appeared to have it all—visionary leader, well-articulated mission, well-defined and efficient organization, inspirational worship, numerical growth, and more. But when a major storm of conflict erupted, the church revealed its weak spiritual condition as it fell apart.

I recall a church that was known for its successes. The senior pastor received acclamation for his church's accomplishments. The church built a huge new sanctuary to accommodate the growth in worship attendance. Staff were added to serve the expanding membership. New ministries were established to care for people within the church and out in the community. People came from across the country to learn how this church achieved such triumphs. It was viewed as the ultimate model of a successful, healthy church.

But when conflict came, the church's proud veneer cracked. In a matter of weeks, their worship attendance dropped by more than one-third. Many staff members resigned. Lay leaders walked away. The associate pastor led former staff and church members in establishing a new church nearby. They called it a mission plant from their former church, though the mother church never acknowledged them. The remaining faithful were in shock.

At one time, this church had been known for its biblical teaching. Leaders and members knew God's Word because they were committed to studying it. But over the years, other areas took precedence. By the time the conflict erupted, many had neglected regular study of the Word. Staff and lay leaders had bought into worldly means to achieve new heights. Instead of looking primarily to God's Word for direction, leaders put more faith into psychological philosophies and new organizational concepts. They still reflected characteristics of a healthy church, but they were no longer grounded upon the Rock. The storm of conflict revealed that the church was built on shifting sand.

The people responded quickly to biblical teaching. They once again increased dependence upon Christ and His Word and less upon their visionary leader or other attractive traits. Their journey to restored health began again.

SPIRITUAL MATURITY IN OTHER CULTURES

I have witnessed this dynamic not only in American churches but also in churches in other countries and cultures. In India, the church leaders with the most serious conflicts were those who were not regularly studying God's Word. This was in spite of the fact that Indian Christians showed great respect for the Bible. However, when it came to knowing the Word well and applying it, those in the most severe conflicts revealed biblical ignorance and resisted guidance from Scripture. Instead, leaders within factions fought with legal action and power struggles to get what they wanted.

In Africa, I observed that Christians held God's Word in high regard. Yet, cultural norms and long-term tribal wars would often dominate unless the people were committed to Bible study and regular devotions. Because of their high regard for the Bible, when they were shown what God's Word taught concerning their situation, they responded immediately. I witnessed tribes set aside centuries of cultural norms to practice confession and forgiveness.

In Ukraine, churches that suffered from severe conflicts were those whose people did not depend on the Bible for addressing their issues; rather, they relied upon the societal norms that remained from years as part of the Soviet Union. Some of the techniques I observed included staunch denial, demonstrations of power and threats, quiet undermining of reputations, and insiders who "report" (or spy) on opponents. Ukrainian churches with more people in Bible study dealt with their disagreements with greater spiritual maturity and overcame what had been normalized from the past.

As I met with leaders in South America, it become obvious that the more people were in God's Word, the more spiritually mature they were and the healthier their churches.

Working with churches in Canada, I saw these same principles at work. Australian churches and schools exhibited similar patterns, as well as Korean churches here in the United States and in Canada. The healthiest churches were those in which the people knew God's Word and applied God's Word to themselves.

THE FINAL AUTHORITY

Should we be surprised that a common thread for spiritual maturity across all cultures is directly related to abiding in God's Word? The Bible attests to its own power.

> Your word is a lamp to my feet and a light to my path. (Psalm 119:105)

> But [Jesus] said, "Blessed rather are those who hear the word of God and keep it!" (Luke 11:28)

> And now I commend you to God and to the word of His grace, which is able to build you up and to give you the inheritance among all those who are sanctified. (Acts 20:32)

> I write to you, young men, because you are strong, and the word of God abides in you, and you have overcome the evil one. (1 John 2:14)

More important than personal observations or surveys are what the Scriptures teach. God's Word instructs us. We are called to be grounded in God's Word so that we can fight the spiritual battles of this life, cultivate lifestyles of reconciliation, and serve in the mission of our Lord. The Means of Grace, Word and Sacrament, nourish us and equip us for the spiritual battles to come.

Paul admonishes us to forgive one another and abide in God's Word:

> Put on then, as God's chosen ones, holy and beloved, compassionate hearts, kindness, humility, meekness, and patience, bearing with one another and, if one has a complaint against another, forgiving each other; as the Lord has forgiven you, so you also must forgive. And above all these put on love, which binds everything together in perfect harmony. And let the peace of Christ rule in your hearts, to which indeed you were called in one body. And be thankful. Let the word of Christ dwell in you richly, teaching and admonishing one another in all wisdom, singing psalms and hymns

We are called to be grounded in God's Word so that we can fight the spiritual battles of this life, cultivate lifestyles of reconciliation, and serve in the mission of our Lord.

and spiritual songs, with thankfulness in your hearts to God. (Colossians 3:12–16)

Paul mentored the young pastor Timothy:

But as for you, continue in what you have learned and have firmly believed, knowing from whom you learned it and how from childhood you have been acquainted with the sacred writings, which are able to make you wise for salvation through faith in Christ Jesus. All Scripture is breathed out by God and profitable for teaching, for reproof, for correction, and for training in righteousness, that the man of God may be complete, equipped for every good work. (2 Timothy 3:14–17)

Those rooted in God's Word recall their identity as children of God:

For as many of you as were baptized into Christ have put on Christ. There is neither Jew nor Greek, there is neither slave nor free, there is no male and female, for you are all one in Christ Jesus. And if you are Christ's, then you are Abraham's offspring, heirs according to promise. (Galatians 3:27–29)

We are nourished in the Lord's Supper, remembering Christ's sacrifice for us, proclaiming His death until He comes.

For I received from the Lord what I also delivered to you, that the Lord Jesus on the night when He was betrayed took bread, and when He had given thanks, He broke it, and said, "This is My body, which is for you. Do this in remembrance of Me." In the same way also He took the cup, after supper, saying, "This cup is the new covenant in My blood. Do this, as often as you drink it, in remembrance of Me." For as often as you eat this bread and drink the cup, you proclaim the Lord's death until He comes. (1 Corinthians 11:23–26)

God's people trust Christ's forgiveness in relationships. We view one another not just as members of the same club, but rather as new creations, related by Christ's blood as brothers and sisters, reconciled to God.

From now on, therefore, we regard no one according to the flesh. Even though we once regarded Christ according to the flesh, we regard Him thus no longer. Therefore, if anyone is in Christ, he is a new creation. The old has passed away; behold, the new has come. All this is from God, who through Christ reconciled us to Himself and gave us the ministry of reconciliation; that is, in Christ God was reconciling the world to Himself, not counting their trespasses against them, and entrusting to us the message of reconciliation. (2 Corinthians 5:16–19)

Peter challenges his readers to set aside sinful behavior and instead mature as believers:

So put away all malice and all deceit and hypocrisy and envy and all slander. Like newborn infants, long for the pure spiritual milk, that by it you may grow up into salvation—if indeed you have tasted that the Lord is good. (1 Peter 2:1–3)

The Bible asserts that our spiritual growth and health depends on our connection to Christ through His Word. Those who dwell richly in that Word demonstrate spiritual maturity and health, individually and corporately. The Bible is our final authority on what makes a church healthy.

When our hearts place their trust or affection in anything else more than God and His Word, we are guilty of false worship. The underlying cause of our spiritual sickness is revealed—we are struggling with spiritual heart disease.

Reflection

Reflection

Considering this chapter, discuss the following questions with the leaders in your congregation.

1. Although the following characteristics do not in themselves define whether a congregation is healthy, they may prove beneficial. Which ones describe your congregation?

   a. We have developed and communicated a clearly defined mission.

   b. We maintain a well-organized structure as documented in the constitution and bylaws, policies, and job descriptions.

   c. We benefit from bold, visionary leadership.

   d. We are experiencing numerical growth (e.g., in membership, attendance, or offerings).

   e. We offer inspiring worship services.

2. Which of the above characteristics do you believe are important for your congregation?

   In which areas do you think your congregation should improve?

3. Review the following Bible passages listed from this chapter. Which of them impacted you the most? Why?

a. Psalm 1:1–4

b. Psalm 119:105 – P 69

c. Luke 11:28

d. Acts 20:32

e. 1 John 2:14

f. Colossians 3:12–16

g. 2 Timothy 3:14–17

h. 1 Peter 2:1–3

4. Place your congregation on the sliding scale in Diagram 1. How satisfied are you with where your congregation is on this scale? Discuss.

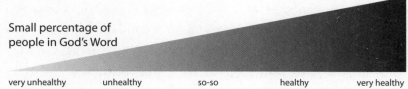

Large percentage of people in God's Word

Small percentage of people in God's Word

| very unhealthy | unhealthy | so-so | healthy | very healthy |

5. What do you think would improve the health of your congregation more than any other factor? Why?

6. If you desire to increase the number of people engaged in God's Word, with which leaders should you first discuss your ideas?

CHAPTER 4

IDOLATRY: SPIRITUAL HEART DISEASE

> Jesus, grant that balm and healing
> In Your holy wounds I find,
> Ev'ry hour that I am feeling
> Pains of body and of mind.
> Should some evil thought within
> Tempt my treach'rous heart to sin,
> Show the peril, and from sinning
> Keep me from its first beginning. (*LSB* 421:1)

What causes conflict among God's people? Misunderstandings can lead to confusion, which then results in conflict. Differences in viewpoints, gifts, backgrounds, and values can create friction in relationships. As people compete for limited resources, clashes can arise. Many factors contribute to our disputes.

James identifies the underlying source of conflict:

> What causes quarrels and what causes fights among you? Is it not this, that your passions are at war within you? You desire and do not have, so you murder. You covet and cannot obtain, so you fight and quarrel. You do not have, because you do not ask. You ask and do not receive, because you ask wrongly, to spend it on your passions. (4:1–3)

Not all passions are sinful. But when we demand that our desires be satisfied, whatever the cost, conflict results. Such passions wage war between the saint and sinner natures in our heart. Selfish gratification puts us at odds with God and with others.

Spiritual heart disease evidences itself when we are willing to sin to satisfy our wants.

A FIRST COMMANDMENT ISSUE

Conflict ultimately reveals the false gods of our hearts. It happens when we don't get what we want.

Conflict ultimately reveals the false gods of our hearts.

Case Study: First Church

Consider First Church in a small town. A fight arose over whether the church should continue operating its Christian school. The school had been struggling financially for years. Enrollment had waned, meaning that tuition income had dropped while expenses increased. School supporters desperately wanted the school to continue operating without reducing staff. Those opposed pointed out that the church could no longer afford to subsidize the school's losses. After much heated debate, the congregation decided by a narrow margin that it would allow the school to remain open for the next year, provided sufficient funds could be raised by a certain deadline.

Sheila cherished the school because of how her son was benefiting from it. During the decision-making process, she had become so anxious that she could not sleep for nights. Without talking to anyone from church or school leadership, she sent out a mass mailing to the entire community (more than just the church), trying to encourage support for the school. Her letter declared that God directed First Church to keep the school open. People needed to give generously because it was God's will, meaning she was judging those who were opposed to keeping the school open as going against His will. Imagine the firestorm her letter sparked!

Was her desire inherently wrong? No. But in her heart, she determined to do whatever it took to get what she wanted. She sinned against God and others to save a precious ministry. She failed to check with those in leadership before acting. God instructs us to respect those in authority, which He instituted (Romans 13:1–2). She declared that she knew God's will, exhibiting sinful pride and judging anyone who disagreed with her as living contrary to God's will (James 4:11–12). She failed to trust God, and used her own wisdom to try to get her way (Proverbs 3:5–8). Her letter discredited the public witness of the church by writing to the community, including some who were likely unchurched (1 Peter 2:12).

Her spiritual heart disease was revealed. The school had become a false god for her. She was willing to use sinful means to satisfy her passions. Her unauthorized attempts to encourage people to support the school could have resulted in upsetting people to the point that those opposed to the school would have even more reason to argue for closing it.

In his Small Catechism, Luther explains the First Commandment, "You shall have no other gods," saying, "We should fear, love, and trust in God above all things." Anytime we fear someone or something more than God, love someone or something more than God, or trust someone or something more than God, we are guilty of idolatry. We have a false god. Our heart has replaced the true God with a false one. We have spiritual heart disease. If left untreated, it can result in serious harm to ourselves and others.

Reflecting on the First Commandment, we'll focus on three kinds of spiritual heart disease that are revealed in conflict—the idols of fears, cravings, and misplaced trust.[8]

FEARS

The first kind of spiritual heart disease is idolatrous fear. These fears reveal themselves when we experience anxiety or desperation over losing something precious. When we express, "I'm afraid that _____," what fills the blank may be an idolatrous fear.

In the illustration about the church/school conflict, Sheila was afraid the school might close. Instead of fearing God above all things, she feared losing the school more. She became so desperate to keep the school open that she was willing to employ sinful means to get her way. Sheila's underlying false god was revealed—she worshiped the school.

Not all fears are idolatrous. God expects us to be vigilant to avoid danger. Fear can serve a godly purpose. But when that fear becomes so great that we sin to protect something we perceive as precious, we cross the line. We are no longing fearing God above all things. That fear has evolved into an idol.

Consider fears that can develop into false gods, such as these:

- Losing one's job or status
- Losing financial security
- Losing a home
- Failure
- Change

Notice that each of the above items may be appropriate concerns for a conscientious person. But should one become so fearful that it leads one to employ sinful means, the fear becomes an idol.

A common idolatrous fear is specifically identified in Proverbs 29:25: "The fear of man lays a snare, but whoever trusts in the LORD is safe."

Two kinds of fear are contrasted here: the fear of the Lord (whoever trusts in the Lord is safe) and the fear of man (whoever fears people more than God). A theme throughout Proverbs emphasizes that the fear of the Lord is the beginning of wisdom.

The fear of man, however, is described as a trap. This fear is being overly concerned about what others think. It is proper to be concerned about how you present yourself to others, especially in how you affect them. But when your fear of people's thoughts about you overshadows your fear of God, you have crossed the line into idolatry.

"People-pleasing," "peer pressure," and "codependency" are terms that describe the fear of man. When we transgress against God's laws to gain favor with others, we are guilty of the fear of man. How often have most of us struggled with this idol of the heart? The fear of man correlates to our pride as we attempt to make ourselves look good before others.

To help uncover idolatrous fears of the heart, ask these questions:

- What do you want to preserve or avoid at almost any cost?
- In this situation, what or whom do you fear most of all?

The idols we fear require sacrifice. False gods always demand sacrifice. In protecting her fear, Sheila sacrificed her integrity and reputation, her relationships with the people in her church, respect from her leaders, and her public witness to Christ.

Most important, note the ironic tragedy of idolatry. Left unchecked, idolatry results in destruction or death—of the idol and/or the person worshiping it.

That's the consequence of believing Satan's lies. The deceiver tempts us with the alluring promise that if we worship this false god, we will be happy, secure, and fulfilled. But the truth is that the end result of idolatry is death.

In the case study above, should Sheila have continued to serve her idol and refuse to repent of her sinful ways? Her pursuits to save the school were sure to inflame conflict. People might have become so angry that the majority decided to close the school. Then the very idol she meant to serve would have been destroyed. Those whose idols are destroyed may lose more. They are often devastated, which can lead to depression, anger, and bitterness; in Sheila's case, she could possibly have left the church. If she continued down this path, she could have lost her soul. Unchecked idolatry leads to death.

During the economic depression beginning in 2008, the news media reported about a man who had built his own home but was losing it in foreclosure. He feared someone else would benefit from his hard labor. So he burned his house to protect his fear. Of course, his criminal action led to consequences, including imprisonment. His idolatry led to destruction of both the home and his freedom.

In another news report, a woman feared losing her home in foreclosure. She could not face the shame of such a loss (fear of man). So she hung herself in her house. Her home and her pride had become more important to her than life itself.

Not all fears have such dramatic results. But this kind of spiritual heart disease motivates people to sin in ways that wound themselves as well as others.

CRAVINGS

The second kind of spiritual heart disease is identified in the Bible as selfish desires, passions, or lusts—cravings. This idol begins as a desire and is elevated into a demand.

For example, Paul identifies a familiar craving:

> But godliness with contentment is great gain, for we brought nothing into the world, and we cannot take anything out of the world. But if we have food and clothing, with these we will be content. But those who desire to be rich fall into temptation, into a snare, into many senseless and harmful desires that plunge people into ruin and destruction. For the love of money is a root of all kinds of evils. It is through this craving that some have wandered away from the faith and pierced themselves with many pangs. (1 Timothy 6:6–10)

Notice that Paul describes the potential danger of clinging to this idol—wandering away from the faith and suffering from self-inflicted pain. Untreated spiritual heart disease results in death.

Those who demand what they want, rather than trust God for His provision, seek to serve themselves above all else. The idol takes hold of their heart.

The completion of the statement "Look, all I want is _____" may identify one's idol. It reveals what passion is driving one's behavior.

Cravings abound in our world, and many relate to idolatrous fears. Here are just a few examples of desires that can be elevated into demands:

- Financial security (related to fear of losing financial security)
- Good reputation (another aspect of fear of man)
- Happy marriage or successful children (linked to a fear of an unhappy marriage or children who fail to meet expectations)
- Money or material possessions (related to the fear of losing them)

Addictions are also a form of cravings. Such cravings can include alcohol or drugs, sexual activity, unrestrained use of the Internet for entertainment, unrestrained buying, and work. Some addictions have physiological factors that affect the craving, but they also represent a spiritual issue.

Cravings may be uncovered through these questions:

- What do you find yourself thinking about much of the time? (Or what keeps you awake at night, perhaps for a few nights in a row?)

- What causes you the most worry? How has your anxiety replaced your trust in God?

- Fill in the blank: If only _____, then I would be happy, fulfilled, and secure. What does this suggest to you about your trust in God for what you desire?

- When a certain desire or expectation is not met, do you feel frustration, resentment, bitterness, or anger?

- To fulfill your passion, what have you done—or what are you planning to do—that is not pleasing to God?

For Christians, many of the people or things we desire are good gifts from God intended to bless us. But when we love the created more than the Creator, we worship false gods.

In one church I visited, the fight was over money—not because finances were lacking, but because of abundance. The church received a substantial inheritance. The conflict arose because the members could not agree on how to spend the money. Several advocated for their favorite missions. Many disagreed over whether they should support local or foreign missions. Others demanded they pay off debts. Some pushed for unnecessary remodeling projects for their building. Factions feared they might not get their way, so they hired lawyers. The costs of litigation used up the entire inheritance. The church fell apart and closed. Competing cravings drove them to self-destruct.

Just as with fears, the cravings we worship demand sacrifice. The people sacrificed so much to get what they wanted. They sacrificed their witness to Christ, their personal integrity, and the gifts God gave them. And in the end, they lost it all.

MISPLACED TRUST

A third kind of spiritual heart disease is misplaced trust. Instead of trusting God above all things, we place more trust in people or things when we follow this idol. One of the most popular objects of misplaced trust is one's self (see Proverbs 3:5–7). We trust our own judgments, experiences, education, and personal thoughts more than what God teaches. We minimize others' views. Pride fuels this idol. We anoint ourselves god (James 4:11–12).

The result?

We sinfully judge anyone who doesn't measure up. In other words, we condemn those who don't agree with us or help us get what we want.

People struggling with this idol often come across as condescending, and the most common fruit of this idol is gossip.

We recognize gossip as breaking the commandment "You shall not give false testimony against your neighbor." But first and foremost, it is a sin against the First Commandment, "You shall have no other gods."

When we gossip, we essentially set ourselves up as gods. We know what's best. We judge and condemn those who don't meet our expectations. We punish them by undermining their reputations. We seek to make ourselves look better by tearing them down. I have a god, and its name is me!

Gossip is idolatry. It is the idol of misplaced trust.

Misplaced trust can also occur as we place more trust in anything other than God. Examples include things such as financial security, reputation, and hard work. We may place more trust in a person than God. The phrase "I idolize her" aptly describes what happens. When trust is centered more in people or things than in God, we set ourselves up for potential disaster.

Here are some questions to help identify misplaced trust, especially in ourselves:

- How are your expectations of the other person magnifying your demands on him or her and your disappointment in that person's failure to meet your desires?

- How are you judging the other person when your expectations are not met?

- How are you getting even with the other person when your desires are not fulfilled?

- How have you communicated to the other person what you feel he or she must do?

- How have you threatened the other person?

Case Study: My Personal Experience in Misplaced Trust

It's frightening how easily I am tempted by misplaced trust in myself.

My best friend, Dave, and I invested in income properties, including an office building. Dave informed me that he had just leased one of our small spaces. I became concerned when Dave told me the new tenant was opening a new business.

A few years earlier, I had leased a large commercial property to a Christian businessman who was starting a new venture. After a two-month period of free rent, he was to begin paying rent. But he never paid any rent, which led to a long, drawn-out battle to get him removed from the property. We went to court twice and were headed there a third time when he suggested we use Christian mediation to settle the dispute. Eventually, I agreed. After a year of legal battles, we reconciled our relationship and resolved the financial dispute in two weekends with the help of Christian mediators. The miracle of this reconciliation led me to later leave the business world to work full time in reconciliation work. But I was left with a fear that had become an idol. From my idolatrous fear, I progressed to misplaced trust.

I questioned Dave on how he qualified this new tenant.

"Did you get a credit report on the guy?" (I had failed to do that in my earlier situation.)

"No, but I checked his references. He seems like a good risk to me."

"Did you get a report of any unpaid judgments against him?" With the other tenant, I had not done this. If I had, I would have learned he had been successfully sued seventeen times before our agreement and had not yet paid off those debts. Obviously, I should never have signed the lease with him.

"No, Ted. We've never done that on this little building."

Passion showed in my voice. "I can't believe you, Dave. Didn't you learn anything from my experience? Didn't I tell you I ended up spending $100,000 in legal fees because I hadn't checked out a bad tenant? Sure, we eventually resolved our case in mediation, but it was a disaster for more than a year. I can't believe you are so irresponsible!"

Dave and I often argued with each other in reaching a decision. But this time, he got red in the face, he started trembling, and he turned around and walked out on me.

How dare he walk out on me, I thought. What's the matter with Dave, anyway?

Was it right for me to question my partner about qualifying a new tenant? Of course. That's good stewardship. Did I do anything wrong in my questioning him? Of course.

My attitude and words manifested my pride. I expected Dave to have learned from *my* great knowledge, *my* learned experiences, *my* proven wisdom. And since he didn't learn from that, I declared my friend irresponsible. I trusted my own accomplishments, using my sharp tongue to set myself up as judge over my friend.

Luther's description of idolatry from his Large Catechism convicts people such as myself.

> So, too, whoever trusts and boasts that he has great skill, prudence, power, favor, friendship, and honor also has a god. But it is not the true and only God. This truth reappears when you notice how arrogant, secure, and proud people are because of such possessions, and how despondent they are when the possessions no longer exist or are withdrawn. Therefore, I repeat that the chief explanation of this point is that to "have a god" is to have something in which the heart entirely trusts. (I 10)

In my spiritual heart disease, I entrusted my heart to me. How irresponsible is that!

Unlike fears and cravings, this idol requires more than sacrifice—it demands an execution. On the altar of my pride, I executed my friend Dave.

What made this scene even worse is that I belittled him in front of his secretary, whom I knew well. She was taken aback at my disrespect and arrogance. She felt awkward being caught in the middle.

I went back to my office to sulk, but God's Spirit worked on my diseased heart. I began to see the real problem. What's the matter with Dave? No—what's the matter with Ted?

What have I done? Who am I to judge? Dave has signed many more sound leases than I have. Dave supported me when I was in financial hardship. He covered my share of partnership expenses without ever hounding me for payment. Who supported me in my trials? Who really is the irresponsible one here?

I approached my Christian brother to confess my sin. Immediately, Dave forgave me, showing which of us demonstrated more spiritual maturity that day. I also confessed my sin to Dave's secretary. She also forgave me. My confession and their forgiveness brought healing to the offenses caused by my idolatry.

So many churches suffer when misplaced trust brings about destruction and injury. Proud of his own successful business career, one lay leader treated his pastor as his own employee. When the pastor didn't meet his expectations, he was quick to point out that just like his own employees, the pastor ought to remember who pays his salary. The lay leader didn't trust God's wisdom but instead trusted his expertise as a business owner.

In another situation, a pastor openly criticized his church in front of other pastors and people in town. He judged his members as worthless and ignorant because they did not meet his standards of a faithful flock. He thought he deserved better. He refused to meet with the leaders in mediation but instead continued to rule over his dominion by intimidation. He used sermons to shame people, and he treated the church staff terribly. Those who worked closely with him feared retribution, so they tried to appease him, hoping someone would soon rescue them.

Another congregation suffered from a different form of misplaced trust. They needed help in their conflict but felt they could not afford the fee for four hundred hours of reconciliation assistance. They had more than ten times the fee amount in unrestricted savings, but they refused to access that fund. Many years prior, they had struggled to pay bills. It took them eight years to repay old debts and build up a safety net. Never mind that conflict was tearing the place apart and people were leaving again. It's not that bad, the leaders determined. They survived the last conflict, even when a large group left. They would do it again. They trusted their own abilities and past achievements: "All we have to do is put our mind to it. Besides, we have enough in savings to weather the storm." Their security was in their bank account.

Misplaced trust is an ugly false god.

THE DEVELOPMENT OF AN IDOL[9]

Spiritual heart disease can be deceiving. One may appear spiritually healthy as long as one is not tested. But as a person neglects God's Word and depends more on worldly wisdom than godly wisdom, a silent disease undermines the person's health.

The same dynamic applies to congregations. Conflict reveals true health—or the lack of it. Idols of the corporate body become exposed when conflict tests the spiritually immature.

Idolatry usually catches us by surprise too. It may begin with a reasonable apprehension, a godly desire for His blessings, or an appropriate trust in someone. But when we elevate that fear, desire, or trust into a demand, we begin to slide down a slippery slope.

DIAGRAM 2

THE DEVELOPMENT OF AN IDOL

Fear
Desire
Trust
Demand
Unmet expectations
Frustrations
Judge
Punish

End Result:
Destruction or Death

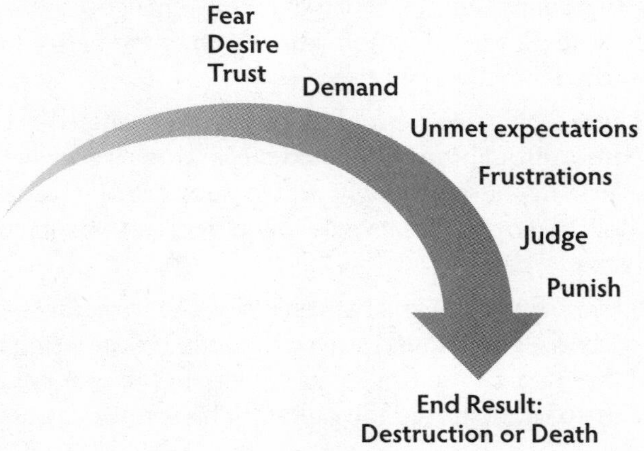

If demands are not fulfilled, unmet expectations lead to frustration or outright anger. Next, we sinfully judge those who prevent us from getting what we expect. We punish them with angry words, the silent treatment, or gossip. If left unchecked, the idolatry results in destruction or death of the idol and/or the person worshiping it.

Holidays have a way of bringing out the worst in families. And that includes church families.

Case Study: Holiday Stress

When the new pastor arrived in January, the congregation welcomed him warmly. But when he began to change long-cherished practices, they began to turn against him. Tensions grew between the pastor and the elders. The last straw came at Christmas. The church had a long tradition of decorating the sanctuary in early December with extensive trimmings, including twelve huge banners that reached from the high ceiling to the floor. Four banners were hung behind the altar, and four banners were hung on each side of the sanctuary. The pastor believed the decorations were gaudy and detracted from the worship of the Christ Child. He especially resented the banners behind the altar that covered the large stained glass window of Jesus. Throughout December, the pastor and the elders had several arguments about the decorations. The Saturday night before Christmas, the pastor and a couple of his friends removed all the banners, placing them around the fellowship hall. Too long for the walls, the lower third of the banners lay on the floor. When people came for worship on Sunday morning, they were shocked. The elders were outraged. That afternoon, the elders rehung the banners in the sanctuary. They changed the locks on the church to keep the pastor out. A note addressed to the pastor taped to the front door warned him to not interfere again.

On Monday morning, the pastor found their note when his key wouldn't work. He peered through the side windows and realized what had been done. He called anyone he thought would support him, reporting what those evil elders had done. Meanwhile, the elders were contacting the old guard to rally the forces.

Christmas Eve service began at seven o'clock Wednesday evening. The church was packed. People loved seeing the little children sing their songs and play out the parts of the Christmas nativity as the older children read from Luke 2. The pastor entered the pulpit for his sermon, stood quiet for a moment, and then said, "I can't do this." He stepped down and walked out of the church. The service erupted into chaos. People left in tears.

‖‖

Apply the development of an idol to this case. The elders resented change. They loved their traditional decorations. Desires turned into demands that the traditions be honored, even if their pastor believed that they negatively affected worship. The battle line was drawn with the fight over the beloved banners. When the pastor failed to meet their demands, their anger led to judging him and punishing him. While they justified themselves for protecting the church, their actions brought destruction. They did not show respect or love for their pastor or try to live in peace (1 Thessalonians 5:12–14).

The pastor also struggled with his idols. Instead of taking time to teach and work closely with his leaders, he argued with them when they refused his demands. When they failed to meet his expectations, his frustration escalated into anger. He judged them as evil, punishing them by acting on his own and slandering them. His behavior also harmed the congregation. He lorded it over his people, failing to provide a Christlike example to his flock (1 Peter 5:3).

Both the pastor and elders sacrificed their integrity, their reputations, their examples as leaders, their congregation's welfare, and their church's witness. Neither side applied what Paul taught:

> Do nothing from selfish ambition or conceit, but in humility count others more significant than yourselves. Let each of you look not only to his own interests, but also to the interests of others. (Philippians 2:3–4)

Not all church conflicts involve this much drama. Nonetheless, key parties in church disputes often act out with sinful responses to serve hidden idols that expose their spiritual heart disease.

THE CURE FOR IDOLATRY

Although spiritual heart disease can result in suffering for many, healing can be found in the confession of sin and the forgiveness of

God. King David was one whose idols led to gross misuse of authority, adultery, murder, and denial of sin (2 Samuel 11). Although what David had done displeased the Lord (2 Samuel 11:27) and caused grief for many, God still loved David and sent Nathan to restore him (2 Samuel 12:1–13). David intimately knew the inner struggle of the old Adam and the shame and guilt born of contrition. When David confessed, Nathan proclaimed God's forgiveness. David rejoiced in God's salvation and praised Him for the renewal of health and youth that forgiveness brings, as he reflects in the Psalms:

> Bless the LORD, O my soul,
>   and all that is within me, bless His holy name!
> Bless the LORD, O my soul,
>   and forget not all His benefits,
> who forgives all your iniquity,
>   who heals all your diseases,
> who redeems your life from the pit,
>   who crowns you with steadfast love and mercy,
> who satisfies you with good
>   so that your youth is renewed like the eagle's.
> (Psalm 103:1–5)

Reflection

Reflection

Praise be to our God for His undeserved grace found in our Savior, Jesus! In the next chapter, we'll explore more about the cure for idolatry and the healing that follows.

AN EXERCISE IN SELF-EXAMINATION

Spiritual heart disease affects more than all "those other people." As creatures living with sinful natures, we are *all* tempted by the idols in our hearts.

This exercise in self-examination can help you identify one or more of your idols. As you examine your own heart condition, you are being prepared through repentance for the healing power found in the cross of Christ. Use the space provided to record your observation and answers.

Think of a specific conflict where you acted inappropriately. You may have felt these emotions:

- Anger
- Bitterness
- Pride
- Fear
- Jealousy
- Defensiveness
- Judgmentalness

With that situation in mind, reflect on the following questions to examine your heart.

1. To recognize idols related to fears, ask yourself these questions:

    a. What did you want to preserve or avoid at almost any cost?

Reflection

Reflection

b. In this situation, what or whom did you fear most of all?

2. To recognize idols related to cravings, ask yourself these questions:

   a. What did you find yourself thinking about much of the time? (Or what kept you awake at night, perhaps for a few nights in a row?)

   b. What caused you the most worry? How did your anxiety replace your trust in God?

   c. Fill in the blank: If only _____, then I would be happy, fulfilled, and secure. What does this suggest to you about your trust in God for what you desire?

   d. When a certain desire or expectation was not met, did you feel frustration, resentment, bitterness, or anger?

   e. To fulfill your passion, what did you do that was not pleasing to God?

3. To recognize idols related to misplaced trust (e.g., trusting yourself as "god" and judging others), ask yourself these questions:

   a. How did your expectations of the other person magnify your demands on him or her and your disappointment in that person's failure to meet your desires?

b. How did you judge this other person when your expectations were not met?

c. How did you get even with the other person when your desires were not fulfilled?

d. How did you communicate to the other person what you felt that he or she must do?

e. How did you threaten the other person?

4. Considering your answers, identify the following:

a. What idols were you serving in that conflict? Write down whether they were fears, cravings, or misplaced trust. (You may identify more than one—idols often overlap and relate to one another.)

b. Indicate what or whom you sacrificed or executed to get what you wanted.

c. What will be the end result if this idolatry remains unchecked?

5. Meditate upon 1 Peter 2:24. What hope is there for healing from your spiritual heart disease?

PART 2

Restoring Health and Nurturing Spiritual Wellness

Although a church may outwardly appear healthy, she may be suffering from hidden spiritual heart disease. She may lack leaders who nourish themselves regularly in God's Word. A majority of her members may suffer from biblical illiteracy. Even a healthy congregation may have a number of members who lack spiritual vitality.

The church may appear strong because she possesses qualities similar to successful clubs or service organizations. However, human reasoning may be taking precedence over being in God's Word when key decisions are being made. Without realizing it, hidden idols are replacing worship of the true God. Reasonable apprehensions, godly desires, and judicious trust may have developed into idols of fears, cravings, or misplaced trust.

Unless the congregation changes her ways to improve her spiritual health, she will likely experience a health crisis when the stress of conflict arises. Her idolatry will be revealed, and the congregation will suffer major losses.

Healing begins by treating the idolatrous heart through confession and the proclaiming of God's forgiveness. The collective faith of church members is nourished as individuals become more connected with God's Word, equipping them for spiritual battle. Unrepentance among the leaders and members, a fix-it mentality, and biblical illiteracy can threaten the spiritual wellness of the church.

Healthy churches benefit from pastors and other leaders who take advantage of the opportunities to hear God's Word of forgiveness proclaimed to them directly, specifically, and personally. Leaders and members proclaim a living faith as they confess their sins to one another and forgive as they have been forgiven.

The proclamation of God's forgiveness among His people restores health and nurtures spiritual health and wellness.

CHAPTER 5

TREATING THE IDOLATROUS HEART

Create in me a clean heart, O God,
    and renew a right spirit within me.
Cast me not away from Thy presence;
    and take not Thy Holy Spirit from me.
Restore unto me the joy of Thy salvation;
    and uphold me with Thy free spirit. Amen. (*LSB* 956)

Case Study: Zion Church

Zion Church earned a reputation as the fighting church in town. For years, the community heard about divisions among members and criticisms of one another. Even the local paper featured articles about the battles during congregational meetings. People inside and out knew that Zion Church was unhealthy.

Healing for the congregation began with a mediation between two congregational leaders who had polarized the church.

After establishing ground rules for mediation, the reconciler asked Larry and Judy for their opening statements. In just two or three sentences, they were to each identify their hopes and expectations. Judy laid out her expectations.

When it was Larry's turn, he pulled out three hand-written pages. He read a detailed confession of his sins to Judy. She had been ready to blast him for his offenses, but she was totally unprepared for his contrition. Forgiving him in tears, she confessed her sins to Larry. He came around the table to hug her as he, too, declared forgiveness.

Having been reconciled, these two leaders wanted to confess their sins before the entire congregation. They acknowledged the harm their open conflict had caused for so many others. They reported their reconciliation to stunned listeners. They asked for forgiveness because of the hurt they had caused. The reconciler led the congregation in pronouncing God's forgiveness.

The unexpected demonstration of contrition and forgiveness between two respected leaders led other members to share forgiveness with one another. Churchwide healing was set in motion with forgiveness in Christ.

As the leaders of Zion Church studied the reconciliation team's report, they began to recognize the depth of their congregation's spiritual weakness. They had fewer than 10 percent of their average worship attendance in adult Bible study. Those who were rooted in God's Word encouraged other members to join them in Bible study, and new studies were offered. In just a few months, Bible study attendance quadrupled. The congregation's spiritual health was improving.

A test of their improving health came when the church was sued by a neighbor for a dispute over the property line and some tree limbs that hung over into the neighbor's yard. During a congregational meeting, the members discussed hiring an attorney to defend their cause.

Then Larry asked a question: "Remember what we learned from our past? Instead of going to court, how can we show Jesus' love to our neighbor?"

The discussion took a major turn. The church leadership invited the plaintiff to join them in Christian mediation. In the end, the church and her neighbor not only resolved the property boundary issue and tree encroachments out of court but the congregation also gave witness to the God they worshiped in the way they responded.

What a transformation! In just a few years, Zion Church had become a healthy congregation. Their reputation in the community now reflects the Prince of Peace they worship.

DENIAL LEADS TO BLINDNESS

Spiritual blindness obscures the need for healing.

In 2 Samuel 11, we learn how King David became blind to his own spiritual heart disease. One sin led to another in his attempts to cover up a mess of sins.

Spiritual blindness obscures the need for healing.

Rather than leading his men into battle as king, David sent Joab to lead the troops while he remained comfortably at home in Jerusalem. One day, from the roof of his house, he watched a beautiful woman bathing. Although he had many wives and concubines, David lusted after this one. He inquired of her and learned that her name was Bathsheba, the wife of Uriah, who was serving the king in battle. He summoned her, satisfied his sexual craving by having relations with her, and then sent her home.

When Bathsheba sent word that she was pregnant, David should have repented then. Instead, he chose to deny the depth of his sin and attempted to conceal it. He knew what he had done was wrong. But idolatry has a way of blinding us to our own sinfulness.

He requested that Joab have Uriah leave the battlefield and come to Jerusalem to report on the battle. When Uriah finished his report, David sent him home, thinking that Uriah would take the opportunity to lie with his wife. Then everyone, including Uriah, would think that the baby was his. But Uriah refused to go home to his wife while his fellow servants remained in battle away from their wives. He stayed with the king's servants.

David should have realized his plot had failed. Once again, he should have confessed. But his heart became more clouded as he devised another plan. He detained Uriah, inviting him to a feast and getting him drunk. Surely, Uriah would then give in to the desire for relations with his wife. But Uriah resisted and remained with the king's servants.

After two repeated failures, one would think David would have seen the light and repented. However, his heart was blinded by self-justification and denial. The desire to protect himself from the shame of his sin was great, likely fueled by fear of man. What would people think of their king? If people really knew what their king had done, would he retain his position and thus his wealth and power? Rather than trusting God, he placed more trust in his own ability to protect his reputation. David was guilty of fears, cravings, and misplaced trust.

The worst evidence of misplaced trust came when David determined to get rid of Uriah. He executed an innocent man, a loyal servant with

Idolatry has a way of blinding us to our own sinfulness.

integrity, to hide his own wickedness. He sent Uriah back to Joab with a written message. Joab was ordered to arrange for Uriah to be killed in battle. Because Uriah died on the battlefield, no one would suspect that Bathsheba's baby was not his. When Uriah's death was reported to the king, he still remained unrepentant.

After the time of mourning was over for Bathsheba, David married her. He must have thought he had been successful in concealing his horrific sins. In reality, several others must have recognized some of the king's dark deeds: Bathsheba, the messenger from David who first summoned her, Joab, those who served Uriah the wine, the servants who kept the king informed about Uriah not going home, and anyone whom these people told.

Of course, God was not deceived. "But the thing that David had done displeased the Lord" (2 Samuel 11:27).

Whom was David fooling? How could one so close to God blind himself to the horror of his sin? He was guilty of adultery, murder, abuse of authority, deception, and self-justification. He traded worship of the true God for numerous idols, including himself.

Before you judge David too harshly, ask yourself, "Am I so different from David?" Perhaps we may try to comfort ourselves in that we are not guilty of physical adultery or arranging for someone's death. But the slippery slope of sin works the same way. Our idolatry obscures our vision of our Redeemer. Our old Adam seeks to cover up our sins and pretend they don't exist. Our own idols seem so precious to us that we often fool ourselves about how desperately we cling to them. We attempt to deceive others to protect our sins from being discovered. We convince ourselves that we're really not so bad. The human heart can justify almost any sin it craves. And that leads us to replace God with the idols we think will satisfy our every desire.

Denial is a powerful force of misplaced trust. This idol promises to provide security, safety, and fulfillment as the sinner proclaims himself god. But if left unchecked, idolatry results in death and destruction.

John identifies denial of sin as denial of Christ. He writes, "If we say we have no sin, we deceive ourselves, and the truth is not in us. . . . If we say we have not sinned, we make Him a liar, and His word is not in us" (1 John 1:8, 10).

Note how John defines "the truth" through Jesus' own words in John 14:6: "Jesus said to him, 'I am the way, and the truth, and the life. No one comes to the Father except through Me.'" *Jesus* is the truth.

John identifies Jesus as "the Word" in John 1:1, 14: "In the beginning was the Word, and the Word was with God, and the Word was God. . . . And the Word became flesh and dwelt among us, and we have seen His glory, glory as of the only Son from the Father, full of grace and truth." *Jesus* is the living Word.

If you replace *Jesus* for the words "the truth" in 1 John 1:8, and if you substitute *Jesus* for "His word" in 1 John 1:10, the revised passages interpret what happens when we deny our sin: "If we say we have no sin, we deceive ourselves, and *Jesus* is not in us. . . . If we say we have not sinned, we make Him a liar, and *Jesus* is not in us."

When we deny our sin, we deny our need for a Savior. We deny Christ and His atoning work on the cross. That's what self-justification means. Those who declare themselves righteous deny their need for Christ. Remember what Jesus taught regarding the self-righteous? "I came not to call the righteous, but sinners" (Mark 2:17).

Peter explains that those who do not manifest the fruit of the Spirit are blind because they have forgotten the source of their justification in the forgiveness of sins. "For whoever lacks these qualities is so nearsighted that he is blind, having forgotten that he was cleansed from his former sins" (2 Peter 1:9).

David blinded himself to his own sin. In the development of his idols, he lost sight of who his Redeemer was. Instead, he trusted his own attempts to cover up his sin to protect his idols—reputation, position, power, authority, wealth, and more. David was headed down a path of destruction.

Each one of us can fall down the same slippery slope. For we are all sinners.

Congregations are made up of people—people who were conceived in sin and who live out their sinful nature in what they think, say, and do. Corporately, congregations can fall into the same trap. Churches can also serve their idols and sin by what they collectively think, say, and do. But God provides a path that leads to restoration.

OVERCOMING SPIRITUAL BLINDNESS

Praise be to God that He provides the cure. John proclaims good news: "The blood of Jesus His Son cleanses us from all sin" (1 John 1:7). He contrasts denial of sin with the righteousness we receive through repentance: "If we confess our sins, He is faithful and just to forgive us our sins and to cleanse us from all unrighteousness" (1 John 1:9).

But the sinner often needs help to overcome spiritual blindness.

Although God fully knew David's depth of sin, He still loved David. David could not see his sin through his attempts to self-justify, so God sent a messenger to restore David.

Nathan engaged David by describing a crime that occurred in the kingdom. He appealed to David's sense of justice with the story of a rich man and poor man. The rich man had many sheep and cattle, but the poor man owned only a single lamb, who was like a daughter to him. When the rich man welcomed a traveler into his home, he went over to his neighbor and stole the poor man's sole lamb to serve to his visitor.

Immediately, David became enraged and declared judgment. Nathan identified David as the real offender: "You are the man!" (2 Samuel 12:7). As Nathan's message removed David's blinders, David repented, "I have sinned against the Lord," and upon his confession, Nathan proclaimed God's forgiveness, "The Lord also has put away your sin; you shall not die" (v. 13).

Whenever God's people are blind in their own sin, they need help to see. Those whom He sends use the Scriptures to confront sin, overcome denial, and declare God's grace to the repentant. The Holy Spirit works through God's Word to change hearts and heal spiritual disease.

As a congregation heals, it is necessary for her to understand the distinction between *conflict resolution* and *reconciliation*.[10] In conflict resolution, we may negotiate to find mutually acceptable solutions for substantive or material issues (as described in Philippians 2:3–4). Or we may present the substantive issues for adjudication to someone in authority, such as a parent, manager, or judge (e.g., submitting to authorities, as in Ephesians 6:1–3, 5–8; 1 Corinthians 6:1–8). *Material* or *substantive* issues involve *what material matter or process* is in dispute. This includes such things as disputes over money, contract interpretations, role definitions, authority, and property. Conflict resolution works to solve material issues, but it fails to mend broken relationships.

In reconciliation, we address personal issues and seek to restore relationships. *Personal* or *relational* issues involve *how* something is done and people are treated. This includes broken trust and relationships damaged by sinful thoughts, words, and deeds. God reconciled us to Himself through Christ (Romans 5:1–11; 2 Corinthians 5:16–21). He calls us to reconcile with others through confession and forgiveness (Matthew 5:23–24; James 5:16; Colossians 3:13; Ephesians 4:32). Reconciliation works to restore broken relationships.

In most conflicts, both conflict resolution and reconciliation are necessary.

Conflict resolution is much easier than reconciliation because we find it easier to deal with material issues. Reconciliation, on the other hand, requires confession and forgiveness. Most people find it difficult to admit wrongdoing or to forgive offenses. We naturally prefer to find a solution to the material issues and simply move on. It's easier to diagnose, and it's much easier to fix.

The problem with this perspective is that when relationships are damaged, trust decreases and negotiation becomes strained. It's difficult to agree on material issues when you don't trust the other party.

Many advisers serving congregations focus on conflict resolution but neglect reconciliation. They recommend solutions to fix the church's problems: replace specific leaders, adopt a specific structure, define the mission, focus on outreach, and so on. It's far more challenging (and unpopular!) to help leaders and members recognize their sins against one another, teach and lead them to confess, teach and lead them in proclaiming forgiveness, and admonish them to replace their idols with the worship of the true God. Ignoring reconciliation fails to help the church overcome her spiritual blindness.

Conflict resolution works to solve material issues, but it fails to mend broken relationships.

I know of a number of congregations who previously had people help them with conflict resolution but fail to assist them in reconciliation. These churches implemented the recommended solutions but fell back into their sinful patterns and found themselves fighting again.

Case Study: Faith Church

To address her conflicts, Faith Church adopted the new governance model recommended to her. The new structure streamlined the church's decision-making process and freed up the professional staff for planning and implementation. Following the adviser's counsel, they appointed new leaders and called a new senior pastor. Hope increased as new expectations were established. People seemed to rally around the vision cast by their senior pastor.

However, no one had helped the leaders and members understand their underlying weakness. While they had worked extensively on conflict resolution, they never learned to reconcile relationships. They clung to old idols and developed some new ones, neglecting to see their spiritual disease. They adopted worldly ways to improve their organization, yet their corporate commitment to studying the Bible remained weak. The new leadership worked hard to fulfill their responsibilities, but they didn't see the necessity to prioritize time for being in God's Word.

At first, things seemed to blossom under the new direction. The congregation experienced moderate growth in attendance and finances. They developed plans for expanding their building. New staff were hired. Excitement and pride in their church swelled among the membership.

But underneath the fresh start, the underlying spiritual disease once again began to spread. Governing board members criticized the senior pastor behind his back because expectations were not being met. Rumors began to circulate about different leaders. Some staff resigned; others were terminated. Worship attendance leveled off and then dipped. An influential group of longtime members organized to solve the church's problems in the same way as before. They sought to get rid of the senior pastor. They were bent on taking back control of their church.

The battles that followed were ugly. By the time a reconciliation team arrived, the damage was extensive. Attendance was declining and finances were strained. The new building plans had been scrapped. Lay leaders had resigned. Several of the old guard had left. The senior pastor was struggling with depression.

> Reconciliation works to restore broken relationships.

The reconciliation team could have made several recommendations for resolving the conflict: terminate the senior pastor and call a new one to set a new vision, elect a new governing board, amend some of the structural problems, and more. But what they really needed was the spiritual healing that comes from reconciliation.

The reconcilers initiated treatment with a full-day Bible study on what it means to be reconciled to God and to one another. Having introduced a new paradigm for addressing conflict, the team met with leadership groups and then with individual leaders and member families. The meetings were not just to gather information. They also served to coach everyone in what they could do to be reconciled with others. Everyone can be part of a church's restoration. Each individual interview began with sharing Scripture, praying, listening, collecting written information, and then coaching. God's forgiveness was proclaimed. Each person was challenged with God's Word to confess, forgive, restore another gently, or pray. A few began to reconcile without any more assistance.

Through this process, the team identified key influencers who divided the congregation. In a second visit, the team met with key parties for more coaching. With their agreement, the reconcilers brought opposing leaders together in mediation. A few declined to participate. In mediation, the team guided the willing parties to agree on certain ground rules based on Scripture. With facilitation, the parties shared their stories, including their perspectives, their hurts, their disappointments, and their desires for healing. When one person confessed, the other side softened. They were shown how to declare God's forgiveness to one another. They then offered personal forgiveness. They were reconciling their relationships.

Spiritual blindness was being overcome. As they experienced the healing power of forgiveness through God's Word, hardened positions fell away. The pastor no longer wanted to be rid of certain "alligators." Most of the organized old guard affirmed their pastor instead of running him out.

The pastor prepared a written confession, which he then made before the entire congregation during worship. Both supporters and detractors sat in amazed silence as their pastor admitted his failures and confessed his idols. The reconciliation team led the congregation in proclaiming God's forgiveness to him, using the promises found in several Bible passages.

The reconcilers reminded the members what the Bible teaches regarding peacemaking. The people reflected on what they had learned from the initial Bible study and individual coaching sessions. This day they were witnessing what it means to live lifestyles of reconciliation.

The team shared with them what the sharing of God's peace meant to the Early Christian Church. Before Communion, each person was encouraged to go to another to share the kiss of peace with the words "The peace of the Lord be with you." The person receiving this greeting responded, "And also with you." Today, this greeting is shared with a handshake, whereas in the Early Church it was accompanied with a kiss.[11]

This was much more than a casual greeting for the ancient church. The kiss of peace meant that the relationship between two believers was healthy. If anyone could not approach someone for sharing the peace, the service stopped. Those who needed reconciliation were excused while the congregation waited. Once they had reconciled, they were welcomed back, and the church celebrated the Lord's Supper in peace with one another.

The reconcilers told the people that today they would follow this ancient practice. The service would be suspended and Communion delayed until they had opportunity to reconcile. Through all their meetings, the reconcilers knew many had not spoken to one another for months. The members were urged to seek one another out to share God's peace. Following the example of their pastor, they could then confess their sins to one another and share God's forgiveness and personal forgiveness. The people could take whatever time was necessary.

At first, people were hesitant. Then a couple of brave souls moved across the aisle. Soon the entire congregation was afoot. One could hear crying and laughter as people reconciled. One of the leaders who opposed the pastor and declined mediation sought him out to confess his sins. They reconciled with tear-filled hugs. Forty-five minutes passed before the people returned to their seats.

As people came to the altar to receive Communion, more tears were shed. Spiritual blinders had fallen off. People saw their Savior and one another in a new light. Hope replaced discouragement. Although the service took more than two hours, no one complained about the length.

The team followed up with a written report offering observations and recommendations. In addition to describing different conflicts, observations identified corporate sinful behaviors, using the Ten Commandments. A major focus was on the members' limited knowledge of Scripture and sin against the command "Remember the Sabbath day by keeping it holy." Luther explains this commandment: "We should fear and love God so that we do not despise preaching and His Word, but hold it sacred and gladly hear and learn it." The report included recommendations for substantive changes, but most addressed relational and spiritual heart issues.

The congregation worked to improve Bible study attendance. The governing board led the way by starting every meeting with a Bible study. Each board member hosted home studies, inviting others to join. Biblical literacy increased as more members engaged in the Word. Accordingly, the congregation's spiritual health improved. This time, the pastor and lay leaders remained in their positions.

APPLYING THE CURE

God provides the cure for spiritual heart disease: forgiveness through our Lord Jesus Christ.

As Christians, we confess faith in Jesus, who grants forgiveness of sins. In worship, we practice corporate Confession and Absolution. We hear our pastor proclaim the Gospel from the pulpit. We understand we receive the forgiveness of sins in the Lord's Supper and Holy Baptism. Yes, we know we are forgiven. But how is our forgiveness through Christ lived out in our relationships within our families, at work or school, and in our communities?

We often take our forgiveness for granted in the ways we interact with one another. We deny our daily need for forgiveness when we deny our sin. Another way we take Christ's forgiveness for granted is by minimizing sin. Instead of using biblical language to acknowledge our faults, we adopt the world's way of minimizing sin. In reality, it's just another way to self-justify. Here are some common ways we minimize sin:

- It was just a mistake.
- I made an error in judgment.
- It's only a little white lie.
- Everyone does it.

Luther points out the danger of this: "The more you minimize sin, the more will grace decline in value."[12]

When sin is minimized, there is little need to forgive. Once again, we adopt the world's language to respond to the phrase "I'm sorry."

- That's okay.
- No problem.
- Don't worry about it.
- You should be sorry! Don't ever do it again.

What hope is in these words? "Sin is never *okay*. Sin is never *no problem*. There is only one cure for sin—forgiveness through our Lord Jesus Christ."[13]

Why does the world respond this way? Unbelievers have no hope in Christ. They must self-justify to protect their self-image. Their identity is found in their own self-worth, and therefore they must work to protect that worth.

But Christians ought to know better. We hope in Christ. We do not need to self-justify, because we have One who has made justification for us (Romans 5:1–5). Our identity is found in *whose* we are, adopted children of God, because of *what* God has done for us through Jesus (1 John 3:1). Christ purchased and won us, not with gold or silver, but with His holy blood (1 Peter 1:18–19). We are precious in God's eyes, and therefore we need not deny sin to protect our own self-worth (Isaiah 43:4). Confession and forgiveness are daily necessities for Christians. We sin daily, and therefore we need God's forgiveness every day. Hearing God's forgiveness proclaimed to us is necessary for keeping us spiritually healthy. Unless we confess our sin, we do not acknowledge our need for God's love through Christ, and His redemption has no place in our heart.

Reflection

PRACTICING A HEALTHY LIFESTYLE

As much as we confess our faith in Christ and God's plan of salvation, we frequently fail to live out that faith in daily practice with one another.

To encourage you to practice this healthy lifestyle, I am providing you with an opportunity for personal application.

In the previous chapter, you had opportunity to examine your heart, identifying some of your idols. In this chapter, I encourage you to seek out someone to proclaim God's forgiveness to you.

1. Find someone who will confidentially hear your confession to God and then proclaim God's forgiveness to you. You may go to your pastor, or you may select another Christian who is mature in the faith. You may choose to use the self-examination questions from the end of the previous chapter to prepare you.

2. You may wish to use the form in Appendix A, *Proclaiming God's Forgiveness*, to guide both of you. If you go to your pastor, he can provide a form for private confession and absolution. Be certain that the person hearing your confession understands that you want God's forgiveness specifically proclaimed to you. (The form will guide you both.

3. You may be specific or general in your confession. God knows more about the specifics of your sin than you will ever know! However, if a particular sin troubles you, you will find that by naming the sin out loud in the presence of another person, you will *own* your sin. Then, when you hear God's forgiveness proclaimed, you will be comforted in a wonderful way for that specific sin you named.

4. You may also wish to use the form in Appendix B, *God's Word Proclaiming Forgiveness*. The person proclaiming God's forgiveness reads one or more of the Bible verses of God's promise, inserting the other person's name in the verse.

5. Pray together with the person. Include thanksgiving to God for His gift of forgiveness, and ask for His strength to amend your sinful ways.

6. Reflecting on this exercise, what difference would it make in your church if your leaders practiced proclaiming and receiving God's forgiveness with one another on a regular basis?

CHAPTER 6

Equipping the Saints for Spiritual Battle

Stand up, stand up for Jesus;
Stand in His strength alone.
The arm of flesh will fail you,
Ye dare not trust your own.
Put on the Gospel armor;
Each piece put on with prayer.
Where duty calls or danger,
Be never wanting there. (*LSB* 660:3)

"We just need to get rid of _____. Then everything will be back to normal."

How often I have heard these words spoken by a lay leader or professional church worker!

When we meet with people from a conflicted church, they often identify who they think is the major problem and what the main issue is. Their solution? Eliminate the problem person and everything will be okay.

Conflict is rarely that black and white. Harmful conflict in a church results because of a number of different influences. Like a terrible storm, several factors converge to generate the destructive nature of the tempest. As a result, the simplistic solution of getting rid of one or two key people may relieve some pressure, but it fails to truly address the issues. In most cases, those who remain have contributed to the conflict and will likely do so again unless they learn a different way to handle disagreements.

As I described earlier, the solution is not simply to address the material or substantive issues. The problem goes much deeper than that. One must consider the relational issues, which reflect the condition of the heart. In a congregation, that means looking at many hearts. The collective spiritual condition of the individuals is reflected in the corporate body.

To evaluate and then treat the underlying issues, one needs to view the situation in light of the congregation's readiness for spiritual battle.

RECOGNIZING THE TRUE ENEMY

Being able to correctly identify the enemy is crucial in war. Seeing your comrades as the enemy is a trick of the adversary to divert attention away from himself. Peter points out the true enemy: "Be sober-minded; be watchful. Your adversary the devil prowls around like a roaring lion, seeking someone to devour" (1 Peter 5:8).

When we point to brothers and sisters in Christ as the enemies, the tempter has successfully drawn our attention away from the real enemy. Fellow believers are not the enemies. Our pastor, elders, patriarch, and matriarch are not our major adversaries. The devil is our foe. He exploits the world's influence and appeals to our sinful flesh to deceive us and thwart our attempts to bring healing and wholeness back to our communities of faith. The devil, the world, and our sinful flesh threaten the health and vitality of our congregations.

Understanding how our own flesh has contributed to conflicts provides a place to begin.

People being coached through conflict often stumble over this question: "How have you contributed to the conflict?"

Case Study: Chairman Brad

Brad called a reconciler for help. He served as chairman of the board of elders. The pastor had just resigned, and Brad blamed several in his church who had treated the pastor shamefully. Not only were they disrespectful, but they also had attacked the pastor with verbal assaults to his face and gossiped to others about him. Vandals had painted graffiti on the pastor's house and slashed his car tires. Brad concluded it was the wicked people from their church who ran the pastor off.

He convinced the rest of the lay leaders that an outside consultant would affirm their conclusions about the problem people and assist in removing them. He felt confident this would solve the problem.

In conversations with Brad, the reconciler noticed that his description of their disputes always depicted him and the elders as innocent. They had done nothing wrong in any of the confrontations. The root of their troubles was all about those few people who were destroying their beloved church. Brad declared that these people were enemies of the church.

Brad's perspective is not unique. Those who seek assistance in conflict want help in fixing someone, and it's nearly always the other person. In more than twenty years in this work, I can remember very few people who asked for help in getting the log out of their own eye. It's just not our nature. That's why Jesus uses hyperbole to highlight this point:

> [Jesus said,] "Why do you see the speck that is in your brother's eye, but do not notice the log that is in your own eye? Or how can you say to your brother, 'Let me take the speck out of your eye,' when there is the log in your own eye? You hypocrite, first take the log out of your own eye, and then you will see clearly to take the speck out of your brother's eye." (Matthew 7:3–5)

Our nature leads us to deny personal responsibility. A practical application of denial is to shift blame to someone or something else.

Blame shifting is a spiritual issue. By shifting blame, we deny our sin and therefore deny our need for Christ. Instead, we depend on our self-justification and trust in our own wisdom. Proverbs warns against such thinking:

> Trust in the LORD with all your heart,
>> and do not lean on your own understanding.
> In all your ways acknowledge Him,
>> and He will make straight your paths.
> Be not wise in your own eyes;
>> fear the LORD, and turn away from evil.

> It will be healing to your flesh
> and refreshment to your bones. (Proverbs 3:5–7)

Notice that healing and refreshment come from trusting in the Lord, not from depending on our own wisdom and understanding. Trusting God includes trusting His Word when He admonishes us to first take the log out of our own eye.

Reconciliation for Brad's church began with a full-day Bible study on reconciliation. To prepare for an interview with a member of the consultation team, each church member completed a form with several questions. One of the last questions asked, "How have you contributed to this conflict?"

At first, Brad simply wrote, "I haven't," and he thought through his defense. But by the time he met with a reconciler, his rationalizations seemed feeble to him. The Holy Spirit had begun to work on his heart.

"I need your help. Will you help me get the log out of my eye?"

The reconciler perceived he already knew the answer. "What kind of log are you struggling with?"

Brad's eyes teared up. He admitted his faults, specifically recounting a public offense that hurt many in the church. When God's forgiveness was proclaimed to him, tears filled his eyes. "I've been a Christian all my life. But I have never experienced forgiveness like this before!" Later, Brad led his congregation through a healing process where he was among the first to make a public confession. He had identified the real enemy. The devil, the world, and his sinful flesh had tempted him to take his eyes off of Jesus, the founder and perfecter of his faith. Through confession and forgiveness, his sight was restored. He demonstrated spiritual leadership through dependence on Christ.

BLAME SHIFTING—A NATURAL RESPONSE

In India, I gained new appreciation for how language can reinforce the natural desire to shift blame. Nearly 80 percent of India claims to be Hindu. I've been told by Indians that forgiveness is difficult to grasp, since the multitude of Hindu gods do not grant the kind of forgiveness Jesus gives. If a person sins in this life, he will be reincarnated as a lower life form for punishment. The path to nirvana requires sinless living in each successive life so that one can eventually earn the right to nirvana.

Thus, Hindi languages support blame shifting so that a person won't need to admit any fault and consign himself to a lower position in the next life.

For example, if you cut your thumb with a knife, you wouldn't say, "I cut my thumb." Instead, Hindi language teaches you to say, "The knife cut my thumb." If you step on a nail, you wouldn't say, "I stepped on a nail" but rather "the nail pierced my foot." Imagine how hard it is for a converted Hindu to admit sin!

But is our Western culture really that different? We have developed our own phrases to avoid taking responsibility and to shift blame. "I may have messed up a little, but you made me so mad!" "I wouldn't have called you names if you hadn't called me stupid!" Interpretation? Yeah, *you* caused me to sin, so *I* am innocent.

It's not our Indian or American heritage that moves us to shift blame. We inherited this trait from our first father, Adam. "Yes, Lord, I ate the fruit, but it was the woman whom *You* gave me." When we shift blame to others, we accuse God. John states it this way: "If we say we have not sinned, we make Him a liar, and His word is not in us" (1 John 1:10).

It's someone else's fault that we have sinned. When we blame someone else, we ultimately blame God.

Spiritual threats to the Church include the means through which we are tempted: the devil, the world, and our sinful flesh. These three work together to undermine the health of each individual and thus the Church. Unless we recognize this dynamic at work, we will leave ourselves vulnerable to spiritual weakness.

In the Lord's Prayer, Jesus taught us to pray, "And lead us not into temptation." Luther explains this petition in his Small Catechism:

> God tempts no one. We pray in this petition that God would guard and keep us so that the devil, the world, and our sinful nature may not deceive us or mislead us into false belief, despair, and other great shame and vice. Although we are attacked by these things, we pray that we may finally overcome them and win the victory.

What can we do to strengthen our resolve against the spiritual threats to the Church?

LIFE SUPPORT VS. BATTLE PREPARATION

Nourishing ourselves in God's Word is essential for spiritual battle.

Consider this: the President of the United States is preparing to send his military to war, and to rally the troops, he says, "We're going to equip you with the best training and equipment the world has to offer. And to nourish you for the battle, we will give you one fantastic meal a week. It will be a feast!"

As a solider, what would you think? Ludicrous! No soldier can fight on one meal a week, and no army can win a war on one meal a week, no matter how huge the banquet. Soldiers would starve, and their malnourished bodies would break down in the heat of battle. They would become weak, easy to overcome.

But that's what many in our churches attempt to do. If their only connection to God's Word is in worship on the weekend, then they go on a spiritual fast for six days. And if regular worship attendance is only every other week, then they fast for thirteen days without any spiritual nourishment. If they miss two weeks in worship, they starve themselves for three weeks!

The worship service is a great feast. The preaching, the reading and singing of Scripture, the proclamation of forgiveness, the celebration of the Lord's Supper—all provide spiritual nutrition required to sustain life in Christ. But during the rest of the week, the spiritual enemies of the Church fight against us. The world will shape our attitudes through friends and co-workers and opponents, newspapers and television and magazines, school or work, social media, and more. The devil will tempt us to take good gifts from God and turn them into idols. Our own sinful flesh will elevate our fears, desires, and trusts into false gods that lead us to sin in thought, word, and deed.

One scriptural feeding a week may be enough to keep us on life support, but it's not enough to fight the spiritual battles of life. We leave ourselves open to infection from spiritual disease when we choose to be malnourished, excluding ourselves from the Word of God.

> One scriptural feeding a week may be enough to keep us on life support, but it's not enough to fight the spiritual battles of life.

FORTIFIED FOR SPIRITUAL BATTLE

Paul clarifies what really is at stake in our battles of life:

> Finally, be strong in the Lord and in the strength of His
> might. Put on the whole armor of God, that you may be able
> to stand against the schemes of the devil. For we do not wres-
> tle against flesh and blood, but against the rulers, against
> the authorities, against the cosmic powers over this present
> darkness, against the spiritual forces of evil in the heavenly
> places. (Ephesians 6:10–12)

When we think our enemies are Christians with whom we are in
conflict, we are deceived. When we convince ourselves that our problems can be simply solved by changing leaders, by reorganizing our
structure, or by committing to a defined mission statement, we may
experience some benefit. But attention to our underlying weaknesses
will be drawn away from the spiritual forces of evil.

The Scriptures specify what is most needful in our work together as
God's people.

> Therefore take up the whole armor of God, that you may be
> able to withstand in the evil day, and having done all, to stand
> firm. Stand therefore, having fastened on the belt of truth,
> and having put on the breastplate of righteousness, and, as
> shoes for your feet, having put on the readiness given by the
> gospel of peace. In all circumstances take up the shield of
> faith, with which you can extinguish all the flaming darts of
> the evil one; and take the helmet of salvation, and the sword
> of the Spirit, which is the word of God, praying at all times
> in the Spirit, with all prayer and supplication. To that end,
> keep alert with all perseverance, making supplication for all
> the saints. (Ephesians 6:13–18)

A key to strengthening our congregations is to equip the saints for
spiritual battle. What makes a congregation healthy is that her members are fortified to withstand the evil forces that attack us in everyday life. God's saints must take up the full armor of God. They ground

themselves in Christ and feed themselves through His Word. They pray for God's wisdom and strength.

Applying modern psychology and sound organizational practices to conflict resolution can be beneficial. But we must be wary that these things do not detract us from our foundational needs. Worldly philosophies must not replace our dependence upon the Rock, the living Word.

The Church is not like any other organization on earth. The Church is the Body of Christ, the community of believers who have been brought together for war. While the Church provides comfort and healing for her members, Christ did not build His Church simply to be a country club for those who join and pay dues. The Church is militant, fighting the spiritual battles, strengthening her own, and reaching out to those who are headed to hell.

Sadly, many believe that the local church is just one of several organizations through which we benefit by association. Some people view church through the eyes of a consumer—they seek out a church that can provide them with the most fringe benefits. Others view church as something that good people do—that is, they go to church so they can be viewed as better people. In America, people may attend church because it's socially advantageous.

I once met an Australian pastor who had come to the United States to serve in a large church for two years to learn to be a better pastor. He was assigned to a church in the Bible Belt of the South. I asked him what surprised him most about America. His answer revealed a weakness of American Christianity.

"I had never seen social Christianity before," he replied.

"What do you mean by social Christianity?"

"People in the U.S. go to church because it's the socially acceptable thing to do," he explained. "In Australia, you are looked down upon if you go to church. But in America, going to church can help you socially in business, in politics, and among friends."

I talked with another couple who had just moved across the country. They visited several churches in their quest to find a new church home. Five different pastors followed up with them. Four of the pastors encouraged them to join their church because of the social benefits.

"Our church serves the best chicken dinners in town." "This is the right church to join if you want your business to flourish." "You need our church if you want friends in this town."

Living in affluence presents a subtle but great danger to Christians and their churches. Instead of dependence upon Christ, we trust our wealth and luxuries to meet our needs. We strive for more leisure. Our wants (cravings) morph into needs (demands). Our Christian faith becomes one of life's many segments from which we can select to satisfy our desires. We seek a church that features attractive campuses and offers enticing privileges. (I am not condemning churches that have beautiful buildings or offer many benefits. I am talking about how these great blessings from God can become distractions from Christ and His Word as being central to our faith.) The danger of being richly blessed is trusting more in God's blessings than the One who provides them.

Christ warns about the dangers of affluence: "And Jesus looked around and said to His disciples, 'How difficult it will be for those who have wealth to enter the kingdom of God!' " (Mark 10:23).

When we read Jesus' warning about riches, we rationalize that Jesus didn't mean us. "Well, I'm not as rich as the billionaires of this world." In more appropriate comparison, the average American can be counted among the wealthiest people on earth. Being wealthy compared to the rest of the world is not sinful. But those who live in such communities need to be aware of the spiritual dangers that accompany riches. They need reinforcement to resist the temptations of living in a prosperous society.

A healthy church strives to fortify her members for spiritual war. Her leaders realize that members need more nourishment than once a week to be prepared for the spiritual battles of daily life. Accordingly, spiritually wise leaders provide opportunities and encouragement for being well connected to God's Word. The church may offer many attractive services, but her priorities remain clear. As members are individually equipped for spiritual battle, they serve together as a healthy congregation, armed and ready to fight the good fight. Trials and storms may come that cause damage, but the church stands strong because she is moored to the Rock.

When a congregation loses sight of the spiritual warfare of this world, and thus the need to be fully equipped, she becomes spiritually weak. Leaders may set their priorities on meeting people's needs by offering attractive enticements, neglecting to focus first on getting people into God's Word. Meeting people's needs is part of a church's work. But when a congregation forgets that she is in spiritual battle and needs regular nourishment from God's Word, her foundation is moving away from the Rock and relocating to shifting sand.

> Rise! To arms! With prayer employ you,
> O Christians, lest the foe destroy you;
> For Satan has designed your fall.
> Wield God's Word, the weapon glorious;
> Against all foes be thus victorious,
> For God protects you from them all.
> Fear not the hordes of hell,
> Here is Emmanuel.
> Hail the Savior!
> The strong foes yield
> To Christ, our shield,
> And we, the victors, hold the field. (*LSB* 668:1)

Reflection

Considering this chapter, discuss the following questions with the leaders in your congregation.

1. What percentage of your congregation's members do you think recognize that as Christ's followers they are in constant spiritual battle?

2. If you were to survey your congregation, what do you think would be the most common responses to the question "Why are you a member of this congregation?" How would their answers help you evaluate the spiritual health of your church?

3. Faithful congregations preach the truth of God's Word and rightly administer His Sacraments, which nourish the faith of its members. List the ways your church is currently equipping the saints for spiritual warfare.

4. List the areas in which your church could improve readying the saints for spiritual warfare.

5. How could you help lead your congregation to fortify itself for spiritual battles?

CHAPTER 7

THREATS TO SPIRITUAL WELLNESS

His oath, his covenant and blood
Support me in the raging flood;
When ev'ry earthly prop gives way,
He then is all my hope and stay.
On Christ, the solid rock, I stand;
All other ground is sinking sand. (*LSB* 575:3)

As discussed earlier, the devil, the world, and our sinful flesh work against the spiritual wellness of a congregation.

The devil takes advantage of multiple opportunities to undermine the health of a church. In this chapter, I describe four additional threats to a church's health: the unrepentant pastor, the unrepentant lay leader, the fix-it mentality, and widespread biblical illiteracy among the membership.

Each of these threats can weaken the health of a congregation, sometimes misguiding people to look for congregational health in the wrong places. Instead of clinging to Christ, the solid Rock, people place their hope on earthly props.

THE UNREPENTANT AND THE REPENTANT PASTOR

A pastor or other professional church worker who consistently justifies himself and avoids admitting any wrongdoing leads his flock away from the Good Shepherd.

Case Study: The Unrepentant Pastor

When Our Savior's Church called their new senior pastor, they sought someone with strong leadership skills. Pastor Jamison had a reputation for determination and vision. At first, the people admired their self-confident pastor. But as staff and lay leaders worked with him, they began to resent his arrogance.

In his own eyes, Pastor Jamison could do no wrong. If there was any misunderstanding or disagreement, he made it clear that it was someone else's fault. Staff began to fear him. Several were terminated or resigned and left the church.

After trying to work with him for more than two years, the lay leadership confronted their pastor directly. He repeatedly denied any wrongdoing. They asked for his resignation. He refused, reminding them he had a divine call. Lay leaders indicated they would take the matter before the congregation to have his call rescinded. Pastor Jamison dared them to go ahead. He was confident the lay leaders could not garner the two-thirds majority required to remove him as pastor. Most of the people only knew their senior pastor through his preaching and leading of worship, and he was respected for his gifts in those areas.

The battles that ensued tore the congregation into three factions: those who supported the pastor, those who wanted the pastor to resign, and those who didn't know what was going on. Eventually, the pastor left after a long contest, and most of the lay leaders resigned and left the church. The congregation split into two churches, which when added together were smaller than the whole. No one knows how many left and never attended another church again.

The hypocrisy of a Pharisee-type attitude by the pastor makes a church unhealthy. Such a leader can lead the weak and new in faith to reject the Church and her Christ entirely.

As I described earlier, those who deny their sin deny the need for the Savior. When a pastor takes on such an attitude, he makes himself the messiah. He leads by his own power, wisdom, and strength. He fears that admitting any fault would make him appear weak, foolish, and feeble.

Some worldly philosophies reinforce the notion that leaders should never admit weakness. In order to inspire people to follow, one must lead with strong self-confidence. Some may be deceived into thinking that this approach to leadership is necessary to build confidence and strength in a church. However, replacing trust in the Lord with confidence in one's own abilities leads to arrogance.

The Bible warns against pride and arrogance.

> The fear of the LORD is hatred of evil. Pride and arrogance and the way of evil and perverted speech I hate. (Proverbs 8:13)

> Pride goes before destruction, and a haughty spirit before a fall. (Proverbs 16:18)

> Come now, you who say, "Today or tomorrow we will go into such and such a town and spend a year there and trade and make a profit"—yet you do not know what tomorrow will bring. What is your life? For you are a mist that appears for a little time and then vanishes. Instead you ought to say, "If the Lord wills, we will live and do this or that." As it is, you boast in your arrogance. All such boasting is evil. (James 4:13–16)

The Bible's approach to leadership differs dramatically from the world's view of leading from personal strength. Notice how the apostle Paul describes his own weakness:

> But He said to me, "My grace is sufficient for you, for My power is made perfect in weakness." Therefore I will boast all the more gladly of my weaknesses, so that the power of Christ may rest upon me. For the sake of Christ, then, I am content with weaknesses, insults, hardships, persecutions, and calamities. For when I am weak, then I am strong. (2 Corinthians 12:9–10)

When men arrogantly boast in their own strength, they glorify themselves. Christ is diminished. But when people acknowledge their weaknesses and cling to God's grace, Christ is glorified.

The Bible's approach to leadership differs dramatically from the world's view of leading from personal strength.

In contrast to the picture of the arrogant pastor I described above, I have been blessed to know many pastors who follow Paul's example. They do not feel the need to defend their every action. They humbly listen to criticism and seek to understand. They readily admit their weaknesses, confess their sins, and ask for forgiveness. Such actions confirm their faith and dependence upon Jesus, encouraging others to follow suit.

This includes some pastors who initially fell prey to the fear of man and escalated conflict by self-justifying their actions. I have witnessed pastors who recognized their sin and humbled themselves in confession, bringing healing and health to their flocks.

I am not advocating that a pastor utilize the pulpit as a personal confessional for his deepest and darkest sins. Preaching must focus on proclaiming Law and Gospel based on Scripture. But a pastor who feels he must appear sinless and therefore deny any wrongdoing negates the Word he preaches and discourages the faith of the weak and new believers.

Case Study: The Repentant Pastor

In one church, the pastor was loved by some and despised by others. In disagreements with a few long-term members, he insisted on his way, referencing his authority. Those members disrespected him and worked for his removal. After working with a reconciler, the pastor learned that his fear of man had led him to become defensive in disagreements. He had responded by ignoring the people's requests or discrediting those who opposed him. When he realized his sin in these conflicts, he confessed to the reconciler, who proclaimed God's forgiveness to him.

Having been reminded of God's love in Christ for him, the pastor prepared to confess to his people. There were some he met with one-on-one and a couple others who required the help of a mediator. But he also knew that his public comments had hurt the entire congregation.

He prepared his confession to his church. Before he led the congregation through confession in the worship service, he explained that he first needed to confess his sins to them. The elders were coached to lead the congregation in sharing God's forgiveness with their pastor. Next, the congregation confessed their sins using the familiar words of the liturgy, and their pastor proclaimed the forgiveness of Christ to them.

He thought his confession would mark the end of his ministry. Instead, it became a new beginning for him. His elders assisted him and his opponents in reconciliation through mediation. He ended up serving many more years as this congregation's pastor. As people discussed what happened during that worship service, many exclaimed that they had never seen a pastor confess his sin.

Witnessing a pastor confess sin and receive absolution should not be such an unusual event.

The Early Christian Church utilized an evening prayer service entitled Compline, or Prayer at the Close of the Day. Over the centuries, several church bodies continued the practice with a form of Compline for an evening service. This service often features a mutual time of confession and forgiveness. *Lutheran Service Book* (pp. 253–54) begins Compline as follows (Ⓛ means "leader" and Ⓒ means "congregation"):

Ⓛ The Lord Almighty grant us a quiet night and peace at the last.

Ⓒ Amen.

Ⓛ It is good to give thanks to the Lord,

Ⓒ to sing praise to Your name, O most high;

Ⓛ to herald Your love in the morning,

Ⓒ Your truth at the close of the day.   *Psalm 92:1*

Ⓛ Let us confess our sin in the presence of God and of one another.

Silence for self-examination.

Ⓛ I confess to God Almighty, before the whole company of heaven and to you, my brothers and sisters, that I have sinned in thought, word, and deed by my fault, by my own fault, by my own most grievous fault; wherefore I pray God Almighty to have mercy on me, forgive me all my sins, and bring me to everlasting life. Amen.

C   The almighty and merciful Lord grant you pardon, forgiveness, and remission of all your sins. Amen.

C   I confess to God Almighty, before the whole company of heaven and to you, my brothers and sisters, that I have sinned in thought, word, and deed by my fault, by my own fault, by my own most grievous fault; wherefore I pray God Almighty to have mercy on me, forgive me all my sins, and bring me to everlasting life. Amen.

L   The Almighty and merciful Lord grant you pardon, forgiveness, and remission of all your sins. Amen.

In this service, the pastor or other leader first confesses and receives absolution from the congregation. Next, the people confess and hear God's forgiveness proclaimed to them.

A pastor who admits faults and forgives others leads his congregation in a healthy dependence on Christ.

The unrepentant pastor also leads by example. He shows how arrogance, self-justification, and dependence on one's own ability replace humility, the need for God's forgiveness, and dependence upon Christ. The leadership of an unrepentant pastor threatens the spiritual well-being of a church.

THE UNREPENTANT AND THE REPENTANT LAY LEADER

An elder or board member who refuses to admit his own faults leads with arrogance and personal agendas, steering people away from a solid footing on Christ. Those who follow such a leader become deceived into believing that person's false claims about what is needed to restore the church to health.

Lay leaders carry similar responsibilities as their pastor and other professional church workers. Their personal behaviors sway the members of their church, sometimes even more than pastors do. A strong-willed layperson may exert major influence that affects the church's finances, decisions, and culture.

Some church leaders may hold positional authority (e.g., congregational president, elder chairman). They might rise to these positions because they own businesses or hold positions of authority in other vocations. They are regarded highly by others because of their skills, experience, and education. Their authority flows from their appointed position within the church.

Other lay leaders possess strong personal authority. Personal authority is given by others who respect, trust, or fear someone. These leaders may have held positions of congregational authority in the past. Or they may be the apparent leader of an influential family. People may give them positional power because of their significant financial gifts. Others revere them because of their strong personalities.

Lay leaders who are biblically grounded exercise their influence for good. Their examples inspire others to be in the Word and pursue God's direction for major decisions. Such individuals are known for taking responsibility for their own faults and for forgiving others. Other people seek them out for advice. They earn reputations as being spiritually mature. Their Christian lifestyle contributes to a healthy culture within the congregation.

On the other hand, a strong lay leader who depends on personal strength, arrogance, and intimidation weakens a congregation's health. Such individuals manifest unrepentance in passionate disagreements. Their example teaches others how to trust in personal power and strength and to fear those who hold power. This attitude undermines the health of a congregation.

Case Study: The Godly Lay Leader

I worked with a man who served as CEO of a successful international company for many years. Although he traveled extensively for work, he often served his congregation in key leadership roles. When I met him, he had retired from the corporation and no longer served as an elder or council member. But his pastors and lay leaders regularly sought his counsel. Over the years, he had earned strong personal power.

This man was known for his generosity of time, talents, and finances. His strong influence was not based on what he proclaimed about his own accomplishments and wisdom but on the fact that others held him in high regard. He regularly attended Bible study, and he even led some groups. He knew the Bible well, as was evident in conversations with him. In spite of all he had accomplished in life, he exhibited a humble spirit. He took time to listen, asking insightful questions for clarification. He was known as a man who owned his failures and admitted wrongs.

People would open up to him about their own failings. They knew he would be honest with them, including pointing out their weaknesses with care. But he had earned the reputation of being a forgiving and compassionate person. His leadership brought godly strength and health to his church. In the midst of crisis, his mature Christian faith helped the church stay grounded on the Rock.

Case Study: The Overbearing Lay Leader

I have also known lay leaders whose actions undercut their congregation's spiritual health. One head elder owned a prominent local business that employed several in the congregation. He had given large gifts to the church, and everyone knew it. His grandparents helped found the church, and family members had been in the church for decades. He reminded church staff of how he dealt with employees who resisted his direction. He knew how to wield his power.

Although he attended worship, he never participated in Bible study. Between worship services, he remained at the coffee urn, talking with friends and others while the pastor taught Bible class next door. He utilized this time to reinforce his own agenda. He often used strong language, sometimes crude, to emphasize his position. You learned to expect him to cut you off in mid-sentence so he could make his point. People feared his anger. During meetings or one-on-one, he was known for raising his voice and pounding his fist in judgment.

When reconcilers began to work with his church, he resisted their counsel. He took issue with their emphasis on confession and forgiveness. What bugged him most of all was the use of Scripture to help him recognize his own contributions to the conflict. The reconcilers witnessed his anger a couple of times when meeting with others, and they experienced his attempts to intimidate.

The reconcilers observed that his overbearing personality and overt sinful behavior contributed to significant spiritual weakness in the congregation. They trained other key lay leaders on how to respond to his bullying in firm but loving fashion. Rather than confess his wrongs, he stopped attending worship, waiting to come back into the congregation after the reconcilers left. However, the lay leaders were prepared to resist his attacks.

They learned biblical methods to respond to his tirades. They offered to work with him, encouraging him to join them in Bible study. He ended up resigning his position because he lost the ability to manipulate major decisions. The congregation's health improved.

Note that in this instance, the overbearing lay leader's absence alone was not what enhanced the congregation's health. Other leaders learned to trust God and His Word as they practiced confession and forgiveness. As their trust in Jesus increased, their ability to resist ungodly behavior in leadership matured.

THE FIX-IT MENTALITY

I'm in favor of resolving problems and restoring relationships. But I find that applying a fix-it mentality in a church can compromise her health. Utilizing such an approach detracts people from the underlying relationship issues, misdirecting them in their attempt to address all the issues and restore health to the congregation.

By nature, I'm a problem solver. I like being challenged and finding solutions. But when working on any kind of conflict involving people, I have to resist my own fix-it mentality. People are not problems to be fixed.

There are many like me who like to fix things. Such a characteristic is a gift from God. I look to many professionals who serve me by fixing my car, computer, and home appliances.

But using this gift when helping people in congregations can actually be detrimental. Instead of pointing back to Christ, this kind of thinking can drive people to overlook underlying relational issues and prescribe misguided solutions.

This fix-it mentality can be embraced by pastors, other professional church workers, lay leaders, denominational leaders, and consultants. The danger lies not only with the one who advocates the fix-it solution but also with the people who seek such solutions.

This kind of approach usually latches on to a real issue that does need addressing. The problem often is an obvious one that people can

People are not problems to be fixed.

readily understand and agree with. However, a more thorough diagnosis strives to identify multiple factors contributing to the church's struggles so that they can be proven and prioritized. This includes distinguishing between surface issues and the underlying causes.

Note that a fix-it approach works best with *substantive* or *material* issues. In a congregation, such issues may include confusing communications, an inadequate organizational structure, weak accounting processes, and lack of training. These kinds of issues are important and may be addressed through a fix-it mentality.

But *personal* or *relational* issues are not addressed well with a fix-it mentality. These issues deal with matters of the heart, usually involving spiritual issues such as sin and forgiveness. In disputes, personal issues usually accompany the substantive issues but require reconciliation, not conflict resolution. Because our God is a relational God, He stresses the importance of restoring relationships. Through His own example, He sacrificed His only Son while we were still sinners so that we would be reconciled to Him.

The fix-it approach tends to divert our attention from the underlying spiritual issues and lack of dependence upon Christ. Instead, it focuses attention on material issues that appear easier to identify and resolve. Unfortunately, many congregations suffer from this kind of thinking and act on such advice. When they do, congregational health suffers.

Case Study: St. John's Church

The congregation of St. John's agreed that the church building needed improvement. It lacked handicap access. The sanctuary furnishings were worn and faded. The only restrooms were in the basement. Off-street parking was sorely needed, and the entry to the church was uninviting.

The desires of various people exceeded their financial capabilities. Disagreements arose and camps formed around favorite projects. Clearly, the church was divided.

Leaders came up with the solution. "We can fix it by lumping together key projects into three options, and then decide by majority vote. The option with the most votes wins. This will be a fair way to solve our disagreements."

Obviously, a plan such as that made by the leaders of St. John's is doomed to fail unless the people's hearts are moved to not only accept but also support the final outcome. A decision will be made, but it will likely alienate those whose projects did not win approval. This will only serve to polarize the congregation and worsen its situation. Yet, I have seen many congregations assume similar approaches to all kinds of challenges, all of which end in disaster. Instead of working toward consensus and healing relationships broken by sinful behaviors, leaders look to solve the problems by simple majority vote.

I have encountered congregations that specifically want an expert from outside their congregation to come in and fix things for them. They believe that having an expert analyze their situation and propose or implement the solutions for them is all that is necessary. This professional may be a denominational leader or an outside consultant.

More than once, I met with congregations seeking the fix-it mentality.

Case Study: Fix It for Us

One time, I held a dozen meetings throughout the day with various leaders from a large church. Many of the lay leaders served in top management for large corporations. Everyone I met that day, including the senior pastor, told me they wanted to hire me as a consultant to "tell us what's wrong and fix us." I heard the same words used throughout the day. (It's always interesting to note what words and phrases are repeated in different settings. Such behavior indicates someone with influence has, over time, shaped the culture.)

That evening, I gathered the leaders together to propose a process to address their concerns.

"You have asked me to come and fix your congregation. You want a superhero to swoop in and save the day. I'm here to tell you some good news—I'm not that guy. I'm not your Savior. I did not die for your sins, and I'm not about to. Even if I did die for you, it won't do you any good and it certainly won't do me any good. But if you want our assistance, we will point you to the One who has died, risen, and ascended for you. Jesus Christ came into this world to save sinners like you and me. He promises to be with you always, even to the close of the age. He teaches in His Word how you can restore relationships with your heavenly Father and one another. As you reconcile your relationships, He can lead you to agree on how to handle the material issues. Him you can trust."

This helped them avoid the temptation for a quick fix from the "expert" and, instead, refocus their thinking in support of a reconciliation process.

Another way this mentality reveals itself is when people determine that the ideal solution is to eliminate one or more people. I understand there are instances when certain leaders need to step down. Too often, however, some congregations jump too quickly to this solution in search of an easy fix.

Case Study: Fixed Wrong

I recall a congregation that suffered from years of conflict. Several years before my visit, they engaged an organizational conflict consultant who concluded that they simply needed to get rid of most of the leadership, including the pastor. I thought they may have exaggerated what the consultant said until I saw a copy of his final report. The congregation followed every one of his recommendations. The turmoil and relational damage caused as a result was devastating, and the aftereffects remained for years. The congregation needed extensive Bible teaching and spiritual healing before hope was restored.

Case Study: Fixed to Break

Another church consultant described his own system for fixing conflicted churches. He requires that a church appoint him as the interim senior pastor and give him authority to institute change. In the course of several weeks, he determines who are the major problem leaders and terminates them. Sometimes he removes all in leadership. He takes a few more months to appoint and train a new team of leaders. Once the new team is trained and in place, he vacates the position, believing their problems have been solved. Just imagine the brokenness he leaves behind. Moreover, consider what he has taught the people to do when they encounter conflict again, whether in the church, their family, or workplaces. Fix it by getting rid of the problem people.

Fix-it thinking flies directly in conflict with what the Scriptures teach when working with people. Notice how justice, kindness, humility, reconciliation, confession, prayer, forgiveness, restoring with gentleness, peacemaking, and love are highlighted, while "fixing it" is absent.

> He has told you, O man, what is good; and what does the LORD require of you but to **do justice**, and to **love kindness**, and to **walk humbly** with your God? (Micah 6:8)

> [Jesus said,] "So if you are offering your gift at the altar and there remember that your brother has something against you, leave your gift there before the altar and go. First **be reconciled** to your brother, and then come and offer your gift." (Matthew 5:23–24)

> Therefore, **confess your sins** to one another and **pray** for one another, that you may be healed. (James 5:16)

> **Be kind** to one another, **tenderhearted**, **forgiving** one another, as God in Christ forgave you. (Ephesians 4:32)

> Brothers, if anyone is caught in any transgression, you who are spiritual should **restore** him in a **spirit of gentleness**. Keep watch on yourself, lest you too be tempted. (Galatians 6:1)

> If possible, so far as it depends on you, **live peaceably** with all. (Romans 12:18)

> By this all people will know that you are My disciples, if you **have love** for one another. (John 13:35)

Love is recognized by its actions, which do not include fixing others:

> Love is patient and kind; love does not envy or boast; it is not arrogant or rude. It does not insist on its own way; it is not irritable or resentful; it does not rejoice at wrongdoing, but rejoices with the truth. Love bears all things, believes all things, hopes all things, endures all things. (1 Corinthians 13:4–7)

It can be frustrating working with leaders who are stubborn and hard to get along with. There are times when it is necessary to correct those who are wrong, but that is not the same as fixing people. After futile admonition, it may be necessary to remove such people. Notice what the Scriptures teach about correcting others:

> And the Lord's servant must not be quarrelsome but kind to everyone, able to teach, patiently enduring evil, correcting his opponents with gentleness. God may perhaps grant them repentance leading to a knowledge of the truth, and they may come to their senses and escape from the snare of the devil, after being captured by him to do his will. (2 Timothy 2:24–26)

> Let the word of Christ dwell in you richly, teaching and admonishing one another in all wisdom, singing psalms and hymns and spiritual songs, with thankfulness in your hearts to God. (Colossians 3:16)

Being kind. Teaching. Patiently enduring evil. Correcting with gentleness. Waiting on God to bring about repentance. Meditating on the Word of Christ so that it strengthens and guides you as you teach and admonish. These things are not quick fixes.

There are situations where leaders need to be removed. In those cases, such actions must follow prescribed procedures. In addition, care must be provided for all those affected—the person removed, the person's family, those who supported the person, anyone hurt by that leader, and those in opposition. Simply firing a key leader without caring for those affected in the process will cause wounds that can last for generations.

God calls His children to strive for harmony.

> May the God of endurance and encouragement grant you to live in such harmony with one another, in accord with Christ Jesus, that together you may with one voice glorify the God and Father of our Lord Jesus Christ. (Romans 15:5–6)

He even directs us to our source of hope:

> May the God of hope fill you with all joy and peace in believing, so that by the power of the Holy Spirit you may abound in hope. (Romans 15:13)

WIDESPREAD BIBLICAL ILLITERACY

This book highlights again and again the importance of being in God's Word—for biblical illiteracy represents a major threat to congregational health.

I mentioned before that when I first began working with congregations, the extent of biblical illiteracy shocked me. When I share my experiences with denominational leaders, they often appear surprised as well.

I believe the failure to recognize this weakness among some churches is what leads so many pastors, laity, denominational leaders, and church consultants to propose solutions that fall short. Many of their ideas include valid recommendations. But if biblical illiteracy dominates a church's leadership or membership, even the best guidance will fail to address a congregation's most critical need if it ignores this weakness.

Yes, many churches would benefit from building consensus on a defined mission statement. Appropriate organizational structure can improve how a church functions and eliminate confusion over roles and authority. Training leaders how to develop strategic plans, set goals, improve communications, and lead meetings can make huge improvements.

But if the leaders or members are not being well nourished by God's Word, these things won't address their most important issue: their spiritual health. Untested assumptions about the spiritual maturity of long-term members or well-established churches can cause us to easily miss the underlying issues.

Some congregations tend to look for assistance in preserving their church as a cherished institution or in growing the fellowship.

Others may focus solely on their ability to serve their own members with specialized services. Some strive to protect their proud standing in the community—their status being a top priority. In other words, without knowing it, many churches seek professional assistance in learning how to better serve their idols.

Thus, recommendations for improving a congregation may be well intentioned and may in fact make it a better organization. But such changes may actually serve to reinforce their idolatry.

If a congregation fails to appreciate the need to involve more of its people in God's Word, they may improve some visible aspects of their church. They may even get along better and appear healthy. But their corporate spiritual health will remain vulnerable to disease and infection.

IMPLICATIONS FOR CHURCH LEADERS

Church leaders need to identify the threats to the Church Militant's spiritual health in order to implement defensive and offensive strategies. Recognizing the spiritual causes of a congregation's weaknesses, God's faithful people trust His Word and Sacraments for treatment. The more we make use of the Means of Grace—God's Word, Holy Communion, and Baptism—the more God can transform us into a healthy church.

Reflection

Reflection

Considering this chapter, discuss the following questions with the leaders in your congregation.

1. Think of any leader you've known (in or outside of church) who demonstrated arrogance and generally avoided admitting any wrongdoing. Without naming the person, discuss the following:

   a. How did that person communicate he or she was a strong leader?

   b. How did those under this person's leadership view him or her?

   c. How approachable was this person?

   d. How did that person's leadership affect the culture of the organization?

2. Think of any leader you've known (in or outside of church) who exemplified humility through admitting his or her own faults and who demonstrated compassion with a forgiving spirit when addressing others' failures.

   a. How did that person communicate he or she was a strong leader?

   b. How did those under this person's leadership view him or her?

   c. How approachable was this person?

Reflection

Reflection

d. How did that person's leadership affect the culture of the organization?

3. Think of someone you respect for his or her spiritually maturity. Explain why you view this person as spiritually mature.

   a. How does this person exhibit humility?

   b. How does this person demonstrate compassion and forgiveness?

   c. How well does this person reflect knowledge in Scripture?

   d. What other characteristics reveal this person's mature faith in Christ?

4. Describe a situation from your experience where a fix-it mentality failed to be helpful. What would have made a positive difference?

5. How might improving people's participation in the study of God's Word impact your own congregation?

6. Discuss with other leaders any insights you gained from this chapter as they might relate to your church.

CHAPTER 8

LIVING A CONFESSING FAITH

I lay my sins on Jesus, The spotless Lamb of God.
He bears them all and frees us From the accursed load.
I bring my guilt to Jesus To wash my crimson stains
Clean in His blood most precious Till not a spot remains.

I lay my wants on Jesus; All fullness dwells in Him;
He heals all my diseases; My soul He does redeem.
I lay my griefs on Jesus, My burdens and my cares;
He from them all releases; He all my sorrows shares.
(*LSB* 606:1–2)

I mentioned earlier that I remember very few highly conflicted congregations that exceeded my rule of thumb: more than 20 percent of their average worship attendance participated in adult Bible study. At initial examination, many of these unhealthy churches appeared to be the exception to the rule.

Although these churches' leaders asserted that their members attended Bible study, the people failed to exhibit spiritual maturity in how they treated one another. They failed to apply confession and forgiveness in their relationships with one another. Our reconciliation teams sought to understand the contributing factors to their poor spiritual condition.

In one case, the church reported a large number of people in small-group Bible studies. Investigation revealed that these small groups studied materials that were largely Law based (what God commands) with little or no Gospel (forgiveness through Christ). They focused on how Christians should live (sanctification) but glossed over what Christ has done for us (justification). When church members experienced disagreements, they responded primarily out of a strong sense of self-justification and legalism. They blamed one another and denied any personal responsibility. They did not confess their own sins or forgive one another.

In two other churches, Bible study groups selected their own materials. There was little accountability for what was being taught. Our reconciliation teams learned that some (perhaps most) of the study materials focused on moralism with little or no reference to the Gospel. When disagreements arose, the people did not know how to confess their own sins or forgive others. Instead, they had become self-righteous and accusatory of others.

In one such situation, we learned that the people had been studying humility. When we met with individuals, many boasted how humble they were. And yet, these same people were unable to humble themselves in admitting how they had contributed to the conflicts. Furthermore, they sinfully judged and condemned others who did not live up to their own expectations. With the focus on their own sanctification, they developed self-righteous attitudes rather than practice the humility of confession. They were unable to forgive, since they had forgotten they had been cleansed from their own sins (2 Peter 1:9).

We should not be surprised that some who study God's Word fail to confess sin or forgive as they have been forgiven. In Jesus' day, there were those who also knew the Scriptures but acted out of self-righteous attitudes. Instead of contrition, the scribes and Pharisees self-justified. They did not feel the need for a Savior—they declared themselves righteous by their own deeds (see Luke 5:29–32). Rather than showing compassion and forgiveness for others who sinned, they looked down upon them and judged them. Jesus told the parable of the Pharisee and the tax collector in confronting those with such attitudes (Luke 18:9–14).

Christ noted that the Word they taught should be heard and observed, but He warned against following their examples: "The scribes and the Pharisees sit on Moses' seat, so do and observe whatever they tell you, but not the works they do. For they preach, but do not practice" (Matthew 23:2–3).

Jesus taught we need to do more than just hear God's Word: "Blessed rather are those who hear the word of God and keep it!" (Luke 11:28). This means we should first apply God's Word to our own lives before applying it to others'.

Keeping God's Word also means applying both the Law (what God commands) and the Gospel (what God has done and is doing for us through Christ). Notice that it is God's love (Gospel) that compels us to live for others:

> For the love of Christ controls us, because we have concluded this: that one has died for all, therefore all have died; and He died for all, that those who live might no longer live for themselves but for Him who for their sake died and was raised. (2 Corinthians 5:14–15)

Because Jesus paid for the full punishment of our sins (Gospel), we receive power to resist sin and live in righteousness.

> He Himself bore our sins in His body on the tree, that we might die to sin and live to righteousness. By His wounds you have been healed. (1 Peter 2:24)

Because Jesus has loved and forgiven us (Gospel), we will love and forgive others (Law empowered by the Gospel).

> Put on then, as God's chosen ones, holy and beloved, compassionate hearts, kindness, humility, meekness, and patience, bearing with one another and, if one has a complaint against another, forgiving each other; as the Lord has forgiven you, so you also must forgive. And above all these put on love, which binds everything together in perfect harmony. And let the peace of Christ rule in your hearts, to which indeed you were called in one body. (Colossians 3:12–14)

In healthy churches, I have observed that people who have been studying the Word apply it first to themselves. They speak of God's commands and of the grace they have in Christ. Before I had offered

We should first apply God's Word to our own lives before applying it to others'.

any teaching or coaching in these churches, many of the leaders had already confessed their sins or extended forgiveness to others. They sought out those who disagreed with them for reconciliation. I also noticed in my survey of healthy churches that the pastors often described how people admitted their faults and forgave one another.

After years of working with both healthy and unhealthy churches, I have concluded that those churches whose leadership and members are in Bible studies balanced with both Law and Gospel demonstrate healthy behaviors that the weaker churches fail to exhibit. When disagreements arise among them, many from healthy churches know how to acknowledge their sins and forgive one another as God, through Christ, has forgiven them. Because their confidence is in Christ's forgiveness, they don't feel the need to self-justify—rather, they more freely admit their wrongs. Instead of accusing and condemning others, they demonstrate compassion for those who transgress. The maturity of their faith is evidenced when they practice confession and forgiveness with one another.

A congregation whose members know how to confess and forgive is a healthy community of believers. These folks are recognized as people who live a confessing faith. Jesus taught, "By this all people will know that you are My disciples, if you have love for one another" (John 13:35).

WHY DON'T WE DO THIS MORE OFTEN?

One of the greatest privileges we have as Christians is to share God's love and forgiveness with one another. Personally proclaiming and receiving God's forgiveness demonstrates faith and love for Christ's work on the cross.

Nevertheless, I find it disappointing that sharing God's forgiveness with a fellow believer in the midst of conflict tends to be unusual.

Case Study: The Conflicted Christian College

The conflict among the leadership in one Christian college threatened its continued existence. Although once close friends, board members and

> A congregation whose members know how to confess and forgive is a healthy community of believers.

executive staff had engaged in harsh battles for control. Members of the college president's family served on staff and faculty. His perspective was shared among many who were employed. Board members included alumni and key benefactors, and other donors backed their positions. The college depended upon donors for survival. The stakes were high. If relationships remained unreconciled and control issues unresolved, it was likely that the school would close.

On one side, the president and family members had dug in their heels. On the other side, board members prepared to defend their positions and take necessary action. Hours of individual coaching prepared the parties for a group mediation.

Before mediation, the three Christian mediators listened to the parties' individual stories and coached them in examining their hearts. The parties had been assigned homework designed to help them discover their idols. The mediators helped them consider the fears, cravings, and misplaced trust that contributed to the standoff.

The mediation team brought all the parties together and led them through the first phases of mediation, which took a full day. The next morning, the team summarized what they heard. They reviewed the school's major achievements and challenges. They reminded the parties of days when these leaders cherished one another. They pointed out some of the misunderstandings and differences in values and goals. Finally, the mediators observed how the people's hearts and sinful behaviors exacerbated disagreements, leading to major hurts and mistrust. They encouraged the leaders to confess their sins to one another and ask for forgiveness. The room fell quiet for a moment.

Bethany broke the ice. She had taken to heart the homework and coaching, and she was prepared for this opportunity. She had written her confession, using guidelines for confession the mediators had taught her. Bethany admitted her faults to the others at the table. She not only confessed specific sinful behaviors but also revealed her heart's idols. People on both sides looked down to avoid eye contact. Many of her words could have been confessed by others in that room.

When she finished reading, she addressed a few people by name and confessed specific sins to them. Bethany wrapped up by asking for forgiveness.

The response was silence. Bethany's brothers and sisters in Christ were unsure how to reply.

The mediation team handed out a form for confession and forgiveness (similar to Appendix A). They reminded the group of God's promises to all of us. "If we confess our sins, He is faithful and just to forgive us our sins and to cleanse us from all unrighteousness" (1 John 1:9). They invited the rest of the table to join them in proclaiming God's forgiveness to their sister in Christ, using the words on the form. All joined together in declaring God's grace to Bethany.

Next, the mediators taught the people how to proclaim God's forgiveness by reading a Bible passage with Bethany's name inserted in the verse (Appendix B). Anyone who wished to do so could read a passage to her.

The first to read was a friend from Bethany's side. But then people from the opposing side took their turns. As they experienced sharing God's grace, fear and reluctance turned to joy. Bethany's tears reflected relief and peace. Everyone wanted to share a Bible passage with her. Several also forgave her for personal offenses.

Following Bethany's example, each one took opportunity to confess. They longed to hear the Good News proclaimed to them. They had seen what a gift was given to Bethany, and they all wanted to experience it. The group took the rest of that day for confession and forgiveness. The following day, they worked out the substantive issues. The final agreement fell into place rather quickly because relationships and trust were being restored. Once an unhealthy leadership, they were recovering from spiritual weaknesses, ready to work together again! The college not only survived but also grew as they implemented their agreed-upon solutions. The spiritual maturing experienced by the leaders led to sharing with all the staff and faculty what they had learned.

One of them expressed, "I have never experienced God's forgiveness like this before. Why don't we do this more often?" The rest agreed with that person.

Practicing confession and proclaiming God's forgiveness brings health and vitality to maturing Christians and the communities in which they serve.

PROFESSING FAITH THROUGH CONFESSION
AND FORGIVENESS[14]

A sign of a healthy church is one where leaders and members profess their faith through confession and forgiveness.

The Greek word for *confess, homologeó* (from the root word ὁμολογέω), means "to say the same thing."

In the Letter to the Romans, Paul utilizes the word *confess*:

> But what does it say? "The word is near you, in your mouth and in your heart" (that is, the word of faith that we proclaim); because, if you *confess* with your mouth that Jesus is Lord and believe in your heart that God raised Him from the dead, you will be saved. For with the heart one believes and is justified, and with the mouth one *confesses* and is saved. (Romans 10:8–10, emphasis added)

When we confess with our mouth, we say the same thing that God says in His Word: Jesus is Lord. Our *saying the same thing* reflects what we believe in our heart about Christ being raised from the dead.

As we confess our faith in the words of the Apostles' Creed, we *say the same thing* that God teaches in the Scriptures: That the Father created us, Jesus Christ redeemed us, and the Holy Spirit sanctifies us.

John and James also used the word *confess*:

> If we *confess* our sins, He is faithful and just to forgive us our sins and to cleanse us from all unrighteousness. (1 John 1:9, emphasis added)

> Therefore, *confess* your sins to one another and pray for one another, that you may be healed. (James 5:16, emphasis added)

When we confess our sins, we *say the same thing* that God declares: We have sinned in thought, word, and deed, deserving God's wrath and eternal punishment (see Romans 3:10–12, 23).

When we confess our sins, believing in the forgiveness of sins through Christ, we confess our faith in Jesus. The confession of sin and the proclamation of forgiveness is a confession of faith.

The reverse is also true. If we do not confess our sin, we deny our need for Jesus. We profess faith in ourselves, "and the truth is not in us" (1 John 1:8).

A CONFESSING CHURCH

A healthy congregation is one whose leaders and members confess their faith by confessing their sins. They continue to profess faith in Christ as they declare God's forgiveness to one another. A healthy church is a confessing church. Their passions may lead to harsh words as they voice disagreement in meetings. But afterward, opposing parties come together to ask for forgiveness.

An unhealthy church struggles with confession and forgiveness. When disputes divide, members polarize. Self-justification replaces Christ's justification. Self-righteous judgment trumps forgiveness. Relationships are broken. The public witness of the church fails to reflect faith in a reconciling God. Instead of meeting with those with whom they disagree, members associate only with those who agree with them and often slander the others.

Transforming a congregation into a sin-confessing and forgiveness-proclaiming church takes more than an inspiring sermon or Bible study lesson. This kind of change needs more than simple instruction. Such a transformation requires divine power.

Paul tells us what it takes:

> I appeal to you therefore, brothers, by the mercies of God, to present your bodies as a living sacrifice, holy and acceptable to God, which is your spiritual worship. Do not be conformed to this world, but be transformed by the renewal of your mind, that by testing you may discern what is the will of God, what is good and acceptable and perfect. (Romans 12:1–2)

Paul urges the Christian not to be conformed to this world. In disputes, that means not responding to conflict the way the world does. This includes setting aside denial, self-righteousness, blame-shifting, grudges, and so forth. (See Romans 12:3–21.)

Instead, Paul says, "*Be transformed*." Note that he does not say, "Transform yourselves." We are to "*be transformed*" by God through "*the renewal of [our] mind*."

Only God can provide the kind of power needed to make such a divine transformation (see 2 Peter 1:3–4). He works through the Means of Grace, Word and Sacrament, to nurture us to maturity. Between weekly worship services, feeding on the Word of God produces what we are powerless to do on our own.

Remember what Paul wrote to the young pastor Timothy:

> All Scripture is breathed out by God and profitable for teaching, for reproof, for correction, and for training in righteousness, that the man of God may be complete, equipped for every good work. (2 Timothy 3:16)

Scripture equips the child of God for every good work, including living a confessing faith.

When someone is malnourished and in poor physical shape, it takes time to rebuild the person's vitality and to restore health. Likewise, when a person has been on many weekly spiritual fasts away from God's Word, restoring spiritual health will take time. The person needs weeks and months to feed on God's Word and exercise his or her faith.

Practicing faith in action matures our faith and prepares us for spiritual battle.

The Scriptures reinforce the need to put our faith into practice:

> Practice these things, immerse yourself in them, so that all may see your progress. (1 Timothy 4:15)

> What you have learned and received and heard and seen in me—practice these things, and the God of peace will be with you. (Philippians 4:9)

> For everyone who lives on milk is unskilled in the word of righteousness, since he is a child. But solid food is for the mature, for those who have their powers of discernment trained by constant practice to distinguish good from evil. (Hebrews 5:13–14)

By this it is evident who are the children of God, and who are the children of the devil: whoever does not practice righteousness is not of God, nor is the one who does not love his brother. (1 John 3:10)

As a congregation strives to engage its people in Scripture and urges them to practice their faith, there will be setbacks. The devil, the world, and the sinful flesh will all resist the path to health.

Accordingly, the leaders and members of a spiritually growing community need to take advantage of the opportunity for individual examination and healing. One of the ways in which we can exercise our faith is through private confession and absolution.

THE POWER OF PRIVATE ABSOLUTION

Just as King David was guilty of idolatry that led to a mess of sins, faithful church members—including lay leaders and professional church workers—can also fall prey. When David blinded himself, he needed help. God sent the prophet Nathan to privately assist David in examining his heart and provide healing through absolution.

God has provided me with faithful pastors and mature Christian friends who have served as Nathans to me.

Case Study: Pastor Richard Thompson and Me[15]

As a young businessman, I made my living by selling real estate. Additionally, I personally invested in real estate income properties. High interest rates and a drop in oil prices caused economic depression in our region in the early 1980s. Our real estate market tanked. Home foreclosures appeared in every neighborhood throughout our community.

Since both my profession and investments depended on a thriving real estate market, I found myself falling into financial ruin. My solution? Work longer hours. If only I worked harder, I assumed, I could make something happen. After all, my family's well-being depended on me, right? Working seven days a week, often more than twelve hours a day, did little to prevent the inevitable.

Notice how my reasoning depended on *me*. I had made myself a god

146

and placed more trust in me than in the true God. I was blind to my idolatry, and I was headed down a dangerous path.

I fell further behind in business obligations. I could not keep up with the losses in the income properties. When I was unable to make my own house payments, the mortgage lender started foreclosure. Utility companies threatened to shut off services. My wife took on part-time employment in addition to caring for our toddler.

Although I always considered myself a positive person, I fell into depression. I lost thirty pounds though my eating habits did not change. I thought I was sleeping well but woke up each day more tired than when I went to bed. I felt I was a failure in providing for my family. Guilt filled my heart because I could not pay my creditors, no matter how hard I tried to make something happen. I began to wish that I no longer lived.

I knew I was in trouble—not just financially, but emotionally and spiritually. I went to my pastor for advice.

Pastor Richard Thompson listened as I poured out my heart to him. Without my realizing it, he began to examine my spiritual condition. When describing my guilt, I told him I couldn't forgive myself for failing my family and my creditors. One of his questions in particular troubled me.

"Ted, is Jesus' blood not good enough for you?"

How dare he question my faith, I thought. I have been a faithful member of this church since childhood, and he asks me that?

"What do you mean?" I responded calmly, trying not to show my annoyance and giving myself time for a reasonable defense (that is, self-justification).

Pastor Thompson gently showed me that I was not trusting God but myself for the solution to my troubles. By thinking that I had to forgive myself, I was in fact rejecting the forgiveness that was mine in Christ.

Another point of confrontation bothered me.

"I haven't seen you in Bible class lately."

He observed that I had neglected God's Word, making myself more vulnerable to the guilt and depression affecting me.

Once again, my defenses went up. "Haven't you heard anything I've said? I told you I've been working twelve hours a day, seven days a week. I don't have time for Bible study. I still attend worship, you know."

Of course, he discerned what was needed. His patient and gentle guidance helped me see my weaknesses. I began to express repentance.

He then shared God's forgiveness with me. I was experiencing private absolution from my pastor. His kind words, his prayer, and his comfort of God's forgiveness filled my heart, my soul, and my mind.

On the way back home, I realized how sinful I had been. My pastor was right in his confrontation and advice. I took hold of the forgiveness given me and began to work on my attitude. I applied his counsel. Over the next weeks, I eased up on my work schedule, talked directly with my creditors, took some time off, and returned to Bible study.

I was being transformed over time. It's important to note that my financial condition had not yet improved, but my attitude had changed completely. My depression was replaced with new hope and dependence upon Christ.

One evening, I sat outside our home on our front step, reflecting on what God had done for me. My wife came out to see if I was all right and sat next to me. I told her I thought we would lose the house and business, but I said we would be okay. God promises to provide what we needed. She already believed that, of course. But she affirmed her love for me and her trust in Jesus.

That day I prayed the Lord's Prayer with new understanding in the petition "Give us this day our daily bread." I had also learned new appreciation for "Forgive us our trespasses."

In the weeks and months that followed, God provided in ways I could not have anticipated. I made a few real estate sales. Our utilities were never shut off. I didn't lose the business, and by God's grace, we eventually made back payments on the mortgage and retained our home. There was one investment property lost, but my partner covered my debts through the rest of the bad years so that there were no other major losses.

But what was most important to me was knowing that I was forgiven by God. In my depression, I didn't realize that His forgiveness was what I needed most of all. All my complaining and defenses did not deter my pastor from recognizing my sins (and my idols!), helping me recognize them, and then pronouncing God's forgiveness to me. My healing began with absolution.

David also describes healing that comes through God's forgiveness. As you read David's praises to God for all His benefits, note that all those benefits flow from the first, forgiveness from God.

Bless the LORD, O my soul,
    and all that is within me, bless His holy name!
Bless the LORD, O my soul,
    and forget not all His benefits,
who forgives all your iniquity,
    and heals all your diseases,
who redeems your life from the pit,
    who crowns you with steadfast love and mercy,
who satisfies you with good
    so that your youth is renewed like the eagle's. (Psalm 103:1–5)

From forgiveness come healing of our diseases[16], redemption from the pit (such as depression), encouragement from His steadfast love and mercy, and satisfaction of true needs so that our youth is renewed like the eagle's. God's forgiveness provides the vitality and health we need to face the spiritual battles of life!

That was not the only time I have experienced healing or encouragement through private absolution. I praise God that He has given me faithful pastors, a loving wife, and supportive Christian friends who know how to gently restore me with the assurance of God's grace in Christ.

When I work with spiritually healthy leaders who are experiencing significant challenges in their ministries, I often find people who have a practice of receiving private absolution. On the other hand, many leaders who become depressed because of the struggles in ministry have never experienced personal confession and absolution, confessing their sins to an individual and hearing God's forgiveness proclaimed to them.

The healthiest of churches benefit from pastors and other leaders who take advantage of the opportunities to hear God's forgiveness proclaimed to them directly, specifically, and personally.

SPECIAL NEED FOR PASTORS AND OTHER PROFESSIONAL CHURCH WORKERS

We laity have the privilege of going to our pastor for private absolution. In his ordination vows, he pledges to maintain the confidentiality of private confessions. He knows how to proclaim God's forgiveness in corporate worship services and in private settings with individuals. Most pastors are trained to recognize when someone needs help in examination and when to pronounce absolution.[17]

But for pastors, finding someone who will hear their confession and pronounce God's forgiveness can be challenging. Originally, I assumed that preachers could go to their ecclesiastical supervisors. But because such a person has authority over their professional status, many fear being vulnerable with him. I have suggested that pastors go to a neighboring pastor. But if there is no one near him he trusts as a confessor, this also becomes a barrier.

Other professional church workers, such as principals, teachers, directors of Christian education, directors of outreach, and deaconesses can experience similar fears if their pastor serves in a supervisory role. This is especially true in cases where conflict has strained relationships and trust is low.

For those of you called to serve as church workers, I encourage you to intentionally seek someone whom you can trust for private confession and absolution. Ask him if he will prayerfully consider serving you in this way. Tell him you want someone who will hear your confession to God, proclaim God's forgiveness, protect your confidentiality, and pray for you. You may also ask him to help you examine your own heart. If necessary, show him what to do, using a form for confession and absolution.[18]

I have served a number of weary pastors who have lost joy in pastoral ministry. Their ministries began with great excitement and joy to share God's peace. Over the years, they declared God's grace to the people in corporate Confession and Absolution. They preached thousands of sermons to God's people, assuring them of His love and forgiveness. They taught the Word of God to countless adults and children. They administered the Sacraments. They provided pastoral care to people in crisis. They regularly declared the promises of God to others.

But who says to the pastor, "I have good news for you; your sins are forgiven"?

I have met many pastors who have never received private absolution or who have not provided similar comfort to others. Likewise, I have met a number of other professional church workers who suffer in similar ways. They pour themselves out in caring for others, but they, too, need to hear the Good News proclaimed to them.

Furthermore, for a pastor to prepare for hearing another's confession, he himself ought to be a penitent.[19] Through confessing his own sins, he will learn to resist the temptation of prying into unnecessary details of a penitent's transgressions. He will be much less likely to judge another or be shocked by the ugliness of a particular sin. He will be conditioned to pronounce God's forgiveness because he himself will know the hunger for it in private confession. He will appreciate even more the need for confidentiality. But most important, he will be infused with the love and forgiveness of Christ that builds him up to be better equipped to care for souls.

Allow me to describe a fictional case that reflects what I have personally witnessed.

Case Study: Pastor Jack Brook

Pastor Jack Brook, who had been ordained for more than twenty years, suffered from depression and anxiety. Although he had faithfully served several churches, most of which flourished, his current call had exhausted him. He came under severe attack from a small group that opposed him. Because he was human, he had responded with anger, even preaching against his opponents in sermons. (He didn't specify their names, but everyone in his church knew whom he was talking about.)

Pastor Brook sought comfort from a Christian brother. His friend listened to Jack's hurts and disappointments. Jack needed spiritual care. His brother took time to share Scripture and pray with him. With Jack's permission, his friend asked questions to assist Jack in applying Scripture for examining his heart. Jack saw his sin and recognized his idols. Tears and words of confession reflected his contrition. His friend proclaimed God's forgiveness to him, using passages of Scripture. Jack's eyes watered as he heard good news proclaimed to him specifically, directly, and personally. After prayer, Pastor Brook thanked his friend and exclaimed, "I have been a pastor for twenty-five years, and no one has ever done that for me before!"

Imagine a pastor or other professional church worker serving for twenty-plus years before experiencing God's grace in such a personal way. What a difference it can make for such dedicated servants! And yet, many pastors and other professional church workers go years, even decades, without experiencing the healing power of private absolution. Consider the impact for these leaders and their churches if private absolution became part of their spiritual health practice.

Pastoral counselor and seminary professor Rev. Dr. Bruce Hartung specializes in church worker health and care. He urges lay leaders to be intentional in providing for the physical, emotional, and spiritual needs of their professional church workers, including the need for private absolution. "Churches can encourage their workers to find a confessor to whom they take specific sins, name them, confess them, and then hear the wonderful words of absolution."[20]

THE SECRET SIN—A HIDDEN CANCER

One of the most dangerous spiritual weaknesses is a secret sin. Even though we think that no one else knows, it is possible that someone may know. God certainly does. We convince ourselves that we can control it. Thus, we deny ourselves the opportunity to confess the sin and receive absolution for healing. Like a hidden cancer, it grows untreated and quietly weakens one's spiritual health.

Holding a sin secret slowly undermines our spiritual mooring. It may be a long-kept secret about something we consider unspeakable—a past affair, an abortion, or knowingly letting someone drive drunk who died or hurt someone else. It might have been a shameful act, sexual or otherwise. It may even be a pesky habit that we know violates God's commands and increases our guilt. Maybe it's a long-term pattern of idolatry—an addiction we're trying to hide, such as gambling or alcohol or Internet pornography.

King David went a long time with his "secret" sin. The reality was that different aspects of his sin were likely noticed by several others, but he remained self-deceived. As one who knew what a secret sin can do to one's spiritual health, David penned these words:

> For when I kept silent, my bones wasted away
>> through my groaning all day long.
> For day and night Your hand was heavy upon me;
>> my strength was dried up as by the heat of summer.
> (Psalm 32:3–4)

David also confessed in Psalm 51:

> For I know my transgressions,
>> and my sin is ever before me.
> Against You, You only, have I sinned
>> and done what is evil in Your sight,
> so that You may be justified in Your words
>> and blameless in Your judgment.
> Behold, I was brought forth in iniquity,
>> and in sin did my mother conceive me.
> Behold, You delight in truth in the inward being,
>> and You teach me wisdom in the secret heart. (vv. 3–6)

Whether it be in my personal life, or in my working with others, I have witnessed the destructive power of a secret sin. Because you know better than to commit such sin, guilt eats away at you. You try to minimize its effects on you. You look for ways to hide it from others. Eventually, it will sear your conscience and you will begin to justify what you are doing. Spiritual heart disease is taking its toll on your most inward thoughts.

But as one who experienced the effects of a secret sin, David also experienced the cure. He prescribes treatment.

> I acknowledged my sin to You,
>> and I did not cover my iniquity;
> I said, "I will confess my transgressions to the LORD,"
>> and You forgave the iniquity of my sin. (Psalm 32:5)

Having been restored to God through confession and forgiveness, David was better equipped to lead Israel in repentance and reconciliation.

> Restore to me the joy of Your salvation,
>> and uphold me with a willing spirit.
> Then I will teach transgressors Your ways,
>> and sinners will return to You. (Psalm 51:12–13)

Private absolution is a safe place to pour out the secret sins of your heart. As you hear God's assurance of forgiveness proclaimed to you, you become transformed through the renewal of your mind.

"Bless the LORD, O my soul" (Psalm 103:1). Bless Him indeed!

Reflection

Over the years, our reconcilers have developed a simple tool that helps assess relational health within a congregation (see Appendix C). This is especially helpful in congregations that have denied the need for studying and practicing confession and forgiveness. A summation of the answers can indicate a need for study and application in reconciliation within a congregation's midst.

To assess relationship health within your church, duplicate and hand out the form from Appendix C on a half sheet of paper, providing a blank at the end of each question. Ask people to estimate the numbers to the best of their ability, and then fold the sheet in half and hand it in.

Tabulate the totals for each question, and then add all the totals. Report the results of each question's number and the summation of all totals to the group. This exemplifies a number of hurting relationships that need healing through confession and forgiveness.

This is not a precise tool that reveals which individuals need the most help. But it is useful for showing the congregation's overall need for study and help in this area.

Whether or not you use this simple assessment form, discuss these questions with other leaders:

1. How well do the members of your church confess their faith by the way in which they take responsibility for their own contributions to conflict?

2. Are the members of your church known for how they forgive one another?

3. How many families in your church practice confession and forgiveness in the home?

Reflection

Reflection

4. How well do your members understand what the Bible teaches about confession and forgiveness?

5. How many of the leaders of your church have a practice of privately confessing sins before another believer and hearing God's forgiveness proclaimed to them?

6. What ideas from this chapter would be most helpful to implement for strengthening the health of your congregation?

PART 3

HEALTHY SPIRITUAL LEADERSHIP

As I've mentioned before, the Church is more than a club or service organization. As the Body of Christ, she needs to be equipped for spiritual battle as she puts on the whole armor of God.

A spiritually healthy church depends upon spiritually healthy leadership, as alluded to in the previous chapter. Without nourishment from God's Word, a church will lose her distinction as Christ's Body among her members. Regular feeding on the living Word is crucial for building up her leaders and sustaining the congregation's health.

Professional church workers sacrifice in their service to the Church. Just like the members they serve, they also need to be cared for and well fed. The lay leadership has the privilege and opportunity to minister to the ministers so they can remain healthy together.

If a church is not spiritually healthy, changing its organizational structure will not make it healthy. However, while organizational structure does not guarantee church wellness, well-defined roles and authorities do help to reduce unnecessary conflict. Healthy leaders commit themselves to defining how they serve together, seeking not only their own interests but also the interests of others.

This section highlights the importance of building and maintaining spiritually healthy leaders.

CHAPTER 9

NOT JUST ANOTHER ORGANIZATION

We are God's house of living stones,
Built for His own habitation.
He through baptismal grace us owns
Heirs of His wondrous salvation.
Were we but two His name to tell,
Yet He would deign with us to dwell
With all His grace and His favor. (*LSB* 645:3)

"This is *my* church."

"Look, I pay my offerings. And I expect that *my* church will provide what *I* want."

"You can't tell me what to do in *my* church."

"*My* grandparents founded this church. You're just the pastor, and in a few years you'll be gone. But I'm here for life. Don't expect *my* family to support your changes."

"Unless you have three generations buried in this church's cemetery, your opinions don't count here."

These reflect the attitudes of real people from churches I have served. Amazingly, these folks acted as if their church was a privately owned club or secret society. You had to earn the right to offer your opinion.

It's understandable how people can become so attached to a church or even to the church building itself. For those who have belonged for years, even generations, think of the important life events that have taken place in their church: Baptisms, confirmations, marriages, funerals, pastoral care, prayers, and anniversary celebrations. This is where they have received the Lord's body and blood. It is here that they have been fed and nourished with God's Word. The church is where forgiveness of sins has been proclaimed. Long-term friendships and family connections were formed in the church.

In response to God's love, many have given years of service to their church. They have contributed financial offerings, including major gifts for special projects and for memorializing loved ones.

Once again, the devil can turn our blessings into idols. As a result of years of dedicated service and sacrificial gifts, some can be tempted to believe they have earned or purchased certain rights. Because of the important life events that have taken place there, people may treasure the building, the sanctuary, the altar, or baptismal font with a greater significance than God's eternal gifts.

WHAT DISTINGUISHES THE CHURCH FROM OTHER ORGANIZATIONS?

The Church is the Body of Christ in which God Himself dwells—not just another social or philanthropic organization. In Ephesians 2, Paul describes this spiritual collection of God's people:

> So then you are no longer strangers and aliens, but you are fellow citizens with the saints and members of the household of God, built on the foundation of the apostles and prophets, Christ Jesus Himself being the cornerstone, in whom the whole structure, being joined together, grows into a holy temple in the Lord. In Him you also are being built together into a dwelling place for God by the Spirit. (vv. 19–22)

Peter also described the Church as a spiritual building:

> You yourselves like living stones are being built up as a spiritual house, to be a holy priesthood, to offer spiritual sacrifices acceptable to God through Jesus Christ. (1 Peter 2:5)

Membership in a club provides certain privileges and earthly benefits in return for the members' devotion, which often includes fees or dues. Membership in the Church is attained by faith in the One who paid the ultimate price.

> Christ loved the church and gave Himself up for her, that He might sanctify her, having cleansed her by the washing of water with the word, so that He might present the church to Himself in splendor, without spot or wrinkle or any such thing, that she might be holy and without blemish. (Ephesians 5:25–27)

Belonging to a club can give us prestige, status, and even identity. We may attain greater recognition by our achievements in the organization or service as officers or board members. Membership entitles us to special benefits. In some ways, the Church can offer similar earthly benefits. But she offers much more than any temporal entity.

Membership in Christ's Church entitles one to a new status before God. "For our sake He made Him to be sin who knew no sin, so that in Him we might become the righteousness of God" (2 Corinthians 5:21). As part of His Body, we are transformed from the condemned to the justified (Romans 8:1).

Our identity is not found on the member roster of a local congregation, but rather in the name of our God. Baptism christens us with a new name: Child of God. "See what kind of love the Father has given to us, that we should be called children of God; and so we are" (1 John 3:1).

Unlike membership in worldly organizations, membership in the Body of Christ entitles one to an eternal benefit: "For God so loved the world, that He gave His only Son, that whoever believes in Him should not perish but have eternal life" (John 3:16).

Congregations possess certain characteristics similar to worldly organizations. For example, they may own valuable assets such as real estate and buildings. They receive financial revenues, employ people, and pay salaries and other expenses. They benefit the communities in which they exist by extending aid to those in need. In the United States, a church must be incorporated to be recognized as a charitable non-profit organization. This favorable status relieves the church from paying income taxes and allows its donors to deduct contributions from

Our identity is not found on the member roster of a local congregation, but rather in the name of our God.

their taxes. Incorporation also protects the officers and members from being individually responsible for legal liabilities of the organization. The church has responsibilities to manage all of its physical assets and people resources in accord with civil laws.

Nevertheless, these do not define what churches are ultimately about. The earthly organizational attributes must not overshadow the spiritual responsibilities of churches and their elected leaders.

The Body of Christ gathers together to serve eternal purposes. The Church is given the unique responsibility and authority to preach repentance and forgive or retain sins. She is called to make disciples of all nations, baptizing and teaching people to obey all that Jesus taught. She equips her members to fight the spiritual battles of this world and reach out to unbelievers with the Good News of forgiveness in Christ.

The Church is unlike any other organization on earth. Thus, those chosen to lead her need to be uniquely qualified.

SERVING GOD AS A CONGREGATIONAL LEADER

Because organizations are composed of people, conflict is inevitable, even in churches. In Acts 6, Luke writes about the growth of the Early Church and a dispute that developed:

> Now in these days when the disciples were increasing in number, a complaint by the Hellenists arose against the Hebrews because their widows were being neglected in the daily distribution. (v. 1)

The apostles could have stepped in to solve the matter (conflict resolution). But they utilized this conflict as an opportunity to become more effective in their mission. They prioritized their own responsibilities for preaching the Word and prayer, delegating social ministry matters to lay leaders.

> And the twelve summoned the full number of the disciples and said, "It is not right that we should give up preaching the word of God to serve tables. Therefore, brothers, pick out from among you seven men of good repute, full of the Spirit and of wisdom, whom we will appoint to this duty. But

The Church is unlike any other organization on earth. Thus, those chosen to lead her need to be uniquely qualified.

we will devote ourselves to prayer and to the ministry of the word." (vv. 2–4)

Scripture records those who were chosen:

And what they said pleased the whole gathering, and they chose Stephen, a man full of faith and of the Holy Spirit, and Philip, and Prochorus, and Nicanor, and Timon, and Parmenas, and Nicolaus, a proselyte of Antioch. These they set before the apostles, and they prayed and laid their hands on them. (vv. 5–6)

As the Early Church expanded, more structure was needed. It organized by appointing different people for certain responsibilities.

Note that the apostles did not ask for volunteers. Rather, they asked the church to pick persons with specific credentials. "Therefore, brothers, pick out from among you seven men of good repute, full of the Spirit and of wisdom, whom we will appoint to this duty" (v. 3). The first one mentioned is Stephen, "a man full of faith and of the Holy Spirit." We remember Stephen as the first martyr of the Church, killed because of his courageous witness to Christ (Acts 6:8–7:60).

If the apostles were seeking people for administrative functions, why not require business acumen or governing skills? The apostles recognized that leadership in a church is unique. Even administrative functions in a church require spiritual maturity. To manage fairly and have the support of the people, lay leaders need to have good reputations and be known for their strong faith and godly wisdom.

Because the Church is not just another organization, her leaders need to be spiritually qualified.

BIBLICAL QUALIFICATIONS

Paul lists qualifications for leadership in Christ's Church.

The saying is trustworthy: If anyone aspires to the office of overseer, he desires a noble task. Therefore an overseer *must be above reproach, the husband of one wife, sober-minded, self-controlled, respectable, hospitable, able to teach, not a drunkard, not violent but gentle, not quarrelsome, not a lover of money.* He *must manage his own household well, with all dig-nity keeping his children submissive,* for if someone does not know how to manage his own household, how will he care for God's church? He *must not be a recent convert,* or he may become puffed up with conceit and fall into the condemna-tion of the devil. Moreover, he *must be well thought of by out-siders,* so that he may not fall into disgrace, into a snare of the devil. (1 Timothy 3:1–8, emphasis added)

The word translated "overseer" refers to the pastoral office. Because of his noble task, the pastor wields great influence with the flock by his character and example. The calling of qualified men for this service requires careful examination and selection.

Paul continues to describe how lay leaders must meet similar qualifications:

Deacons likewise *must be dignified, not double-tongued, not addicted to much wine, not greedy for dishonest gain.* They *must hold the mystery of the faith with a clear conscience.* And *let them also be tested first;* then let them serve as deacons *if they prove themselves blameless.* Their *wives likewise must be dignified, not slanderers, but sober-minded, faithful in all things.* Let deacons each be the *husband of one wife, managing their children and their own households well.* For those who serve well as deacons *gain a good standing for themselves and also great confidence in the faith that is in Christ Jesus.* (1 Timothy 3:8–13, emphasis added)

Every Christian is called to live a godly life. Therefore, because the Church is a spiritual house whose Head is Jesus Christ, those who serve in leadership must exemplify spiritual maturity in their daily lives.

I received a call from a panicked pastor one day. His congregation was preparing to elect new officers. One candidate had been nominated for president who had not been in worship for more than a year. The nominee had also made it clear he intended to force the pastor out.

I asked the pastor, "What do your bylaws require to be nominated as an officer?"

"The only requirement is that they be members of the church."

"Is he a member?"

"Yes."

"Does the church have any policies requiring that lay leaders meet certain spiritual qualifications based on Scripture?"

"I'm afraid not. That's it."

Unfortunately, this church had not adopted written guidelines for qualifying people for leadership. I suggested that the pastor make a respectful appeal to his congregation before elections, reminding them of biblical qualifications for service in the church. However, in the end, the church elected the man who had not been in worship. He had standing in the community and a long family history in the church. In any other organization, that would be sufficient. Through its election process, the congregation displayed her lack of interest in selecting spiritually mature leaders. Not surprisingly, the pastor ended up being pressured to resign.

One who serves in church leadership must exhibit self-control and gentleness and be respectable. A person who earns a reputation for losing his or her temper fails these requirements.

One lay leader known for losing his temper became so angry in a congregational meeting that he literally jumped up and down, shaking his fists and raising his voice. In another church, a council member intimidated others by getting red in the face, screaming over others until they agreed with her. A pastor lost respect from his lay leaders because on several occasions he lost his temper, yelling and using coarse language. Parishioners described cases where this pastor stormed out of meetings, sometimes throwing aside a chair or kicking an object in his way.

When confronted about their anger, each of these people denied wrongdoing, defended his or her actions, and blamed others. Their lack of repentance confirmed faith in their own strength rather than in Jesus and His righteousness.

In the world, some rally around people who use angry behavior to control or manage others. CEOs, political candidates, coaches, foremen, and others who earn reputations for angry outbursts may be regarded as powerful bosses who exude strength and confidence.

Scripture stresses that spiritually wise leaders control their temper. In selecting people to serve in positions of authority, God shows preference: "Whoever is slow to anger is better than the mighty, and he who rules his spirit than he who takes a city" (Proverbs 16:32).

The Bible warns against the dangers of anger and calls for a different approach:

> Be angry and do not sin; do not let the sun go down on your anger, and give no opportunity to the devil. . . . Let all bitterness and wrath and anger and clamor and slander be put away from you, along with all malice. Be kind to one another, tenderhearted, forgiving one another, as God in Christ forgave you. (Ephesians 4:26–27, 31–32)

The Word refutes those who claim that anger can produce godly fruit: "Know this, my beloved brothers: let every person be quick to hear, slow to speak, slow to anger; for the anger of man does not produce the righteousness of God" (James 1:19–20).

A healthy congregation is one whose members recognize that the Church is a spiritual house, different from worldly organization. As the Body of Christ, they select leaders who are of good repute, full of the Spirit and of wisdom, gentle, and even tempered. Organizationally, the healthy congregation formalizes biblical criteria for leadership in her governing documents to be faithful to God's Word and protect her from appointing spiritually immature leaders.

ACCOUNTABILITY IN THE CHURCH

Membership in the Church is not just about being a part of an earthly organization. Being a member of Christ's Body means that you are part of the communion of saints, who will live together eternally in heaven.

Thus, when someone strays away from the flock, it's much more serious than an organization losing a financially contributing member.

Being a member of Christ's Body means that you are part of the communion of saints, who will live together eternally in heaven.

This becomes a matter with eternal consequences. A person's eternal welfare is at stake.

Holding one another accountable is an important responsibility for pastors, elders, and other church leaders. Christ calls all His followers, young and old, to be self-disciplined:

> But as for you, teach what accords with sound doctrine. Older men are to be sober-minded, dignified, self-controlled, sound in faith, in love, and in steadfastness. Older women likewise are to be reverent in behavior, not slanderers or slaves to much wine. They are to teach what is good, and so train the young women to love their husbands and children, to be self-controlled, pure, working at home, kind, and submissive to their own husbands, that the word of God may not be reviled. Likewise, urge the younger men to be self-controlled. (Titus 2:1–6)

The words *discipline* and *disciple* are derived from the Latin word *discipulus,* meaning "pupil." One who is disciplined is a learner. Thus, all of Christ's disciples are to be students of His Word. Preaching, teaching, and pastoral counseling are all forms of discipline. Disciples who stray away from the teaching of Christ are to be disciplined for their own good.

> My brothers, if anyone among you wanders from the truth and someone brings him back, let him know that whoever brings back a sinner from his wandering will save his soul from death and will cover a multitude of sins. (James 5:19–20)

Exercising discipline must be done with care and love. Leaders in Christ's Church are instructed in how to deal with the erring:

> And the Lord's servant must not be quarrelsome but kind to everyone, able to teach, patiently enduring evil, correcting his opponents with gentleness. (2 Timothy 2:24)

The following summarizes Paul's instructions to Timothy regarding what the Lord's servant ought to do and not do when correcting others.

> ## THE LORD'S SERVANT
>
> From 2 Timothy 2:22–26, notice what the Lord's servant ought to do:
>
> - Pursue righteousness, faith, love, and peace, along with those who call on the Lord from a pure heart
> - Be kind to everyone
> - Be able to teach
> - Patiently endure evil
> - Correct opponents with gentleness
>
> These same passages tell what the Lord's servant should avoid:
>
> - Youthful passions
> - Foolish, ignorant controversies (they breed quarrels)
> - Being quarrelsome

While church leaders have responsibility for holding people accountable, they cannot force repentance. Change of heart is God's job: "God may perhaps grant them repentance leading to a knowledge of the truth, and they may come to their senses and escape from the snare of the devil, after being captured by him to do his will" (2 Timothy 2:25–26).

Change of heart is God's job.

Paul reinforces how the members of Christ's Church are to be treated when they are ensnared in sin. Notice that he does not say that just anyone should restore such a person. He requires that the restorer be *spiritual*: "Brothers, if anyone is caught in any transgression, you who are spiritual should restore him in a spirit of gentleness. Keep watch on yourself, lest you too be tempted" (Galatians 6:1).

People who restore others must use caution lest they also fall into sin. Leaders of the Church need to be self-disciplined and regularly reside in God's Word so that they can hold others accountable in their Christian walk (Colossians 3:12–17).

When church members refuse to repent after much admonition, they are to be disciplined in the hope that they will be restored. Those who deny their sin deny their need for Christ. They are in danger of forfeiting eternal life in heaven. Churches exercise discipline according to Jesus' instructions for restoring the erring:

> [Jesus said,] "If your brother sins against you, go and tell him his fault, between you and him alone. If he listens to you, you have gained your brother. But if he does not listen, take one or two others along with you, that every charge may be established by the evidence of two or three witnesses. If he refuses to listen to them, tell it to the church. And if he refuses to listen even to the church, let him be to you as a Gentile and a tax collector. Truly, I say to you, whatever you bind on earth shall be bound in heaven, and whatever you loose on earth shall be loosed in heaven. Again I say to you, if two of you agree on earth about anything they ask, it will be done for them by My Father in heaven. For where two or three are gathered in My name, there am I among them." (Matthew 18:15–20)

> [Jesus] breathed on [His disciples] and said to them, "Receive the Holy Spirit. If you forgive the sins of any, they are forgiven them; if you withhold forgiveness from any, it is withheld." (John 20:22–23)

The Church is the only organization on earth entrusted with the Office of the Keys. "The Office of the Keys is that special authority which Christ has given to His church on earth to forgive the sins of repentant sinners, but to withhold forgiveness from the unrepentant as long as they do not repent."[21]

This specific assignment flows out of the Great Commission. Churches are to preach repentance and proclaim the Good News that those who believe in Christ will be forgiven and spend eternity in heaven. Because of the eternal consequences, churches exercise a unique form of discipline to restore members who fall away.

LEADING BY EXAMPLE

Children make great recording devices. They observe, remember, and replay.

As a father, I am both pleased with and embarrassed by how much my son imitated me. He repeated things he saw me saying and doing—both good and bad. It does not take long as a parent to recognize how our example as adults significantly influences our children. Even today, I hear my adult son using words or phrases he heard from me when he was a child.

It's no different in Christ's Church. Pastors, other professional church workers, and lay leaders all teach by living as examples. Just as children do, the members of a church learn from their leaders how to live the sanctified life.

Paul's instruction to Timothy applies to church leaders today:

> Let no one despise you for your youth, but set the believers an example in speech, in conduct, in love, in faith, in purity. . . . Keep a close watch on yourself and on the teaching. Persist in this, for by so doing you will save both yourself and your hearers. (1 Timothy 4:12, 16)

Consider what you teach by example. Are you known as a student of God's Word? Your example is teaching. Do people recognize your speech as godly, speaking well of others? People are learning from you. Would people describe you as one who is kind and gentle, or harsh and angry? Either way, you demonstrate how to exhibit those attributes. As leaders, we are frequently unaware of how often people observe our behavior and imitate it.

As mentioned earlier, two critical behaviors for church leaders to exemplify are participation in Bible study and the practice of personal confession and forgiveness.

DIVINE EMPOWERMENT

When you consider all that God requires of leaders in His Church, you might think you could never make the mark. In fact, who among us sinners can truly fulfill the requirements of Scripture?

In spite of our weaknesses, God chooses to accomplish His perfect will and fulfill His Great Commission through forgiven sinners. Those who humble themselves in confession and trust in Christ's forgiveness are empowered to do that which they could never do on their own.

Hebrews 11 recounts many of the heroes featured in the Old Testament. They are highly regarded, yet Scripture recorded for us how they sinned against God and others. Many failed to meet the mark repeatedly.

What distinguishes leadership in God's eyes? "Now faith is the assurance of things hoped for, the conviction of things not seen. For by it the people of old received their commendation" (Hebrews 11:1–2). Throughout the chapter, the author repeats the words "by faith" as he recalls how the saints of old persevered in their faith, despite obstacles and failures.

These ancient leaders of God's people left us an example for today:

> Therefore, since we are surrounded by so great a cloud of witnesses, let us also lay aside every weight, and sin which clings so closely, and let us run with endurance the race that is set before us, looking to Jesus, the founder and perfecter of our faith, who for the joy that was set before Him endured the cross, despising the shame, and is seated at the right hand of the throne of God. Consider Him who endured from sinners such hostility against Himself, so that you may not grow weary or fainthearted. (Hebrews 12:1–3)

"Lay aside every weight, and sin which clings so closely." Set aside the world's distractions, put away your idols, and confess your sin.

"Let us run with endurance the race that is set before us, looking to Jesus, the founder and perfecter of our faith." We serve in a militant Church, fighting spiritual forces. Thus, we need to be armed for battle, sustained with the Word, and focused on Christ.

"Consider Him who endured from sinners such hostility against Himself, so that you may not grow weary or fainthearted." We depend on the One who gave His righteousness to us. He is the source for our strength and our hope for the fight.

We do not lead Christ's Church as just another organization. We need more than what the world seeks in a leader. Because we fight spiritual battles, we need divine empowerment.

God does not call people to tasks without His provision. Peter reminds us that God furnishes what is needed:

> His divine power has granted to us all things that pertain to life and godliness, through the knowledge of Him who called us to His own glory and excellence, by which He has granted to us His precious and very great promises, so that through them you may become partakers of the divine nature, having escaped from the corruption that is in the world because of sinful desire. (2 Peter 1:3–4)

Where do we find this heavenly energy and authority? In God's precious and very great promises. We are empowered by the forgiveness of sins through the Means of Grace. We set aside the nearsightedness of the world as we recall we are God's forgiven children. "For whoever lacks these qualities is so nearsighted that he is blind, having forgotten that he was cleansed from his former sins" (2 Peter 1:9).

The members of a healthy congregation understand that the Church is not just another organization. She is the Body of Christ, a spiritual house, whose Head is Christ Jesus, her Lord. Accordingly, her leaders need to be spiritually qualified for service.

We do not lead Christ's Church as just another organization. We need more than what the world seeks in a leader. Because we fight spiritual battles, we need divine empowerment.

Reflection

Reflection

Because a church is not just another organization, her leaders should be carefully chosen for unique service. She also has unique responsibilities for exercising discipline among members. Consider these questions as you reflect on your own congregation, and discuss the following with other leaders:

1. In light of the fact that all men are sinful (Romans 3:10–12, 23), how would you define "above reproach" in 1 Timothy 3:2? (Consider 1 John 1:8–10 for part of your answer.) Why do you think this is an important characteristic of leaders in Christ's Church?

2. In 1 Timothy 4:12, Paul instructs Timothy to set an example for the believers. Provide practical examples of how this might be applied today in the areas of speech, conduct, love, faith, and purity.

3. Reviewing 1 Timothy 4:16, in what two areas does St. Paul urge leaders to persevere? Which is most important? Why?

4. Divine power is granted to those who remember that they have been cleansed from their past sins (2 Peter 1:3–4, 9).

   a. How can you as a leader remember that you have been cleansed from your past sins?

   b. How can you be better prepared to announce God's forgiveness to those who admit their faults to you?

5. Discuss the importance of discipline in Christ's Church.

   a. How is the Office of the Keys carried out in your congregation?

   b. Are there any areas in which your church could strengthen its responsibilities in the Office of the Keys?

6. List three to five ideas from this chapter that could be implemented in your church. P. 161

CHAPTER 10

FOCUSING ON SPIRITUAL LEADERSHIP

> Speak, O Lord, Your servant listens,
>> Let Your Word to me come near;
> Newborn life and spirit give me,
>> Let each promise still my fear.
> Death's dread pow'r, its inward strife,
>> Wars against Your Word of life;
> Fill me, Lord, with love's strong fervor
>> That I cling to You forever! (*LSB* 589:3)

Consider the spiritual issues related to the following situations:

- A long-term member and former congregational leader builds resentment against the pastor. He writes a letter to the elders explaining that he is recording the pastor's sermons and sending them to the denomination's top leadership so they remove him as pastor.

- Three unhappy parents write a letter to all of the parents in their children's fourth-grade class, complaining about the teacher at your church's Christian school. They are hosting an evening where they can gather and prepare to show up unannounced at a school board meeting to pressure them for his removal. Another parent forwards a copy to you as a leader of the church.

- The guy who plays guitar and leads the worship team has been living with a woman who sings with the team, but they are not married. They just announced to the rest of the worship team that she is pregnant.

- For the last three years, the church has spent more than it has received. Each year, the congregation has borrowed money from the church's endowment plan. The endowment plan was established for capital improvements, stipulating that no funds were to be spent until $500,000 had been raised. The total raised to date is $275,000. The congregation has borrowed $150,000 from it but has not arranged for paying it back. An attorney representing the family whose estate contributed $200,000 to the fund sent a letter demanding that the funds be immediately restored.

Reflection

Instead of inserting application questions at the end of this chapter, I have incorporated exercises and questions throughout. I encourage you to work through this chapter together with other leaders in your congregation. Begin by discussing the following question based on the bullet points above:

1. Identify the spiritual issues in each situation.

2. Remembering that the Church is not just another organization but the Body of Christ, how would you and other leaders address the spiritual issues of these situations? Identify some Scripture passages that could guide you.

CHALLENGES FOR THE CHURCH LEADER

When presenting a lay leadership workshop, I ask participants to think of situations that frustrate them as church leaders. Using a flip chart, I write down as many ideas as they can come up with in a ten-minute period. I find that in each workshop I present, the group can identify at least forty or fifty different items. They include things such as gossip, apathy, financial matters, property maintenance emergencies, and poor worship attendance.

Once the list is complete, I go back through it one item at a time, asking which items have a significant spiritual aspect to them. By their own assessment, 90 to 95 percent involve a major spiritual component.

Then we discuss whether they tend to address these issues from a *spiritual* perspective or a human organizational point of view.

When we forget that the church is not just another organization, we tend to respond to challenges by seeking nonspiritual solutions. Most of the items include substantive issues that deserve attention. But the majority also involve issues that require spiritual care.

As a result, the church's leaders need to be spiritually prepared to address the congregation's challenges.

EXERCISE

Using a flip chart or whiteboard to record responses, ask your leaders to brainstorm in ten minutes as many answers as possible to this question: What frustrates you most in your service as a church leader?

When time is up, go through each item one at a time. With a different colored pen, circle those that have a major spiritual component to them.

Together, discuss whether you as leaders usually address these issues from a *spiritual* perspective or simply from a human organizational point of view. Take a couple of the ideas and talk about how you might consider the spiritual aspects of those issues.

EQUIPPED FOR SPIRITUAL LEADERSHIP

Review the following biblical accounts. Then, using the questions provided, reflect how church leaders should be equipped for providing spiritual leadership.

Note how God directed Joshua to lead the people of Israel into the Promised Land:

> After the death of Moses the servant of the LORD, the LORD said to Joshua the son of Nun, Moses' assistant, "Moses My servant is dead. Now therefore arise, go over this Jordan, you and all this people, into the land that I am giving to them, to the people of Israel. Every place that the sole of your foot will tread upon I have given to you, just as I promised to Moses. From the wilderness and this Lebanon as far as the great river, the river Euphrates, all the land of the Hittites to the Great Sea toward the going down of the sun shall be your territory. No man shall be able to stand before you all the days of your life. Just as I was with Moses, so I will be with you. I will not leave you or forsake you. Be strong and courageous, for you shall cause this people to inherit the land that I swore to their fathers to give them. Only be strong and very courageous, being careful to do according to all the law that Moses My servant commanded you. Do not turn from it to the right hand or to the left, that you may have good success wherever you go. This Book of the Law[22] shall not depart from your mouth, but you shall meditate on it day and night, so that you may be careful to do according to all that is written in it. For then you will make your way prosperous, and then you will have good success. Have I not commanded you? Be strong and courageous. Do not be frightened, and do not be dismayed, for the LORD your God is with you wherever you go." (Joshua 1:1–9)

1. What earthly concerns do you think Joshua and other leaders had at this time?

2. Identify the spiritual issues that faced them.

3. On what did God tell Joshua and the people to meditate as they carried out God's directives?

4. For what reasons did God give this instruction?

5. God anticipated that the people would experience challenges as they entered this new land. What promises did God make to embolden them?

Consider how the people of the Early Church prepared for service:

So those who received his word were baptized, and there were added that day about three thousand souls. And they devoted themselves to the apostles' teaching and the fellowship, to the breaking of bread and the prayers. And awe came upon every soul, and many wonders and signs were being done through the apostles. (Acts 2:41–43)

6. What was happening in the Church during this period?

7. How did the members of this growing Church equip themselves for service to one another and for spreading the Gospel?

8. What were the results?

Paul taught the Colossians how to continue in their work together:

> Put on then, as God's chosen ones, holy and beloved, compassionate hearts, kindness, humility, meekness, and patience, bearing with one another and, if one has a complaint against another, forgiving each other; as the Lord has forgiven you, so you also must forgive. And above all these put on love, which binds everything together in perfect harmony. And let the peace of Christ rule in your hearts, to which indeed you were called in one body. And be thankful. Let the word of Christ dwell in you richly, teaching and admonishing one another in all wisdom, singing psalms and hymns and spiritual songs, with thankfulness in your hearts to God. And whatever you do, in word or deed, do everything in the name of the Lord Jesus, giving thanks to God the Father through Him. (Colossians 3:12–17)

9. List what Paul tells the believers to put on in their work together.

10. What are they to put on above all else? For what purpose?

11. What is to dwell in them richly? What difference does that make for the congregation and her leaders?

12. What do these three texts from Joshua, Acts, and Colossians indicate to you about being equipped to serve as a spiritual leader in Christ's Church?

At times, Christians minimize the importance of God's Word in guiding daily affairs, including the work of their church. They see the Bible as something that one learns about, but they do not view the Bible as God's means for transforming their lives and directing their decisions.

Timothy Mech highlights the importance of church leaders dwelling in God's Word. "Many have disconnected the Word of God from their everyday lives, including elders, and yes, even some pastors. Among laity, many see the Word of God as simply important information to be taught instead of the very means by which God is active in our lives."[23]

Mech warns about the danger of spiritual leaders embracing a casual attitude toward being in the Scriptures.

> Too often what we do in the Church is influenced or even directed by the word of a fallen humanity instead of the Word of the Lord. If the Word of God is not part of the daily diet of both elders and pastors, the way of the congregation will begin to look more and more like the way of a fallen world. When this is the case, there is anger at the mere thought that elders of a congregation would, for example, be expected to attend a Bible class.[24]

While every Christian should abide in the Scriptures, leaders in particular need it for spiritual nourishment so the Word dwells within them richly. Through this regular feeding, they can minimize worldly influences and become transformed. "Do not be conformed to this world, but be transformed by the renewal of your mind, that by testing you may discern what is the will of God, what is good and acceptable and perfect" (Romans 12:2).

In addition to being in God's Word, consider the following instructions to the Early Christian Church:

> Do not be anxious about anything, but in everything by prayer and supplication with thanksgiving let your requests be made known to God. (Philippians 4:6)

> Rejoice always, pray without ceasing, give thanks in all circumstances; for this is the will of God in Christ Jesus for you. (1 Thessalonians 5:16–18)

> First of all, then, I urge that supplications, prayers, intercessions, and thanksgivings be made for all people, for kings and

all who are in high positions, that we may lead a peaceful and quiet life, godly and dignified in every way. (1 Timothy 2:1–2)

Therefore, confess your sins to one another and pray for one another, that you may be healed. The prayer of a righteous person has great power as it is working. (James 5:16)

13. What do these verses suggest that church leaders should be doing as spiritual leaders?

Occasionally, I work with church leaders who are unpracticed in praying. Not surprisingly, these are the same people who lack biblical knowledge. A church led by people who are unfamiliar with the Bible and who are uncomfortable praying will be found unhealthy. When a congregation elects leaders who are spiritually malnourished, the health of the entire congregation suffers, even if the church has members with spiritual maturity.

In contrast, a church whose leadership knows the Scriptures and prays without ceasing fortifies the well-being of their church. A congregation that purposely elects spiritually mature people provides evidence of its spiritual wellness and strengthens her health.

SPIRITUALLY FOCUSED BOARD MEETINGS

Dwelling in God's Word and praying must characterize the work of church leaders, not only during corporate worship and individual devotions, but also during church board meetings. These disciplines reflect dependence upon Christ, keeping the command to have no other gods. They also shape God's people as spiritually focused leaders.

Such disciplines are critical not only for elders but also for any church board. Since most challenges for church leaders have a major spiritual component, each board needs to strive for spiritually focused meetings.

When working with churches, I discover a great deal about leadership habits and priorities by reading two or three years' minutes of board meetings. I learn who regularly attends the meetings and who is irregular in attendance. I observe whether meetings are well organized and planned or whether the members gather without much advanced thought. I see what discussions (or individuals) dominate the meetings, and thus determine the board's priorities. This also allows me to observe themes or patterns in how boards address internal conflict and conflict within the congregation. In conflicted churches, I note how many leaders resigned, how many people left the church, and the boards' reactions.

One more area becomes obvious. I learn if the leaders of the particular church depend on worldly wisdom or Christ's wisdom. Compare the elder boards from two different churches referenced below by reviewing their board agendas and a summary of their minutes.

In Our Redeemer's Church, the elders' typical agenda looks like this (it's not prepared in advance, but this is the routine they follow):

OUR REDEEMER'S CHURCH BOARD OF ELDERS AGENDA

Opening devotion (led by the pastor)
Approval of minutes
Pastor's report of official acts
Putting out fires (discussing current crises)
Old business
New business
Elder's service schedule (for serving at worship services)
Closing prayer (Lord's Prayer)

Their minutes reflect that reports or proposed actions are not submitted in advance. The elders wait until they come together before receiving any reports or learning about situations that require attention. All reports are given orally. Crisis issues ("putting out fires") can take significant time, due to lack of preparation. Even discussions over less-significant issues appear to ramble on. Meetings may last three hours or more. Sometimes the board takes several months to make any decisions, often repeating discussions similar to those in previous months because no work is done between meetings.

The only time spent in prayer is a brief opening devotion by the pastor and a closing with the Lord's Prayer. There is no indication that the elders spend measurable time in the Bible together.

Compare those behaviors with the typical elder board agenda from Good Shepherd Church:

GOOD SHEPHERD CHURCH BOARD OF ELDERS AGENDA

Opening devotion (led by an elder)
Bible study (led by the pastor or an elder)
Approval of minutes
Discussion on pastor's report
Discussion on elder reports
Business to be considered
Questions on service schedule
Closing prayer (each elder prays for people in his assigned area of responsibility)

The minutes from this elder board indicate that the agenda and all regular reports are sent in advance, including the pastor's report of official acts and each elder's report on monthly calls. Instead of receiving oral reports during the meeting, they use this time to discuss the reports as needed. If the pastor or another elder wants to bring a current issue to the board, it is sent with the agenda in advance, with a suggested response under "Business to be considered." Elders are encouraged to pray for difficult agenda items before they come together.

A major difference is the time spent in God's Word and prayer. The elders and pastors at Good Shepherd Church take turns leading devotions and Bible study. In one year, the minutes reflect that they worked through a theological book on the Lord's Supper. In another year, they worked through Ephesians, using a commentary. Elders were expected to read through commentary sections and answer written questions between meetings. When they met as a board, they read the Bible passages together and discussed reflections from their homework questions. Before closing, each elder prays for people in his assigned area of responsibility. At every meeting, one elder is assigned to pray for the pastor and his family.

This elder board has a policy that no meeting lasts later than 9:30 p.m. If not finished at that time, they set an additional time to continue meeting on another day.

It's obvious which elder board demonstrates spiritual leadership and which one leans more on worldly wisdom. Their agendas and minutes reveal the kind of leadership each board provides. Based on the practices of these elder boards, one would expect to find Good Shepherd Church a much healthier spiritual community than that of Our Redeemer's Church.

EXERCISE

Together with your other board members, write down your board's typical agenda. Be sure to include any time spent in devotions or prayer.

Behind the items listed for prayer or devotions or Bible study, note the average time spent on each area. Next, total the number of minutes spent in prayer and the Word for the average meeting.

Take the total number and multiply it times the number of meetings you typically have in one year. This is the annual amount of time that your board spends together in prayer and Bible study.

Compare your board's activities with the results of the two churches I mentioned earlier:

OUR REDEEMER'S CHURCH BOARD OF ELDERS AGENDA

Opening devotion	10 minutes
Approval of minutes	2 minutes
Pastor's report of official acts	12 minutes per meeting
Putting out fires	x 12 meetings per year
Old business	
New business	
Elder's service schedule	
Closing prayer	

144 minutes per year in prayer and God's Word
   (fewer than 2½ hours per year)

GOOD SHEPHERD CHURCH BOARD OF ELDERS AGENDA	
Opening devotion	**10 minutes**
Bible study	**45 minutes (minimum; sometimes more than an hour)**
Approval of minutes	
Discussion on pastor's report	
Discussion on elder reports	
Business to be considered	
Questions on service schedule	
Closing prayer	**15 minutes minimum (up to 25 minutes)**

70 minutes per meeting (minimum)
x 12 meetings per year =
840 minutes per year, a minimum of 14 hours in prayer and God's Word

1. Review your board's responsibilities as listed in your congregation's constitution, bylaws, and policies (such as operating procedures). What is the overall responsibility for this board in your congregation?

2. How well does your board's work reflect commitment to being in the Word and prayer?

3. What changes would you make to your board's work, given the overall responsibility you identified from your bylaws and in light of the Scriptures referenced earlier?

If your board lacks spiritually healthy practices, repent and believe the Good News. For Jesus' sake, you are forgiven. As a board, take comfort in the promises of God: "He Himself bore our sins in His body on the tree, that we might die to sin and live to righteousness. By His wounds you have been healed" (1 Peter 2:24).

Having been reminded of the grace that is yours in Christ Jesus, commit yourselves as church leaders to be transformed in the way you lead your church.

PRODUCTIVE, WORTHWHILE BOARD MEETINGS

Serving on a leadership board in Christ's Church is a serious responsibility. Moreover, those who serve on a board sacrifice time that could be used for other activities, including time with family, work, household chores, or even leisure. Therefore, it is important that boards strive to make meetings meaningful and effective. Board members owe this to one another out of love and respect for their brothers and sisters in Christ (see John 13:35; Romans 12:10; Philippians 2:3–4).

To maximize time together, board members should be committed to their assigned responsibilities and due dates between meetings. The board chairperson is responsible to hold members accountable between meetings by reminding them of their responsibilities.

When training board members to focus on spiritual leadership, I encourage them to prioritize their commitment to God's Word and prayer during their meetings. When I first mention that, some board members complain that their meetings are already too long. Actually, many are too long.

Boards often waste precious meeting time. Much of what boards do during meetings can be eliminated with advanced planning. By preparing information and sending it out in advance, boards can devote more time in Scripture and prayer and avoid squandering time on unnecessary conversations.

Consider these preparations to make board meetings productive and worthwhile:

- The chairperson reminds individuals that reports are due on a specific date (so the agenda and reports can be sent out in a timely manner). The reminders are made both at the meeting and before the next one.

- Reports are written and submitted to the chairperson in advance of the due date, including the following reports:
    - Reports from the pastor (e.g., official reports on worship and Bible study attendance, membership changes, Baptisms, funerals, marriages, pastoral calls), principal, or other key staff.

- Financial and budget reports.
- Elder, council, or school board reports on visits made in their assigned areas of responsibilities.
    - How many calls were completed?
    - Note any ideas, concerns, and prayer requests.
- Committee reports or special assignment reports.
    - What was accomplished?
    - What is planned?
    - Note any concerns and decisions made.
- Any suggested resolutions for action with accompanying information.
- Secretary's minutes from previous meeting.

- The chairperson sends out these items in advance:
    - Agenda
    - Minutes
    - Staff reports
    - Financial reports
    - Board member reports
    - Committee reports or special assignment reports
    - Recommended motions for action, plus any informational attachments
    - Reminder of reading assignments with questions (for Bible study)
    - Board member assignments (e.g., elder Communion schedule)

- Board members read all material in advance and prepare discussion questions and other assignments made by chairman.

Consider the following as a suggested agenda:

AGENDA

Opening devotion (assigned in advance; led by lay leader)
Bible study (reminder of assigned readings and questions)
Corrections and approval of minutes
Discussion on reports (as needed)
    From key staff member (pastor, principal, etc.)
    Financial reports
    Board member reports
Business to be considered (motions, discussion for future assignment and action, etc.)
    Prayer time
- Each board member prays for people in his assigned area of responsibility
- [Assigned board member] prays for pastors and their families [may include other professional church workers; school board prays for principal and teachers]

MAKING BOARD REPORTS RELEVANT

Throughout the years, I've read multiple reports in various congregational meetings that turn out to be completely useless and a waste of valuable time. I have also heard well-meaning people deliver oral reports that contributed nothing meaningful for the group.

"We canceled our meeting time two months ago because John was sick. This month we ended up meeting last Tuesday at Martha's. You know, she makes the best cinnamon rolls ever. We wondered if we should always meet at Martha's. But then we decided to take turns meeting at different people's homes . . ." And the monologue goes on and on.

The entire group is held hostage as someone rambles on about things that don't matter, but no one says anything because there are no standards for what should be reported. It's difficult to hold people accountable if there are no guidelines. Thus, the entire group is responsible for the poor reporting that takes place.

In my service as a congregational president (I served four terms in my church), I realized that many who gave reports were simply following the examples of reports they had seen by others. Most have never been guided on what makes a relevant report.

To respect people's time, implement policies to streamline reporting. Regular reports should be written and distributed in advance. Attached to minutes, they become part of a permanent record. They should be simple, including only those things that need to be reported to the group receiving it. A simple format can guide people in reporting:

- What was accomplished during this past reporting period
- What is planned to be done by the board in the future
- Any special concerns that affect others
- Any recommendations for the group to take action (e.g., resolutions)

Financial reports can take a lot of time, especially if they are lengthy. In most cases, financial reports should be distributed in advance with a summary by the preparer pointing out areas to note. Board members can study them and prepare questions and comments that would be valuable for the entire group to hear.

It is difficult to review detailed financial reports when one receives them for the first time during a meeting. Accordingly, the discussions that follow tend to be surface level or focus on unimportant points. Worse yet, some boards and councils of congregations adopt motions to accept financial reports without adequately reviewing them. (By the way, unaudited financial reports should be not accepted or adopted, according to *Robert's Rules of Order*. In addition, motions "to receive" financial reports are also inappropriate.)

Note that when people receive reports in advance, some questions or comments can be addressed privately. If corrections are needed, the preparer can make them before the meeting, briefly noting changes during the meeting and avoiding embarrassment of being caught off guard. Participants should be encouraged to only bring concerns to the meeting that would benefit the entire group.

If board members are responsible for regular activities (such as member visits), they should report their activity to the chairperson, who can summarize the reports and submit them on a single spreadsheet. This avoids attaching multiple reports to the agenda. See Table 4 for a sample summary report for monthly elder visits.

TABLE 4

MONTHLY ELDER VISITS

Name of Elder	# Phone Contacts	# Personal Visits	Special Concerns	Prayer Requests
J. Smith	6	3	none	Mary S. — Cancer
B. Jones	7	5	Harry T. needs financial assistance; lost job Tom J. hurt at job	Harry T. — Job; finances Tom J. — recover & return to work
S. Tucker	3	3	Sue M. concerned about new worship service Art & Ann W. recently separated; need help from reconciliation ministry team	Praise for Jon & Linda O. for newborn grandson Art & Ann W. — Marriage
T. Schultz	7	3	Rob T. — surgery went well	Pray for recovery
P. Blake	4	2	Met with member whose son is using illegal drugs	Pray for member & son (keeping name confidential)
Totals	27	16		

When reports are discussed during the meeting, there is no need to report what has already been reported in the files distributed ahead of time. Instead, the chairperson should ask if there are clarifications, questions, or comments for the reports attached to the agenda.

Confidential information may be more properly shared orally at the meeting rather than in an advanced written report. This is especially important when reports are shared by website or email, which can be made available to unintended recipients or forwarded to someone outside the confidential group. In such cases, a board member's report should indicate something like "I have something confidential to share during the meeting." The chairperson can then plan for this in the agenda.

MEETING ACCOUNTABILITY

The chairperson is responsible for leading a meeting for the benefit of all in attendance. Accountability is important for achieving this goal.

The value of a meeting reflects on how well the chairperson has prepared between meetings. The chairperson is responsible for holding people accountable for due dates, for collecting reports, and for the preparation of agendas. While meetings should be a place where new thoughts can be shared, the chairperson works between meetings to identify major issues that should be handled in the meeting and then prepares the group to address them.

Occasionally, someone will bring up an unexpected issue during a meeting that is not on the agenda. The chairperson needs to respectfully remind the person that such an item has not been planned for. Unless the issue requires emergency action, the chairperson can indicate that such an item deserves attention and preparation. Then the chairperson can delegate to a certain individual or group to prepare the issue for a specified future meeting.

When people experience well-prepared meetings, they are more likely to attend and do their part between meetings. They come to expect that the meetings will be meaningful and worth their participation.

When meetings are ill prepared and undisciplined, people expect meetings to be a waste of time. People with multiple responsibilities tend to avoid poorly executed meetings.

Leaders of healthy congregations take time to prepare and discipline themselves for meaningful and effective meetings.

FINAL THOUGHT

During the time when I was beginning to write this book, a pastor approached me at a conference. Three years prior, I had taught the principles from this chapter in a regional lay leadership training workshop that his lay leaders had attended.

He shared what a difference these ideas had made for his church. He said that his congregational leaders had been transformed in the way that they conducted church business.

He told me that every board adopted the practice of beginning with Bible study and ending with a purposeful time of prayer. They changed the priorities of their meetings and did more work between meetings. He added that his church's leaders also regularly attend Bible study. Most important, he said, the overall environment of the congregation had improved.

Focusing on spiritual leadership made them much healthier as a congregation.

CHAPTER 11

Ministering[25] to the Ministers

If you cannot be a watchman,
    Standing high on Zion's wall,
Pointing out the path to heaven,
    Off'ring life and peace to all.
With your prayers and with your bounties
    You can do what God commands;
You can be like faithful Aaron,
    Holding up the prophet's hands. (*LSB* 826:3)

Case Study: Pastor Matthew Jefferson

When Matthew got home at 10:30 that night, he found the envelope on his pillow next to where his wife should have been. Pastor Matthew Jefferson trembled as he read Maggie's letter. "I've given up trying to compete against the one who holds your heart. She demands your attention day and night, and you bow to her every whim and fancy. I realized that I'm just an inconvenience in your affair with the church."

Maggie had taken a taxi to the airport that morning after he went to the office. She left to live with their adult daughter and her husband across the country. Matt's world came crashing down around him.

Adored by people in the four congregations he served as pastor, he had found it increasingly difficult to say no as the years went by. With his regular office hours, special counseling appointments, evening meetings, hospital and homebound visits, funerals and weddings, he rarely took a day off during the week. He seldom ate lunch or dinner with his wife, and he hadn't taken vacation time in three years. He took no time for exercise. He had gained thirty-five pounds over the last several years, and with all that was on his mind, he was unable to sleep through the night.

The church had become his false god, demanding more of him. Matt sacrificed relationships with his own family, especially his wife. Often alone at the office, he dabbled with Internet pornography. His sermons and teaching had become more moralistic. He sacrificed his own health and well-being, including his spiritual life. He sacrificed so much precious to him to serve the church.

The idolatry of his work ended in the destruction of his marriage. This also resulted in the end of his career as pastor. He knew that he was no longer qualified to serve. By losing balance with all his vocations and lack of self-care, he lost the church he worshiped most of all.

How could this happen to one who was so talented and acclaimed by many?

The congregation lost a gifted pastor. Could his lay leaders have done anything in caring for their pastor that may have helped avoid this tragedy?

No one at Pastor Jefferson's church had ever taken time to evaluate his work schedule. No one had ever checked to see if he had been taking a day off or vacation time or if he was taking time for his own family. No one had stopped by their home when Maggie's mother passed away. No one seemed to notice that Maggie had not been in worship for the past six months. Although everyone in the congregation was responsible for showing care for their pastor, no one took an opportunity to care for him and his wife.

The marriage difficulties between Pastor Matt and his wife may not have been preventable. However, the lack of personal attention and concern for their pastor's work schedule, his self-care, and his neglect of his wife all contributed to his idolatry and overall decline in well-being.

Over the years, I have met a number of professional church workers who faithfully served their churches and Christian schools for years, only to lose that privilege because they were not cared for in their needs.

Some, such as Pastor Jefferson, idolize their work and lose work-life balance. Others find themselves alone, experiencing the loss of loved ones with no outside care because no one reaches out to them—for they are the professional caregivers. Several sacrifice so much of themselves for others that they seek comfort in secret sins to compensate for the care they crave. A number of faithful workers struggle with depression and burnout. The stresses of ministry show up in physical ailments that prematurely shorten their careers and lives. Guilt or shame or a sense of failure eat away at spiritual and physical health until all joy in ministry is lost. In other words, many gifted church workers struggle to continue their calling because they lack the ministry care they so freely offer others.

Lay leaders of healthy congregations understand that their pastors and other professional church workers and their families need to be cared for just as God's faithful servants care for them. In a spiritually well church, the members demonstrate their love for Christ and one another in the way that they minister to those who are called to serve them.

CARING FOR OUR PROFESSIONAL CHURCH WORKERS

Providing Christian care to the pastor and other church workers is not a new concept. We often remember the apostle Paul for his great passion and endurance. Yet, he suffered significantly for the cause of the Gospel, and he benefited from the care provided by others.

Paul praised God for the unusual support and encouragement given by the Philippians.

> Yet it was kind of you to share my trouble. And you Philippians yourselves know that in the beginning of the gospel, when I left Macedonia, no church entered into partnership with me in giving and receiving, except you only. Even in Thessalonica you sent me help for my needs once and again. Not that I seek the gift, but I seek the fruit that increases to your credit. I have received full payment, and more. I am well supplied, having received from Epaphroditus the gifts you sent, a fragrant offering, a sacrifice acceptable and pleasing to God. And my God will supply every need of yours according to His riches in glory in Christ Jesus. To our God and Father be glory forever and ever. Amen. (Philippians 4:14–19)

He also expressed appreciation for special care shown to him by Onesiphorus.

> May the Lord grant mercy to the household of Onesiphorus, for he often refreshed me and was not ashamed of my chains, but when he arrived in Rome he searched for me earnestly and found me—may the Lord grant him to find mercy from the Lord on that day!—and you well know all the service he rendered at Ephesus. (2 Timothy 1:16–18)

The Church at Philippi supported Paul through prayer, in encouragement, and by providing for his physical needs. Onesiphorus sought out Paul in prison, refreshing him, possibly with food as well as encouragement from prayer and God's Word.

The Scriptures teach us to support our pastors and teachers.

> Let the one who is taught the word share all good things with the one who teaches. Do not be deceived: God is not mocked, for whatever one sows, that will he also reap. (Galatians 6:6–7)

> Let the elders who rule well be considered worthy of double honor, especially those who labor in preaching and teaching. For the Scripture says, "You shall not muzzle an ox when it treads out the grain," and, "The laborer deserves his wages." Do not admit a charge against an elder except on the evidence of two or three witnesses. As for those who persist in sin, rebuke them in the presence of all, so that the rest may stand in fear. (1 Timothy 5:17–20)

> We ask you, brothers, to respect those who labor among you and are over you in the Lord and admonish you, and to esteem them very highly in love because of their work. Be at peace among yourselves. (1 Thessalonians 5:12–13)

God's people have the privilege and responsibility of caring for those who serve them as pastors and teachers. This includes not only salaries and benefits, but also honor, respect, esteem, and love. We are to protect them against false accusations. We also need to demonstrate care

God's people have the privilege and responsibility of caring for those who serve them as pastors and teachers.

for them and the congregation by holding them accountable in love when necessary.

WHAT DO YOU MEAN?

When teaching lay leaders, I ask the question, "How do you minister to your ministers?" Most often, I get a blank look from the group. I wait until someone inevitably asks, "What do you mean?"

I give some examples.

"When the father of your pastor dies, who from the congregation makes a pastoral visit on him and his wife? You know, like how he does for you when one of your loved ones die."

"When the principal's wife is diagnosed with breast cancer, who from the congregation meets with the family to pray for them?"

"When your pastor goes into the hospital, who from the congregation goes to the hospital at 6:00 in the morning to read a psalm and pray with him before surgery?"

"When the pastor or other professional church worker, or their spouses, or their kids, or anyone dear to them suffers in any way, who from the church goes to comfort them with prayer and Scripture?"

In most groups, heads drop in silence. Someone says, "You know, Ted, I guess I never thought about that before."

I find that most lay leaders love their pastors and other professional staff. They express their love and concern for them in a number of ways. They want to be supportive and helpful. But many have not been taught or encouraged to provide care for those who care for them. Although no one taught them to think this way, many subconsciously reason, "Well, he's the pastor. He's the professional. He's been trained at seminary. Who am I to think that I can go and share a Scripture passage or pray with him? I'd be so embarrassed. I wouldn't know what to do."

I also find that pastors don't always invite lay leaders to show such care for them. For various reasons, some don't feel comfortable revealing the depth of their own needs. Pastors often feel awkward in training elders or other lay leaders how to provide comfort for their pastors.

I remember the first time I prayed for one of my pastors in his presence. I was quite uncomfortable. Actually, I feared looking foolish. I was afraid my prayer would be inadequate. I felt he would judge me for my feeble attempt. I thought my poor job might even make him feel worse.

Just the opposite turned out to be true. He thanked me and was touched by my care. I became bolder as I continued to seek opportunities to pray for my pastor in his presence. Since that time, I have taken time to pray for many leaders in churches, including denominational leaders and theology professors. Near the end of a visit, I ask a simple question: "How can I pray for you today?" Sometimes I begin by sharing a brief Scripture passage before praying.

After praying, I often hear similar comments. "Thanks, Ted. No one has done that for me in a long time." One pastor said it this way, "In twenty-five years of pastoral ministry, I don't remember anyone sharing a devotion with me. Not even a brother pastor. Thank you." Several times, the appreciation has been shown in tears. The leaders in our churches and denominations are frequently overlooked in their needs for spiritual care and encouragement.

I am passionate about teaching lay leaders to minister to their ministers. When they learn what they can do, some are fearful. But many feel motivated and emboldened to reach out to their pastors and other church workers.

At a conference, a pastor came up to thank me for a lay leadership workshop I led for his church. He said that in the three years since, he has felt more cared for than any other time in his twenty years of pastoral ministry. Four of his lay leaders regularly seek him out to see how he is doing. They ask about his joys and struggles that week. Then they pray for him and his family. He told me that it has made a huge difference for him and his wife.

Among the roles that different people hold in the church, perhaps one of the most difficult is serving as the spouse of a professional church worker. Spouses support their loved ones in their callings in sacrificial ways. When their church worker spouse is criticized or under stress, they feel the hurt and the pressure. These feelings intensify when the

The leaders in our churches and denominations are frequently overlooked in their needs for spiritual care and encouragement.

worker is under attack. And yet, these spouses have the least amount of influence for changing the situation. When they attempt defense or correction, they usually make things worse for their loved one. Very few individuals understand the unique difficulty that such spouses endure.

I have met with the spouses of many professional church workers who have suffered significantly and who often feel alone and uncared for. I have heard of cases where people specifically seek out a worker's spouse to criticize the worker, expecting that the message will be shared with him or her. This can be devastating to the spouse. Because of their loved one's position in the church, it can often be problematic for these spouses to develop trusting friendships with people in the church. In addition, professional church workers and their spouses often live far away from their own extended families and long-term friends. This contributes to their feeling isolated or forgotten in the challenges of ministry and life.

Caregivers from the congregation may be limited in how close they can become to the spouse of their professional church worker. However, I have found that spouses of church workers greatly value caregivers from the church who are spiritually mature. Just having someone available to listen, to cry and laugh, to pray and share Scripture can make a significant difference. Maintaining confidentiality is key when providing this kind of personal support for church professionals and their spouses.

Just as important is providing care for the children of church workers. I have met adult children of professional church workers who have left the church because of the treatment their parents received. While the parents try to protect them from the challenges of ministry, these children can't help but also experience some of the joys, hardships, and trials their parents experience in ministry.

Even when ministry is going well, the families of the church worker need care and support. Intentional proactive care promotes health for the church worker, the family, and the entire congregation.

WHO'S RESPONSIBLE?

When a congregation within The Lutheran Church—Missouri Synod calls a pastor, they send official call documents that list his primary duties and the congregation's commitment to support him in his call. Among other things, the congregation vows, "We hereby obligate ourselves to receive you as a servant of Jesus Christ, to give you the honor and love and obedience that the Word prescribes, to aid you by word and deed, and to support you with our diligent, faithful assistance and prayers."[26]

These words reflect what the Bible teaches. The entire congregation is responsible for showing care to their pastor and other professional church workers. The church does provide a compensation package that includes health care and housing support. But who actually carries out personal care for the pastor and his family?

Bruce Hartung observes, "When everyone is responsible, no one is responsible."[27]

In many churches, the elders or other leaders are assigned this responsibility in bylaws or policies. Nevertheless, Hartung points out that unless the church intentionally designates people to focus on such care, it often does not happen. Furthermore, he indicates that many pastoral-care resources put the full responsibility for church worker health care upon the church worker, neglecting to incorporate involvement from his own church.

> If the congregation does not have in place supportive policies and a supportive culture, encouragements alone won't be enough. In fact, they can have the opposite effect, putting workers into a situation in which they are encouraged and expected to care for their own spiritual health.[28]

The laity can serve their professional church workers in several areas important to their health:

- Spiritual—How is the church worker seeking to improve personal spiritual health?
- Church/School work—How is the church worker seeking to grow in service to the church or school (e.g., continuing education)?

- Family—How is the church worker intentionally spending time with his or her family (immediate and extended)?
- Physical—How is the church worker caring for his or her physical body (e.g., exercise, diet, medical care, etc.)?
- Mental—How is the church worker seeking to grow mentally outside of the profession?
- Social—How is the church worker investing in friendships and activities unrelated to the professional call?
- Financial—How is the church worker managing personal and professional finances?

An important requirement for providing personal care includes confidentiality. Church leaders and their families serve in public roles and are under constant scrutiny, even in the mundane. People who are critical of their leaders can inflict significant harm to the workers and their families. Those who provide special care for them must be sensitive to maintaining the confidences of their leaders. Without that assurance, the worker and his family will be reluctant to share anything personal.

This is why it is so important that the overall qualifier of a care provider must be spiritual maturity. The care provider must be regularly in God's Word and comfortable in praying for specific requests. These people will depend upon the Spirit for wisdom and discernment in providing care and seeking outside help when needed.

LOVING THROUGH ACCOUNTABILITY

With no accountability, love is incomplete.

Proverbs teaches, "Whoever spares the rod hates his son, but he who loves him is diligent to discipline him" (Proverbs 13:24).

In Hebrews, we see how God's discipline reflects His love for us:

And have you forgotten the exhortation that addresses you as sons?

"My son, do not regard lightly the discipline of the Lord,
nor be weary when reproved by Him.

For the Lord disciplines the one He loves,
   and chastises every son whom He receives."

It is for discipline that you have to endure. God is treating you as sons. For what son is there whom his father does not discipline? If you are left without discipline, in which all have participated, then you are illegitimate children and not sons. (Hebrews 12:5–8)

Wise leaders seek accountability. "Whoever loves discipline loves knowledge, but he who hates reproof is stupid" (Proverbs 12:1).

As part of their care for professional church workers, lay leaders are responsible for holding them accountable in love. This accountability is accomplished by having select lay leaders meet regularly with them, and also through job descriptions and regular evaluations. The congregation and their workers should all have their mutual expectations of one another agreed upon in writing. Job descriptions lay out these details.

Evaluations review the job descriptions and identify what is going well and what should be improved. They should especially highlight what is going well. How can a worker be encouraged to continue doing things that are appreciated if he or she doesn't know what they are? Areas in which improvement is desired should focus on a small number of areas so that specific plans can be developed and checked on.

If the lay leaders most responsible for holding their church workers accountable fail to be proactive in this work, others in the church may fill in the gap. Unfortunately, this is usually done in a sinful and harmful manner. Thus, the healthy congregation outlines who is responsible for church worker accountability and the process for it. Then, if unauthorized attempts to hold a church worker "accountable" are made, the lay leaders have reason to hold the involved congregational members accountable themselves for overstepping their bounds.

Lay leaders have an obligation to protect their called workers from false accusations. "Do not admit a charge against an elder except on the evidence of two or three witnesses" (1 Timothy 5:19). If there is no regular practice for evaluation, the opportunity increases for frivolous and false accusations. Proactive care includes regular accountability.

When developing a system for holding church workers accountable, apply these principles:

- Document in bylaws or policies who is responsible for the task. Assure that anyone responsible for this assignment is spiritually mature.

- Remember the importance of confidentiality.

- Be sure to distinguish between the evaluation of an "employee" versus a "called" pastor, principal, or other worker. Called workers should not be treated as hirelings but rather as the called servants of God. This does not mean they cannot be held accountable, but rather that the manner in which they are treated is consistent with scriptural mandates.

- Develop a system where the church worker evaluates himself or herself as part of the process.

- Reinforce all that is going well. Tell your worker what is appreciated most about his or her work. Make this list lengthy. You want the worker to know what is being done that is valued so that he or she will continue to do it.

- Seek one or two areas for improvement. Then, working together, establish goals.

- Include areas for review in the worker's own spiritual health, physical health, and family's well-being. Incorporate a way to receive input from the worker's spouse to make certain that the worker is making time for family and time away from work.

- Document your evaluations and agreements in writing, and secure those documents in a safe place.

- Review important goals throughout the year to monitor performance for accountability.

- Overall, make the evaluation encouraging. Take time to pray for the worker and his or her family.

- Report to the congregation that care is being given and regular reviews are being conducted so that the members know it is being done. However, don't reveal the details.

Reflection

Considering this chapter, discuss these questions with the leaders in your congregation.

1. What portions of this chapter were helpful to you?

2. Make a list of your professional church workers. Who currently ministers to them and their families? Who *should* provide such care?

3. How can I make a "spiritual care" call on my pastor, principal, or other church worker? on their spouse and children?

4. Read Colossians 3:15–17. Describe how God intends for us to provide accountability.

5. What changes does your church need to make to minister to its ministers?

I recommend a wonderful resource for lay leaders. Bruce Hartung's book *Holding Up the Prophet's Hand: Supporting Church Workers* discusses both the needs and practical applications for caring for and supporting professional church workers.

CHAPTER 12

THE ROLE OF STRUCTURE IN CONGREGATIONAL HEALTH

Lord Jesus Christ, the Church's head,
    You are her one foundation;
In You she trusts, before You bows,
    And waits for Your salvation.
Built on this rock secure,
Your Church shall endure
    Though all the world decay
    And all things pass away.
O hear, O hear us, Jesus! (*LSB* 647:1)

Case Study: Grace Church

The leadership at Grace Church believed that all they needed was a new organizational structure. That would save their church!

It was true that their organizational structure contributed to their disputes. In a few cases, the bylaws themselves contradicted who had authority over certain matters. The church had not adopted any policies to clarify the misunderstandings. Few workers had job descriptions, and those that had been written didn't fully reflect the bylaws. In some cases, the church didn't even follow their written procedures. Obviously, the congregation needed to change their structure.

The congregation engaged a consultant and invested two years in adopting a new structure. The amended bylaws detailed responsibilities and authority for each board, officer, and key staff person. A policy manual provided details not covered by the bylaws. Job descriptions coordinating with the bylaws and policies were written for each staff person. In the end, the church adopted governance documents totaling nearly one hundred pages.

They held their first election for new officers and board members. Confident that their problems were solved, each one began his or her assigned work.

All the while, however, the major issue contributing to the church's poor health remained undiagnosed and, therefore, untreated.

Within the first thirty days after installing new people in positions, the disagreements began. Some were fighting over interpretation of specific bylaws and policies. Others ignored those new governing documents, claiming that their board had always been responsible for certain areas. Gossip began mounting as complaints increased. Instead of the traditional methods of phone and face-to-face, gossip now occurred more expansively through social media, emails, texting, personal webpage posts, and blogs.

Within the first few months, newly elected persons began resigning and even leaving the church. Because their pastor had supported these new changes, he was a target for people's frustrations. Attendance and offerings began declining again. What many had hoped would be the salvation of their church now appeared to be the cause of its demise.

THE STRUCTURAL FOUNDATION
FOR CONGREGATIONAL HEALTH

What went so wrong at Grace Church? After all, advisers pointed out to members the inadequacies of their governing documents. Certainly, changing their structure should have solved their issues, right?

Well-articulated roles and authorities are important for any organization. Without agreed-upon rules of operation, groups operate out of chaos. As Christians, we should understand this better than anyone.

God established rules to live by for our own protection. His commands provide safe boundaries in society so we can live in relative peace. Having a common set of rules to live by is what differentiates organized society from undisciplined chaos where every man is for himself.

The Church is a body of believers, each part with differing gifts. Congregations structure themselves by assigning people with certain gifts and skills to appropriate positions, thus avoiding unnecessary confusion and directing service to Christ in orderly fashion. Paul underlines the importance of this in his admonition to the conflicted Church in Corinth: "But all things should be done decently and in order" (1 Corinthians 14:40).

However, while governing documents define the material issues of how a congregation operates, they do not regulate the heart. When member disagreements are fueled by their heart idols, the church needs much more than structure to avoid conflict. If the leadership looks to governance as the ultimate solution, their focus on Christ as the Head is minimized. Instead of looking to Jesus, the chief cornerstone, they seek earthly models on which to base their hopes.

Church operations must first and foremost be founded on Christ, the Head of the Church. As people turn their heart toward Him and abide in His Word, they are better equipped to work on structure.

I am an advocate of congregations adopting well-defined structures. Inadequate organizational documents can lead to confusion and unnecessary competition.

Nevertheless, I have worked with numerous congregations that have adopted several different forms of improved governance and yet have continued infighting, even to the point of self-destruction. On the other hand, I have met with church leaders whose congregations lacked adequate governing documents but had spiritual maturity so strong that when they had disagreements, they trusted, submitted to, and supported one another in their work. When they caused offense, they reconciled through confession and forgiveness. Despite their poor structure, they were still able to accomplish much good because of their corporate spiritual health.

Although I don't wish for congregations to ignore their structural deficiencies, I am concerned about those that look to improvements in governance to solve all their operational issues. If their hearts are not set on Christ and His Word, the best structures in the world will not prevent conflict or help them navigate through major differences. In fact, it may give them false security that will only contribute to more serious problems.

> Church operations must first and foremost be founded on Christ, the Head of the Church.

THE ROLE OF STRUCTURE FOR PREVENTING AND ADDRESSING CONFLICT

Well-designed and implemented structure can help to reduce conflict. However, organizational structure does not address all issues of conflict.

In chapter 5, I discussed the difference between *conflict resolution* and *reconciliation*. I distinguished between two different kinds of issues that can arise in conflict:

- *Material* or *substantive* issues involve *what material matter or process* is in dispute. This includes such things as disputes over money, contract interpretations, role definitions, authority, and property.

- *Personal* or *relational* issues involve *how* something is done and people are treated. This includes broken trust and relationships damaged by sinful thoughts, words, and deeds.

In most disputes, *both* kinds of issues are involved and *both* need addressing to reach resolution and reconciliation. Yet, different kinds of issues require different approaches.

Organizational structure primarily addresses *material* or *substantive* issues. Bylaws, policies, job descriptions, and other documents proactively limit substantive issues by defining roles, responsibilities, and authorities of various positions. They also establish expectations and ground rules for operations.

Structure can also provide processes for addressing substantive issues in disagreements, often outlining how to handle disagreements.

However, organizational structure does not directly address *personal* or *relational* issues, though it may provide a process or set of guidelines for reconciliation. For example, it may define procedures for how disputing parties are to address offenses or it may provide guidance for processes that can lead to personal reconciliation. Most often, though, formal organizational structure fails to provide much guidance in this area.

Case Study: Holy Trinity Church

Holy Trinity Church had outgrown its facilities. The congregation owned sufficient land, but they lacked the financial resources to build a new sanctuary and convert the existing one to a fellowship hall. The expansion committee proposed selling the front of the property to a commercial developer, who planned to build a two-story office/retail strip center. The church would retain an entrance to the main street but lose most of its visibility. The new sanctuary and additional parking would be built near the back of the property.

The bylaws required a congregational vote by simple majority.

The expansion committee met for three years, preparing plans and financial strategies to make this proposal work. They held several informational meetings for the congregation, which were attended by small groups of interested people. They distributed regular reports to the church through the newsletter and church website. While people asked questions, no one raised significant opposition to the plan.

When it came time for the final vote of the congregation, the committee and the commercial developer were excited to see their plans come to fruition. Average congregational meetings drew about 35 people, but more than 150 showed up for this crucial vote. It became apparent that a group of nine people had been organizing for some time to oppose the plans with force. Most were influential businesspeople in the community who had strong negative opinions about the proposed developer and the church losing its visibility. They brought many members to the meeting who had not attended any previous church meetings, but who had apparently attended two to three of the opposition's secret meetings. A number of the meeting attendees had not even attended worship in the past year.

The church council expected the vote on this major issue to go smoothly without resistance. What happened instead was an angry debate where passions arose on both sides of the issue. People tried shouting one another down. A few employed name calling. Several used inflammatory language. A couple of the opposition leaders used coarse language to push their agenda. After two hours of heated debate, the question was called. The new proposal was defeated, 74 to 71. Committee and church leaders were angry. Some people walked out in tears. The opposition group was high-fiving one another with their victory.

A decision had been made according to the bylaws, but the manner in which it came about resulted in breaking many of God's commands. The outcome? Several people left the church, including building committee members and lay leaders who resigned their positions. So many left that the need for expansion no longer existed. Within six months, the pastor took a new call and left.

In the case of Holy Trinity Church, the substantive issue was decided according to the structure. But the personal issues that remained brought significant harm to the church—spiritually, emotionally, and financially. Relationships among members were deeply strained. Trust in leadership was undermined. Several members avoided one another as they came together for worship. No amount of structural change would heal the wounds caused by the sinful ways they treated one another.

The church leaders never addressed the relational issues. They continued to operate on autopilot, pretending everything was okay. Five years later, with the encouragement of their new pastor, they adopted a new structure that streamlined the number of boards. However, the congregation continued to suffer with poor health. Visitors never heard what had divided the people, but it was evident after just a few visits that Holy Trinity Church was a place with a broken spirit.

To help understand how structure alone can fail to address congregational health, allow me to reflect on how God's people were organized in different times throughout biblical history and what effect that had on them as a people.

GOVERNANCE FOR THE CHILDREN OF ISRAEL

Following the exodus from Egypt, the children of Israel were organized under four basic structures: prophets, judges, kings, and rule by other nations.

PROPHETS

As they were freed from the oppression of Egypt, God's people were led by prophets, beginning with Moses. Moses represented God to the people, and he represented the people to God. Initially, Moses served alone as the judge for people's disputes, which was cumbersome.

Moses' father-in-law, Jethro, recommended a change in organizational structure:

> Jethro, the priest of Midian, Moses' father-in-law, heard of all that God had done for Moses and for Israel His people, how the LORD had brought Israel out of Egypt. . . .
>
> Moses' father-in-law said to him, "What you are doing is not good. You and the people with you will certainly wear yourselves out, for the thing is too heavy for you. You are not able to do it alone. Now obey my voice; I will give you advice, and God be with you! You shall represent the people before God and bring their cases to God, and you shall warn them about the statutes and the laws, and make them know the way in which they must walk and what they must do. Moreover, look for able men from all the people, men who fear God, who are trustworthy and hate a bribe, and place such men over the people as chiefs of thousands, of hundreds, of fifties, and of tens. And let them judge the people at all times. Every great matter they shall bring to you, but any small matter they shall decide themselves. So it will be easier for you, and they will bear the burden with you. If you do this, God will direct you, you will be able to endure, and all this people also will go to their place in peace."
>
> So Moses listened to the voice of his father-in-law and did all that he had said. (Exodus 18:1, 17–24)

This new structure helped Moses better prioritize his ministry, focus on what was most important, and fulfill his responsibilities as leader. Nevertheless, the new structure did not prevent the people from sinning against God under the leadership of Moses. Even while Moses was receiving the Ten Commandments, the people fell back into idolatry.

> When the people saw that Moses delayed to come down from the mountain, the people gathered themselves together to Aaron and said to him, "Up, make us gods who shall go before us. As for this Moses, the man who brought us up out

of the land of Egypt, we do not know what has become of him." So Aaron said to them, "Take off the rings of gold that are in the ears of your wives, your sons, and your daughters, and bring them to me." So all the people took off the rings of gold that were in their ears and brought them to Aaron. And he received the gold from their hand and fashioned it with a graving tool and made a golden calf. And they said, "These are your gods, O Israel, who brought you up out of the land of Egypt!" When Aaron saw this, he built an altar before it. And Aaron made a proclamation and said, "Tomorrow shall be a feast to the LORD." And they rose up early the next day and offered burnt offerings and brought peace offerings. And the people sat down to eat and drink and rose up to play. (Exodus 32:1–6)

Despite the improved structure under the leadership of Moses, the people fell away from worshiping the Lord, resulting in conflict with God and one another. Their most significant need was not new structure, but rather new hearts. As they repented, Moses interceded on their behalf, and God relented from destroying the congregation.

After Moses, Joshua served as the leader of the people. But following Joshua's death, the people fell away from God again, worshiping false gods and breaking God's commands.

JUDGES

After Joshua's service, God appointed judges to lead the people of Israel. "Then the LORD raised up judges, who saved them out of the hand of those who plundered them" (Judges 2:16). In Hebrew, the term *judge* refers to a military leader or a type of ruler or magistrate—one who administrated laws. They were viewed as God's special deliverers from their enemies. Some of the judges ruled over portions of the country, and thus some ruled in overlapping or similar time periods. The judges served as governing leaders.

Still, the people continued to sin against God and worship false gods. "Yet they did not listen to their judges, for they whored after other gods and bowed down to them. They soon turned aside from the way in which their fathers had walked, who had obeyed the commitments of the Lord, and they did not do so" (Judges 2:17). Even some of the judges were godless during their reigns. Conflict with God and within the people of Israel continued.

Kings

After several judges, the people demanded a king (1 Samuel 8). Through Samuel, God warned the people against an earthly king:

> So Samuel told all the words of the Lord to the people who were asking for a king from him. He said, "These will be the ways of the king who will reign over you: he will take your sons and appoint them to his chariots and to be his horsemen and to run before his chariots. And he will appoint for himself commanders of thousands and commanders of fifties, and some to plow his ground and to reap his harvest, and to make his implements of war and the equipment of his chariots. He will take your daughters to be perfumers and cooks and bakers. He will take the best of your fields and vineyards and olive orchards and give them to his servants. He will take the tenth of your grain and of your vineyards and give it to his officers and to his servants. He will take your male servants and female servants and the best of your young men and your donkeys, and put them to work. He will take the tenth of your flocks, and you shall be his slaves. And in that day you will cry out because of your king, whom you have chosen for yourselves, but the Lord will not answer you in that day." (1 Samuel 8:10–18)

But the people insisted, saying, "We also may be like all the nations, and that our king may judge us and go out before us and fight our battles" (1 Samuel 8:20). They were confident that this new form of governance would make them a vibrant nation.

The new organizational structure that the Israelites demanded failed to meet their desires, and it failed to resolve all their conflicts.

Although some exercised godly leadership, the majority of Israel's kings often failed to do so. Under the governance of kings, the Israelite kingdom divided (1 Kings 11–12). Once again, a change in governance did not make the people healthy. Their primary struggle was spiritual, not structural.

RULE BY OTHER NATIONS

Because of their unfaithfulness to God, the children of Israel lost their own land and right to govern themselves. They fell under the rule of others. The people suffered under oppression from other nations, and they were pressured to worship idols and earthly leaders. No matter the form of governance, God's people repeatedly failed to live in accord with God's will.

What the Israelites needed most of all was change of *heart*, not change of *governance*. Unless the hearts of the people were turned toward God and focused on His Word, their different governance structures did not prevent them from falling away from God and turning against one another.

CONFLICT OVER ROLES AMONG JESUS' DISCIPLES

As described earlier, good organizational structure can help minimize conflict over roles. However, it may not eliminate such disputes. When disagreements over roles and authorities are driven by desires elevated into demands (idolatry), structure alone will not solve the problems. The spiritual condition needs to be addressed.

Although Jesus was physically present among them, the disciples argued among themselves as to who was the greatest and therefore qualified to be over others. For example:

- The mother of James and John asked that her sons be seated at Jesus' left and right in His kingdom, leading the other disciples to be indignant (Matthew 20:20–28).

- The disciples argued among themselves as to who was the greatest (Mark 9:33–37).

- Even on the evening Jesus instituted the Lord's Supper, a dispute arose among the disciples as to who was the greatest (Luke 22:24–30).

Jesus confronted the disciples about their bickering over roles and authority. This was a conflict that seemed to repeat itself among them. Even with Jesus as their rabbi, twelve disciples could not avoid controversy. So Jesus demonstrated humble servant leadership by washing their feet. He addressed the spiritual condition of their hearts rather than simply prescribing an organizational structure.

CONFLICT OVER ROLES IN THE CORINTHIAN CHURCH

The Corinthian congregation suffered from numerous conflicts, including divisions over leadership, unchecked immoral conduct, lawsuits among members, disputes over eating food sacrificed to idols, misuse of the Lord's Supper, conflict over worship, and biases toward people.

In his First Letter to the Corinthians, Paul set the priority for how their conflicts should be addressed. Their divisions over leadership could be partially identified as conflict over roles and authority. Yet, Paul approaches their divisions not with advice regarding structure, but rather, with an appeal to the power of the cross of Christ.

> I appeal to you, brothers, by the name of our Lord Jesus Christ, that all of you agree, and that there be no divisions among you, but that you be united in the same mind and the same judgment. For it has been reported to me by Chloe's people that there is quarreling among you, my brothers. What I mean is that each one of you says, "I follow Paul," or "I follow Apollos," or "I follow Cephas," or "I follow Christ." Is Christ divided? Was Paul crucified for you? Or were you baptized in the name of Paul? I thank God that I baptized none of you except Crispus and Gaius, so that no one may say that you were baptized in my name. (I did baptize also the household of Stephanas. Beyond that, I do not know whether I baptized anyone else.) For Christ did not send me to baptize but to preach the gospel, and not with words of eloquent wisdom,

lest the cross of Christ be emptied of its power. For the word of the cross is folly to those who are perishing, but to us who are being saved it is the power of God. (1 Corinthians 1:10–18)

Paul does not suggest changes to their congregational organization. Instead, he contrasts human reasoning ("words of eloquent wisdom") with the cross of Christ. Paul indicates that as the church looks to the world's way of dealing with such issues, "the cross of Christ [is] emptied of its power."

Continuing to read through this epistle, you can see that Paul addressed the spiritual nature of their issues.

But I, brothers, could not address you as spiritual people, but as people of the flesh, as infants in Christ. I fed you with milk, not solid food, for you were not ready for it. And even now you are not yet ready, for you are still of the flesh. For while there is jealousy and strife among you, are you not of the flesh and behaving only in a human way? For when one says, "I follow Paul," and another, "I follow Apollos," are you not being merely human? (1 Corinthians 3:1–4)

When addressing the disputes in Corinth, Paul focused on the hearts of the people, not their structure. Unless they would grow in spiritual maturity, the worldly ways of addressing the conflicts would not lead to peace.

SCRIPTURAL GUIDANCE ON STRUCTURE

The Bible does not prescribe the specifics of what church governance should look like. Congregations may choose different forms of governance to achieve their purposes. However, the Scriptures do provide specific guidance in certain areas of governance.

DECENTLY AND IN ORDER

Organizational structure is important to our God. He brought order out of chaos in His creation. Paul reinforces that God's nature is being orderly: "For God is not a God of confusion but of peace" (1 Corinthians 14:33).

God instructs people in His Church how to conduct themselves: "But all things should be done decently and in order" (1 Corinthians 14:40).

Paul commended the Colossians for their conduct: "For though I am absent in body, yet I am with you in spirit, rejoicing to see your good order and the firmness of your faith in Christ" (Colossians 2:5).

RESPECT AUTHORITY AND EXERCISE IT WITH CARE

God expects us to respect authority: "There is no authority except from God, and those that exist have been instituted by God" (Romans 13:1).

In the explanation of the commandment "Honor your father and your mother," Luther explains that all authority is to be honored and obeyed: "We should fear and love God so that we do not despise or anger our parents and other authorities, but honor them, serve and obey them, love and cherish them."

Of course, God's direction for honoring authority applies to the Church as well, beginning with those God has called to serve as pastors and teachers: "We ask you, brothers, to respect those who labor among you and are over you in the Lord and admonish you, and to esteem them very highly in love because of their work" (1 Thessalonians 5:12–13).

Those who answer God's call to serve as pastor are given specific instructions regarding their position and exercise of authority:

> An overseer, as God's steward, must be above reproach. He must not be arrogant or quick-tempered or a drunkard or violent or greedy for gain, but hospitable, a lover of good, self-controlled, upright, holy, and disciplined. He must hold firm to the trustworthy word as taught, so that he may be able to give instruction in sound doctrine and also to rebuke those who contradict it. (Titus 1:7–9)

Those given authority must employ it carefully:

> Shepherd the flock of God that is among you, exercising oversight, not under compulsion, but willingly, as God would

have you; not for shameful gain, but eagerly; not domineering over those in your charge, but being examples to the flock. (1 Peter 5:2–3)

Similarly, James admonishes those who teach: "Not many of you should become teachers, my brothers, for you know that we who teach will be judged with greater strictness" (James 3:1).

Different Roles, Same Lord Jesus

God has gifted people with unique skills, and He calls people to serve different vocations for service to Christ, His Church, and the world. "And He gave the apostles, the prophets, the evangelists, the shepherds and teachers, to equip the saints for the work of ministry, for building up the body of Christ" (Ephesians 4:11–12; see also 1 Corinthians 12:12–30).

God calls *pastors* to Word and Sacrament ministry and for equipping the saints (Ephesians 4:11–12; 1 Timothy 4:14–16). Also, in Exodus 18:17–20, the prophet Moses was to represent God to the people (teach them God's Law) and carry the people's concerns to God—the duties of a pastor. Luke recorded the priorities of the apostles—pastors—in the Early Church: "But we [apostles] will devote ourselves to prayer and to the ministry of the word" (Acts 6:4).

God calls spiritually mature *laypeople* to serve as leaders who use their God-given gifts and talents, in matters such as judgment of earthly matters, social ministry, and administration (Exodus 18:21–23; 1 Corinthians 6:1–8; Acts 6:1–7; 1 Corinthians 12:12–30). In Exodus 18, lay leaders were chosen based on qualifications: "Look for able men from all the people, men who fear God, who are trustworthy and hate a bribe" (v. 21). Likewise, the Early Church chose leaders who met specific criteria for the apostles to appoint: "Therefore, brothers, pick out from among you seven men of good repute, full of the Spirit and of wisdom, whom we will appoint to this duty" (Acts 6:3).

Because of their example and responsibilities, pastors and lay leaders are called to noble tasks that require specific qualifications (1 Timothy 3; Titus 1). The leaders of Christ's Church must watch not only what they teach but also how they live, since their example influences others: "Let no one despise you for your youth, but set the believers an example in speech, in conduct, in love, in faith, in purity. . . . Keep a close watch on yourself and on the teaching. Persist in this, for by so doing you will save both yourself and your hearers" (1 Timothy 4:12, 16).

MODIFYING CONGREGATIONAL STRUCTURE

Although a congregation may be spiritually healthy, it may still struggle with structural challenges. Changes in congregational structure may be necessary for several reasons:

- Poorly written documents or inadequate designations for roles and authorities, which may lead to unnecessary confusion and conflict
- Growth or reductions in staff and membership
- Additions or terminations of ministries (e.g., day care, school)
- Societal changes that affect laypeople's availability for regular meetings (e.g., both parents working, more one-parent households, people working shifts on evenings and weekends, or parents with children who have scheduling conflicts)
- Certain areas of ministry that require more time and expertise, moving responsibilities from lay volunteers to professional staff
- Changes in financial abilities

As a congregation plans for changing its organizational structure, the following principles can guide the process.

1. Begin by identifying all the existing documents and decisions that establish different roles and authorities, including these:

   - Constitution and bylaws

   - Policy manuals

   - Job descriptions

   - Adopted resolutions or miscellaneous policies that define leadership responsibilities

2. Compare all the governing documents and systems to determine where they agree, where they are inconsistent, or where they may be inadequate.

   Note: As congregations change over the years, especially as staff are added or roles redefined, new policies or job descriptions may be developed that are not consistent with the constitution and bylaws or formerly adopted policies.

3. Determine how your congregation actually works, noting where current practice follows prescribed procedures or is in noncompliance. If noncompliant, decide what you will do to change the following:

   • Actual practice—to be compliant with existing governing documents

   • Documents—to reflect how the church has learned to govern herself (which may include writing new job descriptions or policies where none existed before)

   • Structure and practice—to better reflect the existing mission and challenges

4. If change to structure is needed, assess what works well with existing governing documents and where improvement is needed. Decide if minor changes will meet the needs or if major restructuring is necessary.

5. For major changes, develop a conceptual organizational structure to present for approval before rewriting major documents.

6. Once the conceptual organization plan has been adopted, develop new governing documents. As you do, follow these steps:

   • Seek guidance from your denominational leadership. They often have recommendations that have worked for other churches in your denomination. There may be requirements by the denomination for changes to governing documents.

- Review organizational structures of similar churches who have restructured.

- Seek legal counsel to ensure compliance with government laws and regulations.

- Seek help from consultants who have experience in organizational structure.

- Make opportunities available for input from leaders and members as you develop your plans.

- If adopting a major change, develop a plan for the transition period.

7. Throughout the process, assess what areas require spiritual healing. Address these issues with scriptural guidance, prayer, confession, and forgiveness.

Consider the spiritual qualifications discussed in this book for those who serve in leadership roles. Look for ways to strengthen the spiritual maturity of your leadership. Maintain biblical priorities for pastors, teachers, and other professional church workers (e.g., the apostles' decision "we will devote ourselves to prayer and to the ministry of the word" in Acts 6:4), and delegate administrative responsibilities to spiritually wise lay leaders or staff.

Organizational structure is a tool designed to help the people of God carry out His mission "decently and in order." Well-defined governance is important, but it should never overshadow the need to improve the spiritual health of the congregation.

Reflection

Considering this chapter, discuss the following questions with the leaders in your congregation.

1. When dealing with issues over structure, role definition, or governance, would you describe such issues as primarily *material/substantive* or *personal/relational*?

   a. How should one deal with the material/substantive issues when addressing confusion over structure?

   b. How should one deal with the personal/relational issues when addressing difficulties with structure?

2. Consider the situation where conflict arises among church leadership over roles and authority.

   a. Review 1 Corinthians 3:1–4 and John 13:1–17. In these passages, what spiritual issues are identified in conflict over roles and authority?

   b. What might be the organizational issues in such conflicts?

   c. How would the Scriptures guide you to address such issues?

Reflection

Reflection

3. Complete an assessment to see if your governing documents agree with one another and if your actual practice reflects what is written.

   a. What do you think would be important for your church to do regarding her present organizational structure?

   b. What would be important in assessing and addressing the spiritual needs of the congregation?

4. Review the readings from Exodus 18:1, 17–24 and Acts 6:1–7. Discuss the following:

   a. What were the priorities of Moses and the apostles?

   b. What responsibilities were delegated to lay leaders?

   c. What were the criteria for appointing lay leaders?

   d. Based on your answers, what guidance might you apply in the structure of your congregation?

PART 4

PRACTICAL APPLICATIONS FOR IMPROVING SPIRITUAL HEALTH

How can you guide your congregation to improved spiritual health? Make Bible study a priority. Focus on nourishing the troops so they are prepared for the spiritual battles of daily life. The devil, the world, and our sinful flesh resist scheduling time for Bible study. Leaders in healthy congregations strive to find ways to overcome obstacles and increase people's direct contact with the Word of God.

Strengthen the spiritual health of individuals. As their individual health increases, congregational health improves. Organizing leadership to visit all the church's members regularly provides care for the Body of Christ. Preventive care builds relationships and provides opportunities for engaging people in the Word and prayer.

Establish a reconciliation ministry. Teach and guide people to apply confession and forgiveness in every vocation. Although people may increase Bible study, they may still resort to worldly ways in daily life. Reconcilers can be appointed and equipped to demonstrate personal peacemaking in their own lives, teach others, and guide others through conflict coaching and mediation. When necessary, reconcilers can serve as adjudicators to help Christians resolve material issues in a private and biblically faithful manner. The more her members practice confession and forgiveness, the more a church's health will be enhanced.

This section presents practical ways to improve spiritual health within the congregation.

CHAPTER 13

IMPROVING BIBLICAL LITERACY

Lord, Your words are waters living
  When my thirsting spirit pleads.
Lord, Your words are bread life-giving;
  On Your words my spirit feeds.
Lord, Your words will be my light
Through death's cold and dreary night;
  Yes, they are my sword prevailing
  And my cup of joy unfailing! (*LSB* 589:3)

Case Study: All It Takes Is Two

"You won't get anyone to come to Bible study. We're just not used to it!"

That's the repeated message Rev. Bruce Zagel[29] heard as he visited the members of his new church. They had a long practice of no Bible study on Sunday or during the week.

Their pastor wasn't discouraged. "That's okay. My wife and I will be there. Jesus says, 'Where two or three are gathered in My name, there am I among them.' "

During the first two months of his new call as pastor, Rev. Zagel prioritized his schedule to meet with every household in the congregation. In his visits, he described the four new Bible studies that would be starting and personally invited people to come. During worship, he emphasized the importance of being in the Word.

Despite the naysayers, people did show up at each Bible study. Some may have attended initially out of curiosity, but they came. Over the following weeks, more began coming based on the reports of those who first attended. By the time one year had passed, sixty-five people were attending Bible study in a church that previously had no Bible study.

Encouraging people to change long-term habits of neglecting the Word is challenging. But when it becomes a focus and multiple opportunities are made available, some will meet the challenge.

The good news about biblical illiteracy is that it is curable. The resolution is not complicated—but it's not easy either. It requires persistence and trust in God.

In this chapter, I suggest some ideas for addressing this weakness among Christ's followers. Although you may decide not to use any of them, I hope that they will inspire you to find new ways to engage people with God's Word. After all, we His people need nourishment for the spiritual battles of life.

KNOW YOUR COMPETITION

When encouraging people to attend Bible study, it's important to understand their competing habits and desires—for people have already committed their time to something else.

Work schedules may prevent them from attending Bible study. Some work on Sunday mornings. Others may work in the evenings. Night shifts require people to sleep during the daytime. A few may travel during the week for work and are not in town when Bible studies are offered.

In families with school-age children, parents may be required to provide transportation or to accompany their children to school activities such as sports practices, games, and other extracurricular activities. As teens become employed, the use of family cars becomes limited.

In families where both parents work and children work and participate in school activities, family schedules are hectic and tiring. Adding another hour-long commitment for Bible study often means squeezing in another to-do in an already demanding schedule.

Retired people often busy themselves with part-time jobs, travel, hobbies, or volunteer commitments. They often seek ways to spend time with grandchildren and other family.

A major competitor to Bible study is leisure activity. Watching and playing sports, camping, fishing, boating, skiing, hunting, watching television, keeping up with social media—all these and more compete against people's time for Bible study. On Sunday morning, some people have developed the habit of going to brunch or coffee with friends during Bible study hour. Personal pleasure often wins over Bible study.

Why should people make time for Bible study a priority? Luther explains the commandment "Remember the Sabbath day by keeping it holy" by saying, "We should fear and love God so that we do not despise preaching and His Word, but hold it sacred and gladly hear and learn it."

Prioritizing many other activities, especially leisure, over the study of God's Word is sin.

Prioritizing many other activities, especially leisure, over the study of God's Word is sin.

I became aware of how much our Western society values leisure over God's Word when I first visited India. Christians in India often sacrifice basic needs to make time for God. Many take an entire Sunday just to attend worship. Most walk to church because they don't own cars. It may take one, two, or three hours to walk one way. The average worship service lasts several hours. I was told that if a sermon lasted fewer than forty-five minutes, people were offended.

For some, basic needs require working every day. If they don't work on any particular day, they don't eat that day. They don't have the money to buy food. But in India, I've seen these people give up a full day of working—and, as a result, eating—to be in church. They aren't sacrificing leisure time for worship—they're sacrificing basic necessities of life. Worshiping God is a priority.

When we had developed a close-enough relationship where we could be honest with each other without feeling like we would offend, I asked my Indian pastor friend what surprised him most about the time he spent as a student in America. He shared many positive observations. But one of his thoughts hit me cold. He was disturbed that in America people have only one hour per week to spend in worship with God. And if a worship service extends much beyond that time, even fifteen minutes, people gripe and complain.

I felt ashamed for my culture. Americans are among the wealthiest people in the world. Yet, we find it difficult to spend much more than one hour a week in worship. And as mentioned earlier, many believe that attending worship two times a month is regular worship!

The pursuit of wealth and the leisure it affords compete against people's desire to study God's Word. We choose demanding work schedules so we can earn more money. Both spouses work long hours so we can afford the nicer things in life. We spend time in pleasure activities that are affordable by the well-to-do. America is truly a land for which Jesus' words ring true: "Truly, I say to you, only with difficulty will a rich person enter the kingdom of heaven. Again I tell you, it is easier for a camel to go through the eye of a needle than for a rich person to enter the kingdom of God" (Matthew 19:23–24).

Wow. Is there any way for people in wealthy societies to be convinced to give up some of their pleasures or pursuit of wealth for the study of God's Word? We could ask the same question as the astonished disciples: "Who then can be saved?" (v. 25).

Jesus assures His followers: "With man this is impossible, but with God all things are possible" (v. 26).

Not hoping in men, but remembering that with God all things are possible, churches can compete for people's time to be in God's Word.

Like all competition, it takes deliberate strategizing and work—for people will have to give up something to invest time in Bible study. They will have to be convinced that the benefits are worth the cost. Leaders must strive to make multiple opportunities available for Bible study at times convenient for the attenders. Begin by identifying people's specific roadblocks to attending Bible study. It may be attitude, ignorance, work schedules, leisure activities, and such. Then determine what days and times will work for your members. Although there will never be a time that works for everyone, offering multiple opportunities expands the possibilities. In the end, people will have to make a choice of what's more important.

Learn what will interest people. Make available different studies to meet people where they are. Offer studies for books of the Bible. Plan topical studies. Provide introductory-level learning, as well as moderate and deeper studies. Find out what will help people set aside time for another commitment to start a new practice of Bible study.

Don't depend on bulletin and oral announcements alone to entice people to attend Bible study. People respond better to personal invitations. Ask those already attending a Bible study to personally invite others to join them. When lay leaders and professional church workers make personal visits on members, they should ask what it would take for the members to attend a Bible study. When the church can meet their specific needs, then the leader can connect with the members and invite them.

As people begin to engage, provide ways to grow deeper into the Word. Never assume that once people start they will always continue. Encouraging people to stay in God's Word is a never-ending responsibility of leadership.

ATTEND TO ADULT LEARNING STYLES

Learning is the objective of teaching. It is not important that the teacher satisfy his own desire to present or look important or knowledgeable. In other words, the focus of teaching is the learner, not the teacher.

> The focus of teaching is the learner, not the teacher.

As you and others teach adults, it's important to pay attention to adult learning styles. A common approach to teaching Bible study is lecture (auditory learning), which may be modeled after what Bible teachers experienced in higher education.

Yet, 85 percent of learners are visual or kinesthetic (requiring physical activity). The challenge for teachers is to design presentations to help all those in the class learn. Disciples learn best when the presenter has prepared to appeal to their learning styles. Note what improves adult learning:

- An understanding of how the learning will benefit them
- Verbal and/or physical participation in learning exercises
- Relating new learning to past experiences
- An understanding of how this learning will be practical and applicable to them

Consider how to improve your teaching as you serve the learner:

- Respectful relationships in a safe environment contribute to long-term retention. Building and maintaining trust is crucial in teaching. If there is fear, intimidation, or sarcasm, the learners will likely not retain the desired learning.

- The brain relates new learning to past learning. These connections are fostered when the teacher helps people see application to past and future life experiences. Note how Jesus used parables from everyday life to teach new concepts and practical application.

- Learners need time to process for learning connections to be made in the brain. Too much information without adequate time for reflection wastes the learner's precious time.

- Effective teachers are energetic and enthusiastic. They create curiosity and use a variety of instructional techniques to engage attention. The more senses learners can engage, the better their ability to retain new knowledge. Visual aids with color and movement improve learning for visual learners. Appeal to today's learners with media, including pictures and short video clips.

- If the body doesn't move, the brain doesn't learn. Physical movement tied to the teaching enhances learning. Kinesthetic learners learn best by moving their bodies, activating large or small muscles as they learn. Simple ways to encourage physical movement include requiring the larger group to break up into smaller groups to look up and read passages in the Bible, engaging in small-group discussions, using fill-in-the-blank for key thoughts, and asking participants to write down answers on a common sheet in the small groups before answering them in plenary sessions.

- Regular review and life-application illustrations increase the probability that learning will be recalled and applied successfully. In fact, the entire Bible is made up of stories about people who succeeded and failed to apply what God teaches His people.

Examples of failures provide antitheses to successes that illustrate key teaching points.

- The brain has an approximate attention span of eight minutes, with a maximum of twenty minutes. Break learning time into sessions of twenty minutes or less. Toward the end of each session, highlight the most important information. The brain remembers the first and last things it is exposed to.

Not everyone is naturally gifted as a teacher. To make learning more effective requires thoughtful preparation.

Poor teaching hinders Bible study attendance. People with busy lives tend to avoid studies where the leader fails to prepare adequately. Lecture or extensive rambling by the leader is another way to dissuade attendance. A teacher who asks questions but doesn't provide opportunity for the group to respond discourages people from reflecting and responding to the questions. Effective teachers learn to be comfortable with silence when asking questions because they understand that people need time to contemplate their answers—and eventually someone will answer. An arrogant attitude of "I know what's best" is a surefire way for teachers to reduce Bible study attendance.

Quality teaching improves Bible study attendance. Well-prepared leaders anticipate questions and have resources available to reference. Those who design their teaching to include active participation (e.g., small- and large-group discussion, exercises, writing out comments, and looking up passages in the Bible) increase interest as well as learning. Adults learn best when the teacher requires them to respond with their reflections on application.

AVOID BIBLELESS BIBLE STUDY

In chapter 1, I referenced a church where I was invited to teach the Sunday morning Bible class in a local church. After the pastor introduced me, I asked the group to open to the first Bible passage. Only two of the thirty people present had a Bible. We had to pause the study for about ten minutes until enough Bibles could be found so the attendees could at least share with one another. When we resumed the class, it was evident people needed extra time to look up what I consider to be familiar books of the Bible. I don't know what their normal practice was during their Bible study hour, but it was obvious they did not expect to use Bibles in Bible study.

Although you want to appeal to people's needs, avoid Bibleless Bible studies—those that don't require people to actually use their Bibles.

Teachers may print out all the verses because it saves time. Such a practice results in several disadvantages:

- Removing the opportunity for people to learn how to find books in their own Bibles
- Keeping people from highlighting certain verses or adding notes in the margins of their Bibles
- Encouraging biblical laziness
- Eliminating a kinesthetic activity that improves learning
- Reducing engagement

Some study groups review a book or current events. This focus on nonbiblical sources of information may produce interesting discussions, but it is not truly a *Bible* study. If a book is to be reviewed in the study, the leader needs to build into the review the looking up of Scriptures for comparison. The leader can also encourage people to use their concordance or topical index to search for applicable passages, training people how to search the Bible on their own. No matter how great the book or article may be, man's word does not carry the same power as God's Word.

When choosing a study that features videos, look for those that require people to look up passages in their own Bibles and discuss their application. Watching a video without interacting directly with the Bible robs people of the mental and physical engagement of using their Bibles.

Avoid calling fellowship activities "Bible study." I have worked with churches that utilized extensive small-group ministries that were primarily fellowship groups. Although the purported purpose was Bible study, small-group leaders told me that they opened with a devotion for about ten or fifteen minutes, and then enjoyed fellowship for an hour or more. I also have learned about youth, women's, and men's groups that claimed to be Bible studies with fellowship activities, such as bowling or breakfast groups. In some cases, the main purpose was fellowship, and "Bible study" was minimized to a few minutes.

Fellowship is important, but these kinds of arrangements are not truly Bible studies.

HOMEWORK ASSIGNMENT

An effective way to improve people's learning is to assign work between classes. Homework provides an opportunity for reflection, personal application, review, preparation, and additional engagement with the Word.

The amount of time necessary to complete the assignment should be appropriate for the participants involved. Make assignments too long or too short, and people won't complete them. You may need to experiment for the right design for your group.

Effective assignments require accountability. For example, when assigning work, the next session should include an opportunity for people to discuss what they learned. If the class is large, this is best done in small groups. If there is no accountability, few will complete the task.

Apply these seven tactics to make assignments effective:

- **Design around one major learning objective**. Trying to cover more than one key area loses impact.

- **Focus on application.** As adults apply the Scriptures to their own lives, the learning is deeper and longer lasting. This type of learning increases the desire to continue in the study and encourage others to participate.

- **Keep the assignment simple.** Long reading assignments or multiple questions can confuse or overwhelm a person, which often results in the assignment not being completed or having much impact.

- **Assign something to read** or meditate upon. This should include a Scripture passage or reading from another source that relates to the Bible section being studied.

- **Provide a few questions** that help the person apply the biblical teaching to a specific attitude or behavior.

  - Ask open-ended questions.

  - Avoid questions that are too general or too obvious.

  - Require that the answers be written out.

    — Writing requires a more thoughtful response.

    — Written answers improve accountability.

- **Balance Law and Gospel**. If you assign a passage or question that may convict someone of his or her sin, be sure to include Gospel for comfort.

- **Provide accountability** by discussing the homework at the next session. Instead of asking each person to read all the answers, simply ask, "What did you learn from the assignment?" If you have a group of six or more, divide into smaller groups of three to four so each person can participate in the discussion.

KEYS FOR EFFECTIVE HOMEWORK

- Have only one objective
- Focus on application
- Keep it simple—design for one objective
- Assign a relevant reading that promotes reflection
- Ask open-ended questions that help apply Scripture to participants' lives
- Balance Law and Gospel
- Provide accountability

BEGIN WITH LEADERSHIP

Paul wrote to Timothy: "Let no one despise you for your youth, but set the believers an example in speech, in conduct, in love, in faith, in purity. . . . Keep a close watch on yourself and on the teaching. Persist in this, for by so doing you will save both yourself and your hearers" (1 Timothy 4:12, 16).

Leaders lead by example.

If parents drop their children off at Sunday School while they go to brunch, their example teaches children to do the same when they grow up. If the manager in a business is known for wasting time on her computer, her employees will follow her example. If the lay leaders and staff of a church or Christian school fail to attend Bible study, the message to the rest of the people is clear—Bible study is unimportant.

The staff and lay leadership teach and encourage others by their actions. Educate the leadership on the importance of being in the Word and the difference their examples make. Make plenty of opportunities for Bible study available. Ask leaders who have a practice of being in the Word to assist you in this task; they already understand the need for Bible study.

Several of the healthy churches I surveyed expected staff and lay leaders to be active in Bible study. In fact, their governing documents (bylaws or policies) required it. Those not active in worship and Bible study did not qualify for leadership.

If your church does not have such policies, take time to reinforce the importance of such practices and enact new policies over time.

ENCOURAGE BIBLE USE DURING WORSHIP

In our desire to make worship more convenient, we often print out the Bible passages in a bulletin or on a big screen. In some cases, we depend on people to just listen without reading along. Such practices discourage people from using their Bibles during worship and foster biblical laziness.

While assisting a conflicted church to reconcile, our team met with all the families in the church. We asked people in our meetings to read

> Leaders lead by example.

Bible passages with us. We realized that most of the people could not look up books of the Bible, so we had a Bible on the table for them, open to the Gospel of John.

A recently retired couple sat down in front of me. During their introduction, they told me that they had been regularly attending this congregation for more than twenty years. When I asked them to read along with me in the Bible, I gave them the reference. Although the Bible was open to the right book, they were unable to find the verse. They didn't know the Bible was divided by chapter and verse. Being in worship did little to teach them how to use the Bible.

In contrast, I visited an African American church where the people knew their Bibles. During the opening announcements, the pastor did a quick test with his congregants. He raised his hand holding his Bible: "Adults, Bible check. Bible check."

All the adults raised their hands with Bibles in hands.

"Youth, Bible check. Bible check." All the children and teens raised their hands holding their Bibles.

The church provided Bibles in all the pews, but they appeared unused to me. However, everyone sitting around me held well-worn Scriptures.

When the time came for the Scripture readings, the references were given in the bulletin, but the passages were not printed out. The reader announced each lesson, giving people a little time to look up the passage. The entire congregation participated, including visitors such as myself. During the sermon, the pastor often referenced Bible passages, and the people had been taught to look up the passages with their pastor. I noticed that those around me had passages underlined and highlighted in their Bibles. Several had notes in the margins. These were people who marked, learned, and inwardly ingested the Word of God during worship.

During the Bible study that followed, I was not at all surprised that people had no trouble finding any passage they were asked to reference. These people were biblically literate.

There are congregants who because of age, poor eyesight, mental limitations, or illiteracy are unable to use a Bible during worship. Be creative in finding ways to accommodate them. Some churches ask the people around them to share their Bibles, or they print out readings for these special instances.

There are also visitors or infrequent worshipers who attend worship and may have difficulty in looking up passages. Also, if you begin a new practice of asking people to use Bibles, you may have many in the congregation who struggle to find books and passages in the Bible at first.

Encourage people to take home the bookmarks below for their own Bibles. Announce the readings for the next week's worship service. People will learn to prepare before going to worship.

EXERCISE

Print special bookmarks, each titled for the different readings: Psalm of the Day, First Reading, Epistle, Holy Gospel, Sermon Text, etc. List all the books of the Bible on each bookmark. Place multiple sets of bookmarks in each row of pews or seats.

Be creative. On one side of the bookmark, include a Bible passage on the Word (such as Psalm 119:105; 2 Timothy 3:16–17; or John 20:31). Add a picture or graphic. Today, many churches have the equipment needed to print their own bookmarks. There are also professional printers who specialize in custom printing at reasonable prices. The more attractive the bookmarks, the more likely they will be kept and used. Invite people to keep a set of bookmarks in their personal Bibles.

A few minutes before the service starts, have a leader announce the Scripture readings for the day. If you have pew Bibles, also list the page numbers, while at the same time describing what books come before and after the reading. (Do this until people are comfortable using their Bibles.) Provide time for people to look up the passages and mark them with the bookmarks. Encourage people to assist others around them.

If you have children's sermons, invite older children or parents to accompany younger children and ask them to bring their

Bibles. Encourage the children to look up passages and read them with the presenter.

Even if many don't attend Bible study, they will learn how to use the Bible. The more they handle God's Word, the more familiar it will become to them. At the very least, you hope that regular attenders will learn that the Bible is divided by chapter and verse.

LEADING HOME DEVOTIONS

In chapter 14, I explain that lay leader visits to members should include leading a devotion. I recommend that all members be visited, not just those who haven't attended for more than a year.

Leading home devotions is a great way to encourage people to be in God's Word. Many have not yet practiced the discipline of daily devotions. Leaders of households often have never been shown how to lead a devotion.

The home visit is an ideal time to demonstrate leading a family devotion. The visitor should always have a devotion booklet available to leave with the family and should also carry a Bible that can be left with the family.

Before arriving, the lay leader should inform the member that he will begin with a brief devotion and ask the member to have his or her Bible available for the visit. When teaching people to have family devotions, ask a family member to read the Scripture reading or the meditation or the written prayer. Be prepared to help those who have difficulty reading.

In our reconciliation ministry, we recorded one of our devotion booklets on CD so people could listen to them if they had difficulty finding the time to read. Websites also provide oral devotions. Many resources exist to help people fit devotions into their everyday lives, whether it's listening to them in the car, while they do chores, or while they exercise.

Over time, if one lay leader has repeated visits with the same family, they will come to expect the devotion and be prepared to participate. Moreover, families will actually begin the practice of being in God's Word through daily devotions between visits.

THE YEAR OF THE BIBLE

Adopt a year-long theme, "The Year of the Bible." Prepare months in advance and announce the objective for the coming year—to get people into God's Word at home, at church, and in small groups.

- Provide multiple Bible study opportunities for the coming year. If you do not have several leaders, you will need to appoint new ones and equip them to lead the studies.

- Offer an introductory study on the Bible, describing its history and how the different books were brought together in our Christian Bible. However, make sure to incorporate actual scriptural readings. Teach people to use a concordance and topical index. Ask folks to share notes from their study Bibles. Show them how to note references marked in their Bibles. Even if people grew up in the church and had this information taught in Sunday School or confirmation, many may have forgotten it. Furthermore, many adults attending worship today didn't grow up in the church.

- Before the year begins, ask people to make a commitment to read through the Bible in a year. Prepare a schedule for daily home readings. You can find these in hymnals, online, and in other resources.

- Get your lay leaders involved in the Word. Ask for their commitment to be in the Word and lead by example.

- In the months before the official start, the lay leaders should describe the coming theme in member visits. They can hand out bookmark sets (explained earlier) and describe the new available Bible studies. They should encourage members to prayerfully consider committing to reading through the Bible in a year. They can also hand out a diagram of "The Books of the Bible" bookcase (see Diagram 3 on page 242).

- Utilize the Bible during worship as described earlier, with help from the Bible bookmarks. Encourage people to bring their own Bibles to church rather than use the church Bibles, so they can get to know them better and mark them.

- Use Sunday School, Vacation Bible School, and other children's ministry lessons to teach how to use the Bible. Help kids memorize the books of the Bible. Design contests for the children and teens on knowing the order of the books of the Bible. Hold the contest during an adult Bible study so the adults can test their own knowledge (in their minds) against the kids as they give their answers.

- Build a Bible bookcase and make it visible in the fellowship hall or another place where people gather. Cover sixty-six books or video cases with large binding labels on them to go in the bookcase. (You may wish to make each section its own color.) Arrange the "books" in sections:

  - Old Testament
    - The Law
    - History
    - Poetry
    - Major Prophets
    - Minor Prophets
  - New Testament
    - Gospels
    - History
    - Paul's Letters
    - General Letters
    - Prophecy

- Purchase or prepare a topical index of where to find passages dealing with specific topics. Make the handout small enough to fit inside people's Bibles. These can be handed out during worship, Bible studies, and home visits.
- Focus Bible studies on using the Word, not just another person's meditations or writing.

DIAGRAM 3

THE BOOKS OF THE BIBLE

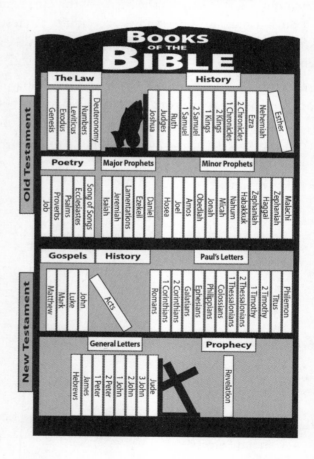

CAUTION! EXPECT TO GO SLOW

Pull back on your personal expectations, and trust God for the results.

Spiritual nourishment takes time. Expect spiritual maturity to be a painfully slow process. It takes persistence and patience to encourage people to engage with God's Word.

Moreover, people who are just beginning to read and study the Bible will not exhibit immediate change. Remember, if they have been spiritually malnourished for a long period, it will take time before the Word will show impact. It may take a couple of years before people demonstrate any effect. Then, expect a gradual process of transformation. You may not even recognize the changes. But the Word will bear fruit. Trust in God's promises about His Word:

> For as the rain and the snow come down from heaven
> and do not return there but water the earth,
> making it bring forth and sprout,
> giving seed to the sower and bread to the eater,
> so shall My word be that goes out from My mouth;
> it shall not return to Me empty,
> but it shall accomplish that which I purpose,
> and shall succeed in the thing for which I sent it.
> (Isaiah 55:10–11)

Note that God does not promise when the fruit will come, through whom it will come, or what it will look like. In fact, God does not promise that we will even recognize it.

Because we live in a temporal world, we often expect immediate results. But God has an eternal perspective. While we hope for instant gratification, God is at work for the eternal welfare of His children.

So often I have been guilty of pressing for results, when all the time God was working in ways far beyond my limited perspective.

Because we live in a temporal world, we often expect immediate results. But God has an eternal perspective.

Case Study: Letting Go of Control

A fellow reconciler, Gary, and I were serving as mediators for several business partners. Their venture was experiencing significant losses, and the partners began turning on one another. Because they had signed a prior agreement for Christian mediation and arbitration rather than litigation, they engaged our services. Their business had limited liquidity, so the managing partner was personally paying for our professional fees and the expenses for the mediation.

The mediation was scheduled for three and a half days. Gary and I had been working ten to twelve hours a day trying to help the parties reach reconciliation and agreement. Late on the third evening, I was tired with a headache and began complaining to my colleague. Actually, I was whining.

"I don't think we're going to get an agreement."

"Ted, that's not your problem."

"Yes, it is, Gary. I'm the lead mediator. Jim has paid for our fees out of his own pocket, and he and the other partners are anticipating an agreement out of this. They expect results!"

"Ted, you're not responsible for these people coming to agreement. Our job is to present God's Word to them as effectively as possible so God can change their hearts. We are just the messengers. Perhaps if you spent more time praying and less time complaining, you might feel differently."

Gary was right. I was looking for an agreement, an immediate result. I wanted to be able to say we had been successful. I wanted to prove I was a good lead mediator. "I" was getting in the way.

That evening, I took Gary's counsel to heart and laid my concern at the foot of the cross. I prayed that God would achieve His purposes and that I would faithfully deliver His message. I slept well that night.

The next morning, three of the partners reconciled. But a fourth person who was key in the relationship refused to see that he had contributed to the dispute in any way. Reconciliation stopped short. We broke for lunch. I called my office, asking them to pray. We only had two hours left before the mediation was over.

In the last moments, the parties reached an agreement on the substantive issues. We quickly drafted a memorandum of agreement that the partners signed on their way out the door.

Gary and I celebrated the agreement. Yes, I finally saw the results I had hoped for. Once again, "I" became the problem. But despite my limited "I" sight, God was working in ways I could never foresee.

Two years later, Jim called me out of the blue.

"Hi, Jim. Great to hear from you. How are you doing? And how is the business doing?"

"Well, I'm okay. The business continues to struggle. The mediation agreement helped some. But I called for a different reason. I wanted to thank you."

"Thank me? For what?" He just said that the business wasn't doing so well. Why would he thank me?

"You may not remember my father because he left after the first day of mediation. He was one of the partners. He had other commitments and couldn't stay for the whole time."

"Yes, I remember him."

"When Dad went home that night, he told my stepmother he needed to reconcile with his children. Each of us adult kids was managing one of his business entities. Dad was a harsh taskmaster, and he had broken relationships with all of us. He told my stepmother that the Scriptures he heard that day reminded him that relationships are more important than business. So he spent the last two years restoring relationships with all of us. Two weeks ago, Dad suddenly died of a heart attack. At the funeral, I was praising God that my siblings and I had reconciled with our father. And I thought back to what started it all. You and Gary shared God's Word with us in that business mediation. Thank you for being faithful servants of the Lord. Keep doing what you're doing. You will never know how God will use you to change people's lives."

I was deeply convicted of my sin. Throughout the mediation, I had focused on helping these men reach an immediate agreement on their business. I wanted a visible result. In the meantime, God was using this as an opportunity to reconcile a family before He called the father home to heaven. Despite my misdirection, God's Word prevailed and a family was healed.

How many times have I been unaware of how God was using His Word to change lives! We often are not privy to God's working in others' hearts.

Perhaps you also become discouraged when you don't see the results you want. Maybe you can relate to the desire of proving that you have been an effective servant for the Lord. There may have been times when you wanted to give up because your labor seemed useless. But the truth is this: only God can see into another person's heart, and you really don't know what fruit He may be producing with the message you have delivered.

I have Good News for you. God knows how you seek after proven results that will satisfy your personal expectations. He is more aware than you of your own personal desires for gratification and for other sins in serving as an ambassador for Christ. But He loves you with an everlasting love. He has chosen you to be His child and His messenger of grace.

Remember His Word of promise for you:

> For our sake He made Him to be sin who knew no sin, so that in Him we might become the righteousness of God. (2 Corinthians 5:21)

> But now in Christ Jesus you who once were far off have been brought near by the blood of Christ. (Ephesians 2:13)

> The blood of Jesus His Son cleanses us from all sin. (1 John 1:7)

> See what kind of love the Father has given to us, that we should be called children of God; and so we are. (1 John 3:1)

Receive God's promise for you. You are His forgiven child.

Be patient when helping people become biblically literate. More important, fear God and trust in His promises. Remember *whose* Church it is and *whose* people you serve. Simply said, be Word-driven in your service as an ambassador for Christ.

> If You, O LORD, should mark iniquities,
>   O Lord, who could stand?
> But with You there is forgiveness,
>   that You may be feared. (Psalm 130:3–4)

Reflection

Reflection

Considering this chapter, discuss the following questions with the leaders in your congregation.

1. What are the major competing factors to Bible study among your members? In what ways can you overcome them?

    a. If you don't know what they are, how can you learn what is competing for your members' time and commitment to Bible study (e.g., incorporating member visits or surveys)?

    b. How can you intentionally overcome people's obstacles to spending time in the Word?

    c. What opportunities can you provide to address scheduling conflicts of congregants?

    d. How are people currently invited to attend Bible studies in your church? How could you improve the ways you personally invite people to participate?

2. How can you strengthen the teaching methodology utilized for Bible studies in your congregation? List the current Bible studies in your church and describe the methods currently applied in each study (e.g., lecture, discussion, handouts, video or projected pictures, or homework).

    a. How well do the participants understand how the learning will benefit them? How could you improve communicating about the benefits of each class?

Reflection

Reflection

b. What methods are intentionally utilized to engage people? How could you improve participation verbally and physically?

c. How often do people actually use their Bibles in the different studies in your church? How can you incorporate more Bible time in studies that are weak in this area?

d. What are you doing to relate new learning to past experiences? Determine a specific way you can do this in your next class.

e. How do Bible study leaders help people apply the learning to daily life? What can be done to improve application of the Word in their lives?

f. How well do you use homework? Discuss among your Bible study leaders how you can incorporate effective homework assignments applicable to each Bible study in your church.

3. What percentage of your church's staff and lay leaders attend Bible study? What can you do to persuade all your leaders to participate in Bible study and lead by example?

4. How are the Scriptures used during your worship services? How might you encourage people to use their Bibles during worship?

5. How can you teach and encourage family devotions? Consider Bible studies, worship, and member visits.

6. What ideas can you implement for a year committed to increasing Bible reading and study? Develop a plan together with the other leaders of your church.

7. In what areas are you most discouraged about increasing Bible study participation? How can you guard yourself and other leaders against discouragement?

CHAPTER 14

Caring for the Body of Christ

Blest be the tie that binds
    Our hearts in Christian love;
The fellowship of kindred minds
Is like to that above.

We share our mutual woes,
    Our mutual burdens bear,
And often for each other flows
The sympathizing tear. (*LSB* 649:1, 3)

I was a young man when I learned to make my first hospital visit to a congregational member.

The church secretary contacted me because Clara had specifically requested I come. Her husband was in the Intensive Care Unit (ICU), and our pastor and neighboring pastors were out of town for a pastor's conference.

"Why did she ask for me?" I asked the secretary in disbelief. I wasn't an elder, and I had never made a member visit of any kind.

"She knows you from choir."

I had begun directing the adult choir when I was a senior in high school. At the time of this request, I was twenty-five. Clara sang alto. She was quiet and spoke with a German accent. She was a dedicated choir member who loved to sing. I enjoyed having her in choir, but I didn't really know her that well and I had never met her husband. She apparently appreciated something about my leading the choir.

On the way to the hospital, I stopped by the church office to pick up a devotion booklet based on the Psalms. I also brought my Bible.

When I arrived, I found Clara alone in the ICU waiting room. Visits to ICU patients were restricted to a few minutes per hour. She lit up when she saw me. She told me about her husband's heart attack. He wasn't expected to live. Because I was from her church, the ICU nurse allowed me to visit Jacob with his wife. He was not conscious, but I knew from family experience that this did not necessarily mean he could not hear us. I remember reading a psalm and offering a prayer, closing with the Lord's Prayer.

I remained with Clara for a few hours, checking in on Jacob when the nurses allowed. I would read a brief Bible verse and say a short prayer. The next day, I met their son who had just flown in. Shortly after that, our pastor returned to town. He invited me to join him for a couple more visits. I had become close to the family in less than twenty-four hours. I also visited them after Jacob passed into eternal life.

Although I felt ill equipped for such a task, the Lord had been preparing me without my realizing it. As a teenager, I had often visited my mother in the hospital and nursing home, where she died after a long battle with diabetes. The hospital environment was familiar to me. Through instruction I received from pastors, teachers, and personal study, I knew more about the Word than I gave myself credit for. While I hadn't experienced specific training for hospital visits, God had been preparing me for this very day for a long time.

Spiritually healthy congregations understand that regular visits to all members serve as preventive care that builds relationships and provides opportunities to engage people in the Word and prayer.

Making calls on members can be challenging for lay leaders, especially if they don't have experience or have never been trained. The most important preparation is to be in God's Word and to be comfortable praying in the presence of others.

In this chapter, I share some ideas on how to make a visit with a congregational member. This is not just for elders but for anyone who has the opportunity. School board members should know how to visit school families. Council members can also be part of the church's visitation team. Even choir directors can make visits! Often I meet people from various backgrounds throughout the congregation who enjoy visiting those unable to leave their homes.

A MINISTRY OF PRESENCE

Ministering to people is not just providing them information about God. Caring for God's flock requires being present with people in their daily lives.

Our God is a God of relationship. He cared so much about us that Christ took on flesh and dwelt among His people. In His earthly ministry, Jesus didn't just study and preach and teach all the time, avoiding contact with people. He was physically present among them in groups and individually. He listened to their cries for help. He spoke with them. He fed them. He touched them. He forgave and healed them.

Today, our Lord is still present with His people through His Word and Sacraments. Christ speaks to us through the Bible. God's Spirit dwells within us. We are made children of the heavenly Father as we are touched in the waters of Holy Baptism. He physically comes to us in His body and blood during His Holy Supper. I love the Communion hymn that reminds us of Christ's presence in the Sacrament:

> Here, O my Lord, I see Thee face to face;
>> Here would I touch and handle things unseen;
> Here grasp with firmer hand the eternal grace,
> And all my weariness upon Thee lean. (*LSB* 631:1)

Moreover, God gives us one another to serve in a ministry of presence.

Today, more than ever, personal contact makes a difference. With the busyness of our society, and with communications becoming more and more digitalized, connecting with someone in person is an unusual blessing.

When I worked for Aid Association for Lutherans, I met in the homes of people from my eight assigned congregations to provide financial planning services, insurance, and investment opportunities. During appointments to discuss their financial needs, we occasionally talked about their involvement in the church. I was told by their pastors that many people who hadn't been to worship in a long time often attended the Sunday following my visit. In the congregants' minds, I represented the church to them (even though I may have attended a different congregation). Even if we didn't discuss their church attendance, my visit meant that someone from the church cared enough to personally be with them.

From my financial services work, I learned the importance of personally visiting people—not only for selling financial products, but also for connecting people to the church.

When professional church workers and lay leaders of a church make personal contact with their members, it strengthens relationships within the Body of Christ. Such contacts provide opportunity to care for one another, share Scripture together, and pray together. It's amazing what one can learn about fellow church members when you take time to visit.

One elder told me that in his visit with a retired couple, he learned that the husband stopped attending worship because the pastor wore a beard. The man had retired from the military and found facial hair on anyone in leadership offensive. A visit from the pastor would not have been welcome. Because the elder cared enough simply to visit, he was able to hear the concern and discuss the issue with the couple. Although there was no pressure from the elder, the husband returned to worship after his elder's visit.

In another case, the elder learned that a family avoided worship because of a misunderstanding about something that happened at church. When the elder heard their concern, he was able to clarify the issue, and the people returned to church.

But it's not just those who miss worship who deserve our attention. Proactive care requires visiting people before something goes wrong. Church leaders who visit active members create the opportunity to show Christian care in areas unknown to the church, including family struggles, financial challenges, health concerns, and work conflicts. I know of a couple of situations where people had just received an unexpected inheritance and wanted to discuss how to bless the church with a special gift. If no one visits them in person, many of these needs go undetected and neglected by the church.

Several years ago, I visited an acquaintance who serves as a pastor in a rural church. He showed me the sanctuary and gave me a walking tour through the church grounds, including the cemetery. As we walked past family markers, he spoke warmly about the families in his church. He knew his people well because of his ministry of presence. He knew what time the farmers began working, because he was up at the crack of dawn to visit them in the fields. He knew when the townsfolk took their coffee breaks, because he visited them in the local café. He knew in advance when his people were undergoing surgery, because he visited them on a regular basis. This man loved his flock—he was present among them in their daily lives.

For most churches, though, there are too many members for the pastors alone to visit on any kind of regular basis. Furthermore, building relationships in the church is not just the pastor's responsibility. Paul directed church members in Corinth and Galatia to care for one another.

> But God has so composed the body, giving greater honor to the part that lacked it, that there may be no division in the body, but that the members may have the same care for one another. If one member suffers, all suffer together; if one member is honored, all rejoice together. (1 Corinthians 12:24–26)

> Bear one another's burdens, and so fulfill the law of Christ. . . . So then, as we have opportunity, let us do good to everyone, and especially to those who are of the household of faith. (Galatians 6:2, 10)

In describing the final judgment, Jesus identified the righteous as those who provided personal care and visitation:

> Then the righteous will answer Him, saying, "Lord, when did we see You hungry and feed You, or thirsty and give You drink? And when did we see You a stranger and welcome You, or naked and clothe You? And when did we see You sick or in

prison and visit You?" And the King will answer them, "Truly, I say to you, as you did it to one of the least of these My brothers, you did it to Me." (Matthew 25:37–40)

The healthy congregations I meet with know how to care for one another. They have adopted formal practices for visitation, providing accountability so they know everyone is being visited. Empowered by God's Word, many also visit one another informally. They have been transformed to be present for one another in times of need and celebration. Interdependence has become more apparent than independence. Because they care for one another, they also demonstrate care for many outside their fellowship. It's part of their DNA.

In unhealthy churches where I have worked, people are disconnected from one another. The leaders know little about the personal joys and struggles of their members. In some cases, the pastor visits those who are sick, homebound, or grieving the loss of loved ones. But the lay leadership lacks accountability for visiting people. Because they have too few people in God's Word, the congregation has little spiritual maturity to drive them to care for one another informally. Independence is valued over interdependence. Without realizing it, many live as if it is every man for himself in his faith walk.

While meeting with a lay leader of a conflicted church, I learned that he had experienced a major heart attack in the previous year. As I talked to him about his experience, he became emotional as he described how it affected his wife, children, and grandchildren. He then shared the struggles of his stress-related job. I asked him who visited him and his family while he was in the hospital and recovering at home. His answer saddened me, as it revealed how his congregation failed to care for its leaders.

"No one."

"No one visited you? What about your pastor?"

"Nope. But that's not expected. I'm a leader. Leaders don't need to be visited."

Very few people in the church even knew about his heart attack. I took the opportunity to share Scripture and pray for him and his family.

He was deeply touched that someone would care for him in that way.

I wish I could say that this was an unusual experience. But unfortunately, I have encountered many churches over the years that don't have a practice of visiting all the members. And many neglect providing care for their professional church workers and lay leaders.

ORGANIZING FOR PERSONAL VISITS

All too often, I meet elder boards who only make calls on those who are absent from worship. Usually, the calls are made to people who have been away for a long time. Some who are contacted resent being called because they no longer see themselves as part of the church. It doesn't take many of these kinds of calls to discourage lay leaders from making calls.

A healthy congregation seeks to make regular personal contact with *all* of its members. Such contacts are often encouraging to the one making the call. Visiting with active members communicates that the church cares about everyone. Making the easier calls on active members provides practice that prepares leaders for making the more difficult ones.

While the pastor and elders have the primary responsibility for calling on all members, organizing for the task divides the work and helps a church be accountable. Households in a congregation should be divided into different groups that are specifically assigned to an elder or others who assist in visitation. Groups may be divided alphabetically, geographically, or by another designation. By organizing in such ways, the number of people for each lay leader to visit is more manageable and easier to track. For example, if a leader is assigned eighteen families in his zone, he can easily visit each family twice year with just three visits per month.

Implement a practice of making calls *without a special need* such as illness, bereavement, lack of worship attendance, or stewardship campaign. Visit members who are active, inactive, hospitalized or homebound, or have children in the church school. Calling on everyone creates a routine in which both the visitor and visited become more comfortable over time. This practice results in a relationship that makes visiting about special needs more ordinary and expected. Of course, new visitors to the church should also be followed up with a visit.

A normal visit should be kept short. When making the appointment, indicate that the visit will only be about 20–30 minutes. When making evening visits, you can schedule two to three visits in the same evening. If something serious comes up in the first visit that requires more time, you can stay longer, and if necessary, call the next appointment to reschedule.

It's important to make an appointment. The layperson responsible may send an introductory note to the members in his zone indicating that he is responsible for visiting everyone in his zone and will be calling in the future for an appointment. Make arrangements when you see someone at church, or send an email or make a phone call. For encouragement, have all the lay leaders meet together one evening a month to make phone-call appointments. Sunday evenings often work well because most people are home.

You may wish to visit in pairs. Having another person present can be beneficial in a number of ways:

- It can provide encouragement, especially if a visitor is apprehensive.

- Having the pastor or another experienced leader present can help train others making visits.

- Avoid meeting one-on-one alone with a person of the opposite sex. Visiting in pairs limits temptation and protects a sole visitor from false accusations.

- Having a spouse with you can also be helpful, especially when meeting with couples or someone of the opposite sex.

There may be times when meeting in person is difficult, such as when scheduling becomes challenging or people are uncomfortable with visitors in their home. Although in-person visits are preferable in most situations, you can complete a visit by phone. With today's technology, you may also consider connecting by video communication.

KISS

A member visit does not have to be complicated. Remember to apply the KISS principle: Keep It Simple, Saint!

Remember the purposes for your visit. You want to connect to another member in the Body of Christ. You do this by being present to provide care and encouragement. This happens as you share a passage from Scripture and pray. Your presence will provide the opportunities to meet other needs.

Consider this outline for a KISS visit:

- At the beginning of the visit, tell the person what you plan to do.

- Share a devotion (five to ten minutes maximum if in person; shorter if by phone).

- Ask if the person has any questions or concerns about the church or his or her personal faith life.

  - You may need to follow up with the pastor or someone else.

  - If a pastoral-care need arises, ask permission to share it with the pastor or another leader (remember to hold confidences).

- Optional: Briefly share about a new or existing ministry opportunity in the church.

  - For example, you might extend an invitation to a new Bible study series, talk about a ministry service opportunity, or remind the person about a fellowship activity.

- Ask how you can pray for the member.

  - Also ask permission to share a prayer request with the rest of your board when you meet.

- Close in prayer.

You may follow up with a short note or email of thanks for the visit, and report on any action you may have taken as a result of your visit.

Below is more instruction on two key components for your visit: praying for people during meetings and leading a devotion.

CARING THROUGH PRAYER IN MEETINGS

In chapter 10, I suggested that leadership boards should devote time during their meetings to pray for people in their assigned areas of responsibility (see p. 189). When you visit people, you will learn of prayer requests, both for celebration and for times of need. In the suggested outline for a member visit mentioned earlier, I included asking permission to share a prayer request with the board.

In spiritually healthy congregations, the leadership boards take time to pray for the specific needs of members and nonmembers. Each person on the board can be given opportunity to pray for the people in his assigned area.

With a simple card, you can demonstrate loving care to the people for whom you pray in a powerful way.

In my congregation, the elders had simple cards made with a drawing of the church on the front and a short Scripture verse on the inside: "First of all, then, I urge that supplications, prayers, intercessions, and thanksgivings be made for all people" (1 Timothy 2:1). You can also purchase inexpensive cards with no print on the inside.

At the end of the prayer, each leader writes a brief note to the person he prayed for. The note indicates that the board prayed for him or her. For example:

- Dear Mary, we prayed for your continued recovery from surgery in our Board of Elders meeting.
- Dear John, your pastor and Board of Elders prayed for you today.

The lay leader who prayed then signs under the hand-written note and passes the card around for each board member to sign. The cards are then mailed to the members.

This simple procedure is another way to connect with people and communicate your care and love for them. When I served as an elder in my church, many of those who received our cards expressed deep appreciation. Our pastor told us that some even responded with tears. As a member, I have also benefited from receiving those cards. It is a huge encouragement to know that your pastor and elders are taking time in their meetings to pray for you.

LEADING A DEVOTION

The devotion is a key component of your visit. First, it is a specific way to share God's Word with the member. Second, it serves as a teaching example for family devotions.

Staying with the KISS principle, keep the devotion simple. This is not the time for an expansive discussion of theology or a major teaching of Scripture. When teaching people for a member visit, my former district president George Wollenburg said it this way: "Your job is to present the Word of God, and then get out of its way!"[30]

We can trust the Word of God to accomplish God's purposes. For He promises:

> So shall My word be that goes out from My mouth;
>> it shall not return to Me empty,
> but it shall accomplish that which I purpose,
> and shall succeed in the thing for which I sent it. (Isaiah 55:11)

A meditation without a Bible reading is weaker than one that incorporates Scripture. Man's words cannot replace what God's Word does. Your devotion should include two components:

- Scripture reading
- Prayer

You may include two optional components, depending on the situation:

- Brief meditation
- Hymn or spiritual song

Consider what you are modeling for the family you are visiting. You need not make up your own devotion. You can find devotional resources from a number of areas:

- Devotion booklets and websites
    - Available through your church's resources
    - Internet websites
    - Publishers or Christian bookstores

- Review all material for doctrinal content before using

- Especially look for the proclamation of the Gospel

- Be aware of errors that contradict Scripture or fundamental doctrines

- Bibles
  - Many have suggested daily devotional readings

- Hymnals
  - Readings of the day or for that week (e.g., from a daily lectionary)

  - Psalms (often available in hymnals)

  - Prayers for certain occasions

  - Hymns
    - Can be sung or read

    - Many are written as prayers

  - Short devotion rites for individuals and families, such as in daily prayer for morning, noon, evening, or end of day

- Catechism (e.g., Luther's Small Catechism)
  - Prayers

  - Scriptures

  - Sections that can be used for meditation (e.g., the explanation of the Second Article of the Apostles' Creed)

As you choose resources, look for those that reference a Bible passage that you can read separately from the meditation. If you use a meditation, be certain that the resource you are using is consistent with the Scriptures. Check with your pastor if you are uncertain about any devotional resource.

Make certain that the devotion you use incorporates Gospel—the Good News that because Jesus died for us, God forgives all our sins. Look for devotions that provide comfort and the assurance of God's promises. You can't guarantee earthly results, but you can assure a sister or brother in Christ of the promises of God. You often won't know what spiritual battle the person may be facing. You also don't know if your visit will provide the last biblical message this person hears before entering eternity.

When an entire board makes calls, the same devotion may be used by all board members for a particular period of time.

For prayers, consider the following resources:

- Prepared prayers from hymnals, catechisms, devotion booklets, Bibles, and other books
- The Lord's Prayer
- Prayers from the heart (*ex corde*)

Reflection

Reflection

Considering this chapter, discuss the following questions with the leaders in your congregation.

1. How often are your church's members visited by anyone from the congregation?

2. When was the last time you were visited by someone in the congregation?

    a. If you received a visit, what did you appreciate most?

    b. If you have never been visited, what disappoints you most?

3. How well is your congregation organized to make certain everyone is visited by someone?

    a. If not well organized, what can you do to implement organization so that the workload is divided and you can be assured that everyone is getting visited?

    b. How can you improve training for people who make visits?

    c. How does your church provide for pairs to visit when working with a person of the opposite sex?

Reflection

Reflection

4. Who visits the pastor and his family? other professional church workers and their families?

   a. If you don't know, whom can you ask?

   b. If no one is making home visits to the pastor, what can you do to change that?

5. What resources are available for you as a leader to lead a devotion?

CHAPTER 15

CULTIVATING LIFESTYLES OF RECONCILIATION[31]

Lord, let me win my foes
    With kindly words and actions,
And let me find good friends
    For counsel and correction.
Help me, as You have taught,
    To love both great and small
And by Your Spirit's might
    To live in peace with all. (*LSB* 696:4)

Case Study: A Family in Need of Hope

Sixteen-year-old Travis had become difficult to handle for both sets of his parents. His biological mother and father were divorced. Each parent remarried, and the new marriages produced two new children for each couple.

When Travis didn't get what he wanted from one set of parents, he moved in with the other. After he had switched back and forth between the households a couple of times, both sets of parents finally determined Travis could no longer move back and forth. He needed to stay in one home or the other and live by that family's rules. Instead, Travis appealed to his grandmother, who invited Travis to live with her. The result was three angry households.

Travis, his mother, and his stepfather were active members of a church with a reconciliation ministry. When his mother asked their pastor for ideas, she was directed to Ron, one of the church's reconcilers. With Ron's encouragement, the four parents, grandmother, and Travis agreed to mediation.

Ron began the meeting by establishing ground rules and describing the process. He read a portion of Scripture and prayed for God's guidance. After each person gave an opening statement, Ron led the parties through storytelling.

When it was Travis's turn, he expressed current pain over his parents' divorce. The only child of that marriage, he felt he no longer belonged to either family. "My hope is that Mom and Dad will remarry and we can be a real family again." Travis's parents were surprised to hear of their son's distress. They assumed their son had adjusted to their divorce and new marriages.

As his parents spoke, Travis began to realize how his behavior hurt his younger half-siblings. His example of disobedience was rubbing off on them. Although Travis held bitterness against both of his biological parents, he cared about his siblings and felt shame that his own actions caused problems for them. Previously, Travis's grandmother had only heard Travis's side of the story. Now she saw how her interference had made matters worse.

Ron shared how much God loved us to send Jesus into the world to die for our sins against God and one another. He described how God's act of love reconciled us to Him, providing hope for healing our broken relationships. He told them that reconciliation begins with confessing our sins to God and to one another. Upon hearing this, Travis and his family members confessed to one another. Ron announced God's forgiveness and encouraged them to forgive one another. Tears and hugs were shared around the room as forgiveness was shared.

Ron helped the family identify what issues needed resolving, and he led them through a brainstorming exercise to come up with solutions. At that point, it didn't take much time to reach agreement.

As they finished, Travis's father, who didn't attend church, said, "Travis, you should feel pretty special because you have people at your church who really care about you. On the weekends you spend with us, I'm going to make sure that you go to church."

Ron excused himself while the family continued to talk. He thanked Jesus for his church's reconciliation ministry and the opportunity to share God's love with people who needed hope.

THE NEED FOR A MINISTRY OF RECONCILIATION

Healthy congregations not only abide in God's Word but also demonstrate maturity in the faith by practicing confession and forgiveness in daily life with one another. A congregation's Reconciliation Ministry can help cultivate lifestyles of reconciliation among its membership.

At times, we take our reconciliation to God for granted. In worship, we praise God for restoring our relationship through Christ, but afterward we often act or speak in ways like nonbelievers in the daily activities of our lives.

This is especially true in conflict. By nature, we tend to say and do things to get what we want rather than work to serve God and others first. The old Adam nature in us embraces the world's message to take care of number one first, referring, of course, to ourselves. James explains what causes our conflicts:

> What causes quarrels and what causes fights among you? Is it not this, that your passions are at war within you? You desire and do not have, so you murder. You covet and cannot obtain, so you fight and quarrel. You do not have, because you do not ask. You ask and do not receive, because you ask wrongly, to spend it on your passions. (James 4:1–3)

God teaches that He ought to be number one in our lives: "You shall have no other gods before Me" (Exodus 20:3). To satisfy our own passions first is to sin against the First Commandment.

In contrast to serving ourselves first, Paul instructed the Corinthians in their conflicts: "So, whether you eat or drink, or whatever you do, do all to the glory of God" (1 Corinthians 10:31). To live in reconciliation means to first seek to glorify God, even in our conflicts.

Reconciliation is not *simply* an event. We can recall specific miracles of reconciliation, ranging from tearful moments of exchanging confession and forgiveness to Christ dying on the cross. But living reconciliation means much more than certain memorable events.

To cultivate lifestyles of reconciliation means to live our lives in such a way that we reflect Christ in everything we say or do. When we sin (and we do so daily), we repent, confessing our failures to God and others. When relationships are hurt, we quickly go to others to reconcile. When others sin against us, we forgive as God forgives us.

As part of making disciples and teaching them to observe all that Jesus commanded (Matthew 28:19–20), Christian parents, congregations, and schools are responsible for equipping children, members, and students for biblical peacemaking. The congregation or school can actively assist parents and enhance its ministry of reconciliation by establishing a reconciliation ministry.

The church proclaims our reconciliation to God through preaching and the teaching of God's Word. Through the sacraments of Holy Baptism and the Lord's Supper, we receive God's forgiveness. The pastor announces God's grace to us in corporate and individual confession and absolution.

And yet, we Christians often struggle to live, proclaim, and cultivate lifestyles of reconciliation in our relationships with others.

LEADING PEOPLE IN LIFESTYLES OF RECONCILIATION

Every Christian is called to be a peacemaker in his or her own life. In each vocation we serve—parent, child, employer, employee, pastor, church member, governor, citizen, and so forth—we live as people reconciled to the Father through Jesus the Christ.

In all our vocations, we are Christian. As such, we continuously serve as ambassadors for the Son of God, who reconciled us to the Father. St. Paul teaches:

> All this is from God, who through Christ reconciled us to Himself and gave us the ministry of reconciliation; that is, in Christ God was reconciling the world to Himself, not counting their trespasses against them, and entrusting to us the message of reconciliation. Therefore, we are ambassadors for Christ, God making His appeal through us. We implore you on behalf of Christ, be reconciled to God. (2 Corinthians 5:18–20)

Conflict presents opportunities for Christ's ambassadors to act so differently from the world that people wonder, "Why did you respond to that conflict in such a way?" God's Word instructs us: "Walk in wisdom toward outsiders, making the best use of the time. Let your speech always be gracious, seasoned with salt, so that you may know how you ought to answer each person" (Colossians 4:5–6).

God has placed many of us in positions of leadership to guide, encourage, teach, and provide examples to others. Leaders may be formal (parents, teachers, pastors, principals, employers) or informal (anyone who influences others to do something). God not only used officially appointed leaders (prophets, judges, kings, apostles, pastors) but He also often used the young (the shepherd boy David), the meek (Esther), the Gentile (the Canaanite woman who sought healing for her daughter), and even those of ill repute (the Samaritan woman at the well) to lead others by their acts of faith. And God continues to use all people today too.

St. Paul encouraged the young pastor, Timothy: "Let no one despise you for your youth, but set the believers an example in speech, in conduct, in love, in faith, in purity. . . . Keep a close watch on yourself and on the teaching. Persist in this, for by so doing you will save both yourself and your hearers" (1 Timothy 4:12, 16). As leaders, we influence others positively or negatively. Thus, we are called to be Christ's ambassadors of reconciliation.

Reconciliation is not an event but a lifestyle. To help cultivate lifestyles of reconciliation, lead others by your own example as a peacemaker. To assist you in this role, help your organization develop a Reconciliation Ministry.

> **Reconciliation is not an event but a lifestyle.**

RECONCILIATION MINISTRY

Every Christian is called to be a peacemaker in his or her own relationships. But not everyone is gifted to be a reconciler. I distinguish "reconcilers" from "peacemakers" as those who are gifted, appointed, and trained to guide others through their conflicts.

A Reconciliation Ministry utilizes reconcilers to equip and assist members in living lifestyles of reconciliation. Congregations, schools, and other organizations appoint reconcilers and provide them with the training and resources necessary to serve in the following roles:

- **Personal Peacemaking**—leading others by example, applying personal peacemaking in one's own life
- **Teaching**—equipping Christians in biblical peacemaking for lifestyles of reconciliation
- **Coaching**—guiding individuals to apply biblical approaches in specific conflicts
- **Mediating**—assisting two or more people in conflict to reconcile relationships and resolve their material issues
- **Adjudicating**—deciding substantive matters through a just and fair hearing

Personal Peacemaking

Cultivating a lifestyle of reconciliation begins with a congregation's leaders. God led the way by reconciling us to Himself through Christ while we were yet His enemies (Romans 5:10). Christ humbled Himself to take on our sins, making peace between God and us, while He Himself was sinless (2 Corinthians 5:21; 1 Peter 2:24). All true peacemaking is based on what God has done for us through Christ. Thus, compelled by Christ's love and empowered by the Holy Spirit, we are taught in God's Word to live as peacemakers in our own lives (2 Corinthians 5:14; Romans 8:9–10; 12:18; James 5:16; Ephesians 4:32).

Teaching

Reconcilers teach biblical peacemaking one-on-one and in groups through devotions, in Bible studies, and in other settings (Proverbs 22:6; Matthew 28:20; 1 Timothy 4:11). Throughout the year, reconcilers lead Bible studies on various topics for applying peacemaking to different aspects of daily life. They make recommendations for creating a culture of reconciliation in the family, church, school, and other organizations, and they make brief presentations on peacemaking to various groups. Congregational members can participate in one of the scheduled studies or invite a reconciler to make brief presentations on peacemaking to their group.

COACHING

When someone experiences conflict in the home, workplace, neighborhood, extended family, or church, he or she may want some help in understanding how to respond to the conflict in a God-pleasing manner. Such disputes may range from small personal squabbles to major matters involving legal issues. A congregation's reconcilers coach individuals by listening to concerns, helping assess the opportunities, and providing guidance through God's Word (Colossians 3:14–17; 2 Timothy 2:24–26; Galatians 6:1–2). They not only coach people to *resolve conflict*, but also to *reconcile relationships*. At times, they may also refer individuals to other professionals for specialized help (such as attorneys or counselors). As coaches, they do not solve people's conflicts for them. Instead, they serve as guides to encourage people to "go . . . be reconciled" (Matthew 5:24).

MEDIATING

When people are unable to resolve conflict on their own, Jesus teaches to "take one or two others along" to assist as witnesses (Matthew 18:15–16). Reconcilers serve as witnesses to Christ when they mediate between parties. Using a process to facilitate godly discussion, they coach all parties to apply God's Word to the conflict. As mediators, reconcilers do not make decisions for the parties but guide them in reaching biblically faithful solutions. They help negotiate material issues, and they encourage people to reconcile through confession and forgiveness. Throughout the process, they proclaim Christ and His ministry of reconciliation (2 Corinthians 5:16–21).

ADJUDICATING

For simple cases, church reconcilers may adjudicate (or arbitrate) disputes. In more complex situations, disagreements may be submitted to professionally trained Christian conciliators for adjudication. Parties submit disputes to the adjudicator and agree to be bound by his or her decision on the matter (1 Corinthians 6:1–8). Unlike mediation, adjudicators act as judges, making decisions on behalf of the parties.

When serving as an adjudicator, a reconciler cannot make decisions on relationship issues such as confession, forgiveness, or love. He or she is limited to making decisions only on material issues.

Instead of lawsuits, which can damage relationships and present a poor Christian witness, adjudication by fellow believers provides a private, God-honoring alternative for Christians seeking just decisions.

ESTABLISHING A RECONCILIATION MINISTRY

Every congregation organizes its specialized ministries in different ways. I suggest that the called and lay spiritual leaders of the congregation identify those in their midst who have special gifts in peacemaking, appoint them, and equip them to serve as reconcilers.

The church's Reconciliation Ministry need not be a special board but might be better organized as a ministry accountable to the elders or other spiritual leadership board. I recommend this accountability because the work of reconciliation often involves spiritual-life issues. By reporting to the congregation's spiritual lay leadership, reconcilers would also be available to serve in situations where the pastor may be a party. Sometimes, however, reconcilers will need to refer people to their pastor or an elder for spiritual care. In addition, the reconcilers as a group should report summaries of their work (excluding confidential information or identification of specific parties) to the congregation, including the pastors, through its spiritual leadership.

After appointing and training reconcilers, the congregation should publicize this ministry to all the members. Reconcilers should be given multiple opportunities to teach biblical peacemaking. Individuals may seek out the reconcilers on their own, and other congregational leaders may refer people to the reconcilers.[32]

SUMMARY

Healthy congregations live out the ministry of reconciliation. Their members practice confession and forgiveness in their personal lives and in their interactions with one another in the church. Reconciliation is more than just an event. Children of God are all called to be peacemakers. "[Jesus said,] 'Blessed are the peacemakers, for they shall be called sons of God' " (Matthew 5:9).

Peacemakers live in such a way that their reconciliation through Christ is reflected in everything they do. "But in your hearts honor Christ the Lord as holy, always being prepared to make a defense to anyone who asks you for a reason for the hope that is in you; yet do it with gentleness and respect, having a good conscience, so that, when you are slandered, those who revile your good behavior in Christ may be put to shame" (1 Peter 3:15–16).

As Christian leaders, we lead by example. We confess our sins and forgive as we have been forgiven. We teach reconciliation in family devotions, Bible studies, school, small-group settings, and sermons. Reconcilers assist others in their conflicts through coaching, mediation, and adjudication. Your congregation can establish a Reconciliation Ministry to cultivate lifestyles of reconciliation and promote health among its members and throughout the community in which they live.

Reflection

Reflection

Considering this chapter, discuss the following questions with the leaders in your congregation.

1. In what ways do you think we as Christians fail to live out our vocations as peacemakers?

2. Learning how to live as a peacemaker can help us realize just how sinful we really are, especially when we think about the times we have failed to apply scriptural truths in past situations. What comfort can we find to be assured that God has not forsaken us, even when we fail to live in peace? (Consider the following passages: 1 John 1:8–9; 1 Peter 2:24; John 3:16–17; Romans 8:1.)

3. How would cultivating a lifestyle of reconciliation make a difference in your family? at your workplace? within your community? in your church?

4. What kinds of conflicts do you encounter with non-Christians? What would be the possible impact to those people if you consistently responded to those conflicts in a biblically faithful manner?

5. How can your church improve its effectiveness in cultivating lifestyles of reconciliation among your members?

6. Identify the situation and kinds of people from your church or school who might benefit from having a reconciler coach them through conflict.

7. What situations exist among your members or employees in their personal or professional vocations where they could benefit from mediation?

8. Because conflict is inevitable, every organization spends time and financial resources dealing with it. What benefits would be derived from teaching biblical peacemaking before conflict erupts? What benefits would be derived from selecting and training reconcilers to serve the congregation and its individual members in conflict?

CONCLUSION: BUILT ON THE ROCK

Built on the Rock the Church shall stand
Even when steeples are falling.
Crumbled have spires in ev'ry land;
Bells still are chiming and calling,
Calling the young and old to rest,
But above all the souls distressed,
Longing for rest everlasting. (*LSB* 645:1)

Case Study: Hope Church

"He did what? Are you sure?"

"Yes, Pastor, we carefully studied the bank statements, reviewed canceled checks, and compared everything to the official records. Over the last two years, our treasurer has taken more than $75,000 of the church's funds using about four different methods of stealing."

If the embezzlement had occurred more than fifteen years ago, this news would have torn the congregation apart. But Hope Church had grown in spiritual maturity. Now, 48 percent of the average worship attendance was involved in weekly adult Bible studies. Because leaders were required to be active in worship and Bible study, 100 percent of the church's leaders attended Bible study. The church had established a Reconciliation Ministry, and the reconcilers had been teaching peacemaking, coaching people in conflict, and mediating disputes for five years. The church was equipped to handle this challenge in a new way. They were ready to live out the ministry of reconciliation in this conflict.

When the treasurer, Daniel, was confronted with the evidence, he at first tried to deflect but then confessed with tears. "I'm so glad this is over. I just didn't know how to stop." Immediately, the two elders meeting with him proclaimed God's forgiveness and assured him that they would walk with him through a process of healing—for him and the congregation. The elders and Daniel met next with Daniel's wife, who amazingly was unaware of her husband's sin. They provided biblical comfort to her as they discussed next steps. The leadership made certain that neither Daniel nor his wife was alone over the next several days to avoid any attempt at self-harm.

Over the next few days, the pastor and elders met with other leaders to explain what was happening. By this time, an agreement had been reached with Daniel, including his resignation as treasurer and agreement for restitution over time. Since congregational funds were involved, a special meeting was called to describe the embezzlement and the proposed plan for reconciliation. The congregation would have the opportunity to approve the agreement or call for changes.

Although the congregation grieved over the moral failing of one of their own, the members overwhelmingly supported the plan for restitution and reconciliation. As part of the plan, Daniel agreed to a specially called service of reconciliation, in which he publicly confessed his sins to the people he served. Pastor Jacobsen proclaimed God's forgiveness to him and prayers were offered for Daniel and his family as well as the congregation. Pastor reminded the congregation that though forgiveness is granted to all those who repent and believe, earthly consequences are also appropriate. He described the plan for restitution as well as the agreement that Daniel would be meeting regularly with a small group of reconcilers throughout the restitution period. Pastor admonished the congregation not to gossip about what was confessed. If anyone had any concerns over how the situation was handled, he or she was invited to speak with the pastor or one of the elders. Anyone who gossiped about this would be confronted by church leadership.

After the service, many approached Daniel to offer their personal forgiveness and encouragement. Many indicated they did not condone what he had done, but they forgave him in the name of Jesus. Daniel was amazed that people could show such mercy and love after he betrayed their trust in such a dramatic way.

Three years later, the congregation met again to review the progress. Daniel had repaid about half of what he owed. He had followed through with his commitment to meet with reconcilers during this time. With the help of marriage counseling, Daniel and his wife remained together as a married couple. They had continued to worship at Hope Church. The congregation unanimously decided to forgive the remaining debt, believing that healing between Daniel and the church had been accomplished.

In the years that followed, a few people questioned some of the things that happened. But during elder visits, the concerns were privately addressed.

One couple complained to their elder, "I think it was awful that the church forced Daniel to confess to the whole church." The elder explained, "Oh, you didn't know? He wanted to do that." "Why would he agree to that?" The elder explained that Pastor had met with Daniel and discussed how confession and forgiveness could bring healing. Daniel felt deep guilt and shame, and he desired to confess to the people he betrayed. Most of all, he wanted the assurance of God's forgiveness proclaimed to him. The couple were amazed by this report. In the conversation with their assigned elder, they learned what reconciliation to Christ meant in a deeper way.

Another person asked his elder why the church didn't prosecute Daniel. The elder explained how Daniel's repentance and desire to make restitution provided accountability without pressing civil charges. He explained that the lay leadership had met with the local district attorney, describing everything that the church was doing. The district attorney supported their actions, indicating that the opportunity to make restitution would be better for both the church and the accused than if he went to jail. However, should the accused stop making restitution, the church would still have a limited opportunity to pursue civil remedy on the basis of the agreement. The person questioning this appreciated knowing that these things had been considered. More important, his elder explained that the church had opportunity through this process to live out the ministry of reconciliation. "Jesus died for sinners like all of us, so that we would become the righteousness of Christ." The church applied both Law and Gospel in addressing this sin and providing for restitution. This member gained new appreciation for Christ's work by the way his church had responded to the embezzlement.

ANCHORED TO THE ROCK

The storms of conflict will continue to press upon our churches. Healthy congregations prepare for those challenges by strengthening their anchor to Christ, the solid Rock. Their leaders commit themselves to abiding in God's Word and encouraging their members to do the same. They provide ample opportunities and invite people personally to dwell in God's Word through worship, Bible study, and daily devotions. Together, they commit themselves to cultivating lifestyles of reconciliation, professing their faith as they confess their sins to one another and forgive as God through Christ has forgiven them.

As they grow in spiritual maturity, they consider organizational changes that help them define roles and responsibilities. They adopt wise principles that promote organizational strength in how they work together.

Weaknesses can be treated for churches suffering from poor spiritual health. Leaders and members can grow in spiritual maturity as they abide more deeply in Scripture. Biblical illiteracy is curable, though it takes time and work.

Healthy churches look to Christ, the solid Rock, for enduring the race set before them. He is their hope and source for remaining vibrant and strong against the temptations of our flesh, the world, and the devil.

> Therefore, since we are surrounded by so great a cloud of witnesses, let us also lay aside every weight, and sin which clings so closely, and let us run with endurance the race that is set before us, looking to Jesus, the founder and perfecter of our faith, who for the joy that was set before Him endured the cross, despising the shame, and is seated at the right hand of the throne of God. Consider Him who endured from sinners such hostility against Himself, so that you may not grow weary or fainthearted. (Hebrews 12:1–3)

Healthy churches look to Christ, the solid Rock, for enduring the race set before them.

PROCLAIMING GOD'S FORGIVENESS[33]

"Therefore, confess your sins to one another." (James 5:16a)

"Be kind to one another, tenderhearted, forgiving one another, as God in Christ forgave you." (Ephesians 4:32)

When someone confesses his sins, whether against God or us or other people, Christians have the privilege of proclaiming God's forgiveness.

Although the Bible does not require a specific form for confession and forgiveness, these forms provide simple ways to confess sin to our pastor, fellow Christian, or family member and receive the good news of God's forgiveness.

THE CONFESSION

Confession of sin is a private matter. A Christian hearing a confession and proclaiming God's forgiveness is obligated to respect the confidential nature of a confession.

When confessing, you may prepare by meditating on the Ten Commandments and by praying Psalm 6, 7, 13, 15, 51, 121, or 130. If you are not burdened with particular sins, do not torture yourself to search for or invent other sins. However, if particular sins trouble you, naming them out loud will help you own your sins. Moreover, it will help comfort you for those specific sins as God's forgiveness proclaimed to you.

NOTE: When confessing sin, it is not necessary to use any specific rite or prepared words. However, some may find it helpful to use the following:

The person hearing the confession begins:

Since Adam and Eve sinned, all people have been born in sin. We sin against God by disobeying His Commandments, and we also sin against others around us. Nevertheless, God promises in the Bible to forgive us when we confess our sins because Jesus died for all our sins (see Psalm 32:2–5 or I John 1:8–9). Thus, you are invited to confess your sins so that you can hear God's forgiveness proclaimed for you.

The person confessing prays:

Heavenly Father,

I know that You created me and love me.

You have taught me in the Bible how to live as Your child.

But I was born a sinner.

And I have sinned against You and others around me,

by what I have done, and by what I haven't done.

I deserve Your wrath and eternal punishment.

I am sorry for my sin, known and unknown.

(*optional***) I am especially sorry for . . .** [mention specific sins that trouble your conscience]

Have mercy on me.

Please forgive me for Jesus' sake.

Help me to live in the way that You teach me.

(optional—you may pray additional thoughts to God.)

In Jesus' name. Amen.

If you sinned against the one hearing your confession, you may also say:

I have also sinned against you, and I ask you for forgiveness too.

Fellow Christian Proclaiming Forgiveness Including for Use within the Family

(When seeking absolution through a pastor, he can provide another form for Individual Confession and Absolution.)

Upon hearing a person's confession, a fellow Christian announces God's forgiveness:

God loves you. He promises to be merciful to you and strengthen your faith. Do you believe that God's promises of forgiveness given in the Bible are written for all God's children, including you?

I do.

Then hear and believe what God's Word promises you (*use one or more Bible verses, including those in Appendix B*).

In 1 John 1:9, God promises: "If we confess our sins, [God] is faithful and just to forgive us our sins and to cleanse us from all unrighteousness."

Through Romans 8:1, the Lord declares: "There is therefore now no condemnation for those who are in Christ Jesus."

In 1 Peter 2:24, God assures us: "[Christ] Himself bore our sins in His body on the tree, that we might die to sin and live to righteousness. By His wounds you have been healed."

Therefore, _____ [name], believe this Good News: For Jesus' sake, God forgives you all your sins.

Amen.[34]

If the person confessing has also asked for forgiveness from the one hearing the confession, these words should also be spoken:

As God through Christ has forgiven both you and me, I also forgive you your sins against me.

Amen.

May the peace of God, which transcends all understanding, guard our hearts and minds in Christ Jesus.

Amen.

A prayer of thanksgiving may follow. Psalms 30, 31, 32, 34, 103, and 118 are also appropriate. The one hearing confession may know additional Scripture passages with which to comfort and strengthen the faith of those who have great burdens of conscience or are sorrowful and distressed. He may include some of the passages listed under "God's Word Proclaiming Forgiveness" from Appendix B.

GOD'S WORD PROCLAIMING FORGIVENESS[35]

When proclaiming God's forgiveness, comfort the person with the assurance of God's love by reading Bible passages that proclaim God's grace. Personalize the promise by inserting in the verse the person's name and personal pronouns as noted in the brackets below.

Blessed is [Name] whose transgression is forgiven, whose sin is covered. Blessed is [Name,] against whom the LORD counts no iniquity, and in whose spirit there is no deceit. (Psalm 32:1–2)

For as high as the heavens are above the earth, so great is His steadfast love toward [Name] who fears Him; as far as the east is from the west, so far does He remove [your] transgressions from [you]. (Psalm 103:11–12)

[Jesus] was delivered up for our trespasses and was raised for our justification. Therefore, [Name,] since we have been justified by faith, we have peace with God through our Lord Jesus Christ. Through Him we have also obtained access by faith into this grace in which we stand, and we rejoice in hope of the glory of God. (Romans 4:25–5:2)

There is therefore now no condemnation for [Name] who [is] in Christ Jesus. (Romans 8:1)

[Name,] for our sake [God] made Him to be sin who knew no sin, so that in Him [you] might become the righteousness of God. (2 Corinthians 5:21)

[Name,] He Himself bore our sins in His body on the tree, so that we might die to sin and live to righteousness. By His wounds [, Name,] you have been healed. (1 Peter 2:24)

[Name], the blood of Jesus His Son cleanses [you] from all sin. (1 John 1:7)

APPENDIX C

ASSESSING OUR CURRENT SITUATION

Please carefully consider each question, and then answer honestly with your best estimate. Answers will be compiled and the summations reported, but individual responses will not be identified.

The phrase "associated with this church" includes both those currently involved and those formerly involved.

1. How many people associated with this church do you have something against and have not forgiven?

2. How many people associated with this church do you believe have something against you and have not forgiven you?

3. How many people associated with this church have differences with you that have built walls between you?

4. How many people associated with this church have you said something about behind their backs?

ENDNOTES

1 Dietrich Bonhoeffer, *Life Together*, translated by John Doberstein. English translation copyright © 1954 by Harper & Brothers, copyright renewed 1982 by Helen S. Doberstein. Courtesy of HarperCollins Publishers, 105.

2 Timothy J. Mech, *Pastors and Elders: Caring for the Church and One Another* (St. Louis: Concordia Publishing House, 2011), 62.

3 Names and identifying information have been deleted or altered to protect confidences. However, statistical information from these surveys is reported as received.

4 Greg L. Hawkins and Cally Parkinson, *Follow Me: What's Next for You?* (Barrington, IL: Willow Creek Resources, 2008), 114.

5 Hawkins and Parkinson, *Follow Me*, 114.

6 Hawkins and Parkinson, *Follow Me*, 116.

7 Hawkins and Parkinson, *Follow Me*, 116 (emphasis in the original).

8 Ken Sande, *The Peacemaker: A Biblical Guide to Resolving Personal Conflict*, 3rd ed. (Grand Rapids: Baker Books, 2004), 109. I owe Ken Sande and many friends from Peacemaker Ministries (www.peacemaker.net) a great debt for the many insights given to me on heart idols. I have been blessed by a number of Christian conciliators over several years who have shared their ideas with me. I have added my own thoughts and applications of Luther's teaching.

9 The ideas in this section have been drawn from several sources.
   - Paul David Tripp, *War of Words: Getting to the Heart of Your Communication Struggles* (Phillipsburg, NJ: Presbyterian & Reformed Publishing, 2000), 56–60.
   - ——— *Instruments in the Redeemer's Hands: People in Need of Change Helping People in Need of Change* (Phillipsburg, NJ: Presbyterian & Reformed Publishing, 2002), 76–80.
   - Ken Sande, *The Peacemaker: A Biblical Guide to Resolving Personal Conflict*, 3rd ed., (Grand Rapids: Baker Books, 2004), 102–9.
   - ——— *Go and Be Reconciled: What Does This Mean?* (Billings, MT: Ambassadors of Reconciliation, 2016), 31.

10 Ted Kober, *Confession & Forgiveness: Professing Faith as Ambassadors of Reconciliation* (St. Louis: Concordia Publishing House, 2002), 19–22.

11 Eric Sahlberg and I wrote an article on this entitled "Moving from the 'Holy Howdy' to the 'Kiss of Peace,' " published in the February 2008 issue of *The Lutheran Witness* (Vol. 127, No. 2). It is reprinted by permission at www.hisaor.org under "Articles."

12 Jaroslav Pelikan, ed., *Luther's Works*, vol. 1 (St. Louis: Concordia Publishing House, 1958), 142.

13 Kober, *Confession & Forgiveness*, 171; emphasis in the original.

14 I present how confessing sin is a profession of faith in my book *Confession & Forgiveness: Professing Faith as Ambassadors of Reconciliation* (St. Louis: Concordia Publishing House, 2002) and in the Bible study *Go and Be Reconciled: What Does This Mean?* (Ambassadors of Reconciliation, 2016).

15 His real identity and my true story.

16 It's important to note that forgiveness may not on its own heal all diseases or cure all depressions. It does, however, bring spiritual healing that can assist in addressing physical and mental ailments, especially those conditions caused by guilt. God provides other blessings through professional medical care and mental health treatments that aid in healing. I have witnessed a number of situations where forgiveness provided partial or total healing for physical and emotional distresses. All too often, we forget about the healing power of God's forgiveness, even when other treatments are necessary for restoring physical or mental health.

17 While many pastors are trained in this area, I have met a number who do not practice going to private absolution themselves. Accordingly, they tend to miss recognizing when others need the same kind of pastoral care. I even had to show a couple of pastors how to absolve me when I confessed, because they lacked personal experience. The forms in Appendixes A and B provide guidance in such situations.

18 For example, use the forms in Appendixes A and B.

19 I learned these ideas from presentations by the late Rev. Dr. Kenneth Korby and the late Rev. Dr. George Wollenburg, both respected pastors who served congregations and their synod at large (The Lutheran Church—Missouri Synod).

20 Bruce M. Hartung, *Holding Up the Prophet's Hand: Supporting Church Workers* (St. Louis: Concordia Publishing House, 2011), 167.

21 Luther's Small Catechism, "What is the Office of the Keys?"

22 The Book of the Law refers to the Books of Moses, the first five books of our Bible. Also known as the Torah, or "instruction," these Scriptures include not only God's commandments but also His promises of His love and mercy through the Messiah.

23 Mech, *Pastors and Elders*, 25.

24 Mech, *Pastors and Elders*, 24–25.

25 When I use the verb *minister* or *ministering*, I am not suggesting that everyone is an ordained pastor. I am using this term as one who administers care to another, just as a nurse or doctor provides medical care. In this context, I specifically refer to providing Christian care.

26 "Supplement to the Diploma of Vocation," The Lutheran Church—Missouri Synod.

27 Hartung, *Holding Up the Prophet's Hand*, 101.

28 Hartung, *Holding Up the Prophet's Hand*, 197.

29 His real name; based on actual events.

30 The late Rev. Dr. Wollenburg shared this with me and others on several occasions while serving as President of the Montana District of The Lutheran Church—Missouri Synod. He served in that position from 1969 to 1977, and again from 1992 to 2006.

31 Content for this chapter is drawn extensively from *Cultivating Lifestyles of Reconciliation* by Ted Kober and Ken Sande (Ambassadors of Reconciliation, 2009).

32 For information on appointing reconcilers, training them, and establishing a reconciliation ministry, contact Ambassadors of Reconciliation at www.hisaor.org.

33 Taken from the pamphlet *Proclaiming God's Forgiveness* (Ambassadors of Reconciliation, 2016). An earlier version of this form can be found in my book *Confession & Forgiveness* (St. Louis: Concordia Publishing House, 2002), 186–88. Other versions are available from the website of Ambassadors of Reconciliation at www.hisaor.org.

34 *Amen* means, "Yes, yes, so shall it be!"

35 Taken from the pamphlet *Proclaiming God's Forgiveness* (Ambassadors of Reconciliation, 2016). An earlier version of this form can be found in my book *Confession & Forgiveness* (St. Louis: Concordia Publishing House, 2002), 181–82. Other versions are available from the website of Ambassadors of Reconciliation at www.hisaor.org.

RESOURCES

Critically evaluate my thoughts and these additional resources as the Bereans did with Paul's message: "Now these Jews [in Berea] were more noble than those in Thessalonica; they received the word with all eagerness, *examining the Scriptures daily to see if these things were so*" (Acts 17:11, emphasis added).

Barna, George. *The Habits of Highly Effective Churches: How to Have a Ministry That Transforms Lives*. Ventura, CA: Issachar Resources, 1998.

Bickel, Kurt, and Les Stroh. *Structure Your Church for Mission*. Orlando, FL: Strobickan Publishing LLC, 2010.

Bonhoeffer, Dietrich. *Life Together*. Translated by John W. Doberstein. New York: Harper and Row Publishers, Inc., 1954.

Commission on Theology and Church Relations of the LCMS. *1 Corinthians 6:1–11: An Exegetical Study*. St. Louis: Concordia Publishing House, 1991.

———. *Church Discipline in the Christian Congregation*. St. Louis: Concordia Publishing House, 1985.

Hartung, Bruce M. *Holding Up the Prophet's Hand: Supporting Church Workers*. St. Louis: Concordia Publishing House, 2011.

Hawkins, Greg L., and Cally Parkinson, *Follow Me: What's Next for You?* Barrington, IL: Willow Creek Resources, 2008.

Kober, Ted. *Confession & Forgiveness: Professing Faith as Ambassadors of Reconciliation*. St. Louis: Concordia Publishing House, 2002.

———. "Policy-Based Board Governance in Lutheran Congregations." Billings, MT: Ambassadors of Reconciliation website. (www.hisaor.org/web-content/Images/PolicyBasedBoardGovernance.pdf)

Kober, Ted, and Ken Sande. *Cultivating Lifestyles of Reconciliation*. Billings, MT: Ambassadors of Reconciliation, 2009.

Korby, Kenneth. "Confession and Absolution." One-hour audiotaped workshop held at Concordia Academy of Peace Lutheran Church, Sussex, WI.

Lockwood, Michael. *The Unholy Trinity: Martin Luther against the Idol of Me, Myself, and I*. St. Louis: Concordia Publishing House, 2016.

Mech, Timothy J. *Pastors and Elders: Caring for the Church and One Another*. St. Louis: Concordia Publishing House, 2011.

Oden, Thomas C. *Corrective Love: The Power of Communion Discipline*. St. Louis: Concordia Publishing House, 1995.

Qualben, James. *Peace in the Parish.* San Antonio: LangMarc Publishing, 1991.

———. *Responding to Sexual Temptation in a High Tech Society* (Bible study and DVD). Billings, MT: Ambassadors of Reconciliation, 2008.

Richardson, Ronald W. *Becoming a Healthier Pastor: Family Systems Theory and the Pastor's Own Family*. Minneapolis: Augsburg Fortress, 2005.

———. *Creating a Healthier Church: Family Systems Theory, Leadership, and Congregational Life*. Minneapolis: Augsburg Fortress, 1996.

Sande, Ken. *Go and Be Reconciled: What Does This Mean?* (Bible study and coaching guide). Billings, MT: Ambassadors of Reconciliation, 2016.

———. *The Peacemaker: A Biblical Guide to Resolving Personal Conflict*. 3rd ed. Grand Rapids: Baker Books, 2004.

Schwarz, Christian A. *Natural Church Development: A Guide to Eight Essential Qualities of Healthy Churches*. 7th ed. St. Charles, IL: ChurchSmart Resources, 2006.

Seinkbeil, Harold L. *Dying to Live: The Power of Forgiveness*. St. Louis: Concordia Publishing House, 1994.

Steinke, Peter L. *A Door Set Open: Grounding Change in Mission and Hope*. Herndon, VA: The Alban Institute, 2010.

———. *How Your Church Family Works: Understanding Congregations as Emotional Systems*. Lanham, MD: Rowman & Littlefield, 2006.

———. *Healthy Congregations: A Systems Approach*. Lanham, MD: Rowman & Littlefield, 1996.

Tripp, Paul David. *Instruments in the Redeemer's Hands: People in Need of Change Helping People in Need of Change*. Phillipsburg, NJ: Presbyterian & Reformed Publishing, 2002.

———. *War of Words: Getting to the Heart of Your Communication Struggles*. Phillipsburg, NJ: Presbyterian and Reformed Publishing, 2000.

Veith, Gene Edward, Jr. *The Spirituality of the Cross*. St. Louis: Concordia Publishing House, 1999.

Walther, C. F. W. *The Proper Distinction between Law and Gospel*. Translated by W. H. T. Dau. St. Louis: Concordia Publishing House, 1929.

Welch, Edward T. *Addictions—A Banquet in the Grave: Finding Hope in the Power of the Gospel.* Phillipsburg, NJ: Presbyterian and Reformed Publishing, 2001.

———. *When People Are Big and God Is Small: Overcoming Peer Pressure, Codependency, and the Fear of Man.* Phillipsburg, New Jersey: Presbyterian and Reformed Publishing, 1997.

FOR MORE RESOURCES:

Ambassadors of Reconciliation offers an extensive array of training, workshops, consultation, reconciliation services, and written and recorded resources. Learn more at hisaor.org or call 406-698-6107.

Concordia Publishing House also offers an extensive array of written and recorded resources. Visit cph.org or call 800-325-3040.

About the Author

Ted Kober is a Senior Ambassador for Ambassadors of Reconciliation (AoR), having served as President from AoR's founding in 2004 through May 2015. In addition, Ted has been a Certified Christian Conciliator™ since 1992, consulting and conciliating in cases ranging from personal disputes to lawsuits and church conflicts. Ted is a frequent guest speaker and teacher at churches, church-worker conferences, schools, universities, and seminaries. He is also an adjunct instructor for Peacemaker Ministries and PeaceWise (Australia). He has equipped church-body leaders from more than thirty-five countries.

In 2004, Montana's governor appointed Ted to chair the first Montana Consensus Council. He has also served in leadership at Peacemaker Ministries and as a reconciler for The Lutheran Church—Missouri Synod (LCMS).

Ted has published articles, Bible studies, devotions, training manuals, and books, including *Confession & Forgiveness* (Concordia Publishing House, 2002) and *Cultivating Lifestyles of Reconciliation* (co-authored with Ken Sande; AoR, 2009).

A lifetime member of Trinity Lutheran Church in Billings, Montana, Ted occasionally plays organ for worship. He and his wife, Sonja, live in Billings. They have one son, David, and two grandchildren.